An Illustrated History
of Mexican Los Angeles, 1781–1985

Antonio Coronel, a leader in both the Mexican and United States eras, served as mayor of
Los Angeles and treasurer for the state of California.

(Courtesy of the Southwest Museum)

ANTONIO RIOS-BUSTAMANTE

AND

PEDRO CASTILLO

An Illustrated History of Mexican Los Angeles

1781–1985

Chicano Studies Research Center Publications
University of California
Monograph No. 12

Editor:	Oscar R. Martí
Series Editors:	Juan Gómez-Quiñones
	Carlos M. Haro
	Ray Rocco
	Emilio Zamora
Contributing Editors:	Max Benavides
	Kate Vosoff
Photographic Editor:	Devra Weber
Cartographer:	Nöel Diaz

Library of Congress Cataloging-in-Publication Data

Ríos-Bustamante, Antonio José
    An illustrated history of Mexican Los Angeles,
1781-1985.

    (Monograph / Chicano Studies Research Center,
Publications, University of California ; no. 12)
    Bibliography: p.
    1. Mexican Americans—California—Los Angeles—
History. 2. Mexican Americans—California—Los Angeles
—History—Pictorial works. 3. Los Angeles (Calif.)—
Description—Views. 4. Los Angeles (Calif.)—History.
5. Los Angeles (Calif.)—History—Pictorial works.
I. Castillo, Pedro. II. Title. III. Series: Monograph
(University of California, Los Angeles. Chicano
Studies Research Center. Publications) ; no. 12.
F869.L89M526 1986   979.4'940046872   86-6824
ISBN 0-89551-053-7

Roping the Bear. Grizzly bears, a threat to cattle and people, were captured by vaqueros for the spectator fights between bears and bulls held in a corral near the placita.

(Courtesy of California Historical Society)

Design by Serena Sharp

Typeset by Freedmen's Organization
Copyright © 1986 by Regents of the University of California
                Chicano Studies Research Center Publications
                Antonio Ríos-Bustamante and Pedro Castillo

Printed in the United States of America

Dedication

This book is dedicated to the Mexican people of Los Angeles,
from the *pobladores*
to the present *hombres y mujeres de exercicio*;
to my mentor, Professor Juan Gómez-Quiñones;
and with love to my parents,
Antonio Ríos-Ochoa and Josefina Bustamante de Ríos.

Table of Contents

Diorama of the founding of Los Angeles. *(Courtesy of Seaver Center for Western History Research, Natural History Museum of Los Angeles County)*

Foreword

I am honored to author this foreword to *An Illustrated History of Mexican Los Angeles, 1781–1985*. This publication provides rare and very important evidence of the contributions that have been made to this city, founded as a Spanish pueblo, by the Mexican community.

It contains more than 150 illustrations, photographs and maps that were quite popular when presented, as an exhibit at the Plaza de la Raza, during the Los Angeles bicentennial celebration in 1981.

An Illustrated History of Mexican Los Angeles, 1781–1985 succeeds in its goal to be a scholarly and comprehensive record of the history of Mexican Los Angeles. I hope it is used extensively as a supplement to educational curriculum in the study of Mexicans, Chicanos, United States and California history. It is certainly a tremendous resource.

Antonio Ríos-Bustamante, visiting lecturer at the University of California at Santa Barbara; Pedro G. Castillo, history professor of the University of California at Santa Cruz; and the Chicano Studies Research Center at the University of California at Los Angeles have compiled what I believe is a unique and interesting manuscript.

Two centuries of history are covered from both a social, and a cultural perspective. It takes the reader from early colonization to expansion and growth to urbanization. And don't miss the sections "A Delicate Balance: the Politics of Survival" and "Depression, War, and Resistance." Both chapters serve to broaden our knowledge of American history.

An Illustrated History of Mexican Los Angeles, 1781–1985 is simply one of the most significantly written works on the subject. I encourage you to read on and enjoy.

Tom Bradley
Mayor of Los Angeles

Acknowledgments

The authors wish to express their appreciation to all the people and institutions who have assisted us in the preparation of this book. We want to thank our generous funders, the John Randolph Haynes and Dora Haynes Foundation for their help in making the research and writing of the manuscript possible, and to Dean Robert H. Gray and the College of Fine Arts, UCLA, for their help in making the manuscript a book.

We also wish to acknowledge the special interest, help, and encouragement shown by Prof. Juan Gómez-Quiñones (former director 1975–1985), Dr. Carlos M. Haro (former program director 1975–1983), Dr. Emilio Zamora (former program director 1983–1985), and Prof. Oscar R. Martí, editor of the Chicano Studies Research Center at the University of California, Los Angeles. We thank William Mason, Los Angeles County Museum of Natural History, and William Estrada, Occidental College, for their help.

Thanks go to the members of our advisory council for their encouragement and suggestions. We also want to thank our research assistants, Ms. Cynthia Orozco, Juan Yñiguez, and Roberto Calderón for their assistance during the research phase. Finally, special thanks are given to Max Benavides and Kate Vosoff for their editing of the manuscript, Devra Weber for her photographic editing, Ernesto Collosi for his friendship, encouragement and the use of his photos, and to Serena Sharp, for her superb help in technical production and design of the book.

India y Indio de Monterey. 1786. *(Courtesy of the Bancroft Library)*

CHAPTER ONE

Raices Indigenas

El Pueblo de La Reina de Los Angeles was formally founded in September 1781, but the history of the city's Mexican community is rooted in events and cultures that stretch back milleniums. In the sprawling metropolis that is today's urban Los Angeles, it is difficult to imagine a land swept clean of freeways, architectural collage, and imported greenery. It is more difficult still to imagine the people who once lived here—the Gabrielino tribe and other California Indians whose social dynamics, even now, remain embodied in the Mexican people of Southern California.

A gradual process of racial, cultural, and social interplay has repeatedly transformed the City of Angels. The first settlers of the area—themselves a group of mixed races and traditions—founded their settlement in the midst of an already established social order. So it is with a discussion of the Indian people they encountered, and with an examination of those early California cultures that we should begin building toward a viable image of the Mexican people who have made this place their home.

THE LAND

The history of Los Angeles and its Mexican community has never been limited by the city's designated boundaries. Rather, it has been a history of the entire Los Angeles region.

In a geologic sense, the area is relatively young. Although scientific opinions vary, many experts contend that it may have been formed only one million years ago. It is certain that ten million years ago most of the present Los Angeles area was under water. Slowly, over several million years, one large crustal plate covering part of the earth's surface (including that which forms the region's huge basin) shifted northward while another (including what is now Santa Barbara and parts of western and northern Los Angeles County) shifted westward. Eventually, these two moving land masses joined together along an enormous mountain range now called the Santa Monica Mountains. Thus, the Los Angeles region was formed.[1]

Although the basin area is defined by many natural features—mountains, valleys, hills, coastline, temperate climate, and natural vegetation— the most important are the large plains of the Los Angeles Basin and its associated San Fernando and San Gabriel valleys. The basin itself is enormous. Extending from Santa Monica on the northwest to San Juan Capistrano on the southeast, it meets the Pacific Ocean on the west. And on the north, east, and southeast, it is bounded by mountain ranges—all of which open into the San Fernando, San Gabriel and San Bernardino valleys. At its broadest point, the plain stretches 100 miles wide. Even at its narrowest, it measures 30 miles across. And while the region's southeast end (now called Orange County) is politically independent of Los Angeles County, its flat plains are geologically the natural extension of one vast basin.[2]

Towering mountain ranges shelter Los Angeles from the harsher continental climate of the Mojave Desert to the east. By insulating the interior valleys from the plain and Pacific Ocean, these mountains also create climatic diversity within the enclosed area. During the Mexican period, the major mountain ranges to the northeast were named the Sierra Madre and were divided into three smaller ranges: the San Bernardino, the San Gabriel, and the Santa Susana. Three other mountain ranges, also important to the geography and history of the area, border the basin. They are the Santa Monica Mountains on the west, which form part of the southern rim of the San Fer-

Reception for French naval officer, La Perouse, at the Carmel Mission near Monterey. 1786.

(Courtesy of the Bancroft Library)

nando Valley; the Verdugo Mountains, also forming part of the valley rim; and the Santa Ana Mountains, to the southeast, marking the limit of the plains in present Orange County.[3]

There are several lesser groups of hills throughout the basin. There are the *lomas de las carretas* (Baldwin hills in what is now the West Los Angeles area); the *lomas de Palos Verdes* (Palos Verdes hills on the Palos Verdes Peninsula); the *lomas de la Puente* (Puente hills near the eastern border of Orange County); and, to the southeast, the San Joaquin and Laguna hills of Orange County.

The year-round availability of fresh water has always been essential to the survival of area inhabitants. Only four rivers flow continually in the Los Angeles Basin: the Los Angeles river (by far the most important to the history of the region), which flows from largely underground sources in the San Fernando Valley; the San Gabriel, and Rio Hondo rivers, which originate from mountain streams in the San Gabriel Mountains east of Los Angeles; and the Santa Ana River, which flows southwest in Orange County.

There are also several perennial arroyos which run throughout the basin, particularly after periods of heavy rain.[4] The most significant of these are the *Arroyo de los Coyotes* (Coyote Creek) near the border of Orange County, and La Ballona that flows from the Baldwin hills to the ocean at the foot of the cliffs of Playa del Rey.

Flooding has been a long-time problem in the lowland areas of the plain and adjacent valleys. During extremely heavy rains, much of the basin has suffered severe soil erosion. In fact, during both prehistoric and historic periods, rivers have actually altered course due to flooding. Since 1781, the Los Angeles, San Gabriel, and Rio Hondo rivers have all changed their courses several times. Understandably, each time such a change occurred, local environment, economic activity, and people's lives have been affected. Of equal impact are recurring cycles of drought that have played havoc with food sources and economic activity since the end of the wetter climate of the Pleistocene era.[5]

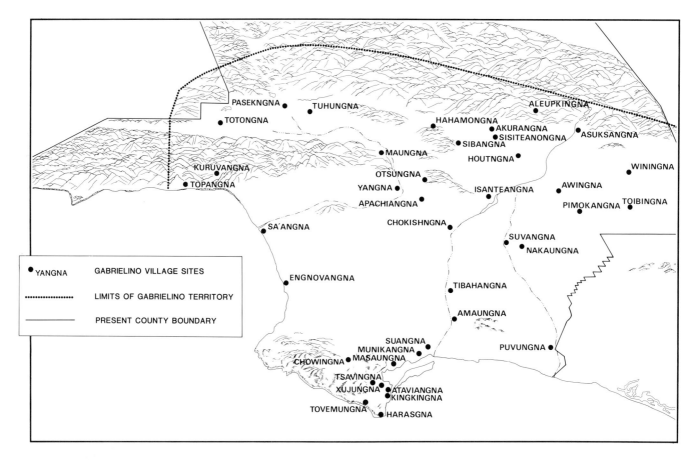

Distribution of Gabrielino Indian villages in the Los Angeles basin and adjacent areas. 1781.

The region's climate is temperate and semi-arid. Never extremely hot or cold, the basin is ideally suited for year-round outdoor economic activity. February is generally the wettest, coldest month of the year; July is typically the driest and hottest. The area is further characterized by a variety of local subclimates. These range from the cooler marine climate (which begins at the coastal range and stretches inland for about three miles) to the somewhat warmer, drier climate of the plains and the harsher continental climate of the inland valleys, from the colder climate of the mountain ranges to the dry, hot climate of the Mojave Desert. This climatic diversity, which results from the variation between sea coast and basin interior, has greatly influenced human activity in the area, especially during Native American prehistory.[6]

The original vegetation of Los Angeles County was very different from that which grows in the city today. Extensive irrigation and the importation of foreign plants have combined to create an artificial environment that belies the region's natural greenery.[7] The greater part of the basin was once characterized by large rolling plains and interior valley floors covered by natural grasses and interspersed with scattered oak trees. Several rivers and streams, bordered on their banks by wooded groves, flowed through the lowland areas of the plains. Sometimes these meandering rivers (especially the Los Angeles River, which prior to 1828 flowed west along the general path of present-day Washington Boulevard but which occasionally flowed to the ocean through Ballona Creek) formed shallow lakes, ponds, or swamps as they traveled along their indefinite course.[8]

Small hills and higher ground rose slightly above the plain. Areas now referred to as the Puente, Baldwin, and Palos Verdes hills were once covered with a thick chaparral. The northern faces of these hills were blanketed with

evergreen scrubs and scrubby trees, while their southern slopes were usually covered by a sparser, parklike vegetation. Coastal areas along Santa Monica, San Pedro Bay, and the coastline of Orange County to the Santa Ana river were even more complex environments that included both salt and fresh water marshes, coastal sand dunes, and sage brush. Finally, rising high above the basin and its associated valleys were the mountain ranges. Those below 5,000 feet were covered by yellow pine forest. Steeper ranges, like the lofty San Gabriels and San Bernardinos, were wrapped in fir forest.

Gabrielina collecting cactus fruit.

(Courtesy of Seaver Center for Western History Research, Natural History Museum of Los Angeles County)

Gabrielino spear fishing.

(Courtesy of Seaver Center for Western History Research, Natural History Museum of Los Angeles County)

NATIVE AMERICAN PREHISTORY

Perhaps more important to the prehistory of Los Angeles than geologic realities is the length of human habitation in the area. Until quite recently, most physical anthropologists thought that human beings had first entered the Western Hemisphere between 10,000 and 14,000 years ago, when a lowering of sea level created a land bridge between the Americas and Asia in the Bering Straits.[9] Then, during the 1970s, a combination of discoveries—including carbon-14 dating of previously discovered human remains—began suggesting that Native Americans had been in the area as early as 100,000 B.C.[10]

In 1936, a group of construction workers excavating a storm drain in West Los Angeles found a bone fragment that turned out to be a mineralized human cranium of modern type.[11] The Los Angeles Man, as the skull would come to be called, was that of a fully modern Homo sapiens.[12] Found several hundred yards away but at the same level as the skull were the remains of mammoths that chemical analysis showed, even then, to date from the same period as the skull.

It was not until 1970 that radiocarbon redating by Dr. Rainer Berger of UCLA showed that the Los Angeles Man was at least 23,000 years old. What's more, other human remains (such as the Del Mar skull from Orange County) have been dated to 48,000 B.C.

The redating of these remains has stimulated more than new discussion over the date of human arrival in the Americas. It has called into question the very origin of modern human beings. Skulls and other remains of modern human beings from California have been dated by carbon-14 analysis to be older than even the oldest remains of modern humans found in Europe, Africa, Asia, or the Middle East. Although no remains of earlier, premodern humans have been found in the Americas, recent discoveries have given rise to the hypothesis that modern human beings may have originated in the Americas, possibly even in Southern California.[13] Without question, scientific evidence indicates that early Native Americans inhabited the Los Angeles Basin at least as early as 50,000 B.C. and possibly before the appearance of fully modern Homo sapiens in the Eastern Hemisphere.[14]

Evidence that might help reconstruct the material culture and lifestyle of the earliest Los Angeles inhabitants is, unfortunately, quite limited. For one thing, relatively recent construction throughout the area destroyed essential archeological data.[15] Even more frustrating, prevailing opinion long held that human beings arrived in the area only 9,000 years ago. As a consequence, many anthropological remains found in California were considered unimportant and were generally ignored or even destroyed. It is to be hoped that re-examination of items found in the past and careful analysis of future discoveries will provide some glimpse into the untold story of Los Angeles human prehistory.

Existing evidence does indicate the presence of a relatively large Indian population in the area for at least 9,000 years. These early inhabitants of Los Angeles are to this day unnamed. However, judging from the remains of discarded artifacts and food stuffs, we do know that they were hunters and gatherers. It appears that their lifestyle was very similar to that of later Indians who lived in the area. They fished, collected large quantities of shell fish, and hunted deer as well as other small land animals.[16] Their material culture was characterized by the manufacture and use of stone spear points, manos, metates, pestles, and mortars for processing seeds and nuts. They may also have constructed and used reed or plank boats as did later Indian people of the Los Angeles coastal area.[17]

GABRIELINO HISTORY

But where does Los Angeles Native American history really begin? Which tribes lived here? How and why did they arrive? These are the questions that beg to be answered as we move toward a clear picture of the city's contemporary Mexican community.

Scientists maintain that at the end of the last Ice Age almost 10,000 years ago, most of what is now the Southwest United States dried up into arid desert. An extensive network of inland lakes that had once made the Mojave area a desirable settlement site disappeared. As a result, large-scale migration began as relatively populous groups dispersed in search of new home sites.[18]

This cycle of settlement, environmental change, and subsequent migration was repeated again and again through Native American prehistory. One such movement—about 1,500 years ago—brought to Los Angeles the ancestors of the Gabrielino Indians, a Shoshonean-speaking language group of the Uto-Aztecan family.[19] It is worth noting that if these Indian people had a tribal name for themselves, it has been lost over time. What seems more likely is that social identification coalesced around distinct villages because many of these community names have survived. The name "Gabrielino" was that given to the group by the Franciscans because Mission San Gabriel served their area.

The natural environment of the Los Angeles basin largely determined the patterns of these California Indian cultures. For example, settlement sites, distribution of resources, and the use of land surrounding each village were all organized around the location and availability of food and raw materials. Similarly, religious beliefs were formed in relationship to the particular characteristics of the natural environment.

By 1769, the Gabrielinos has displaced local Hokan-speaking people (whose descendants would later be known as the Chumash) and had settled between 40 and 50 permanent villages. Occupying land near the best sources of food, water, and those natural resources required by their culture, the Gabrielinos held most of the Los Angeles region as we have defined it.

Topangna (Topanga), in the Santa Monica Mountains, including much of the San Fernando Valley on the north, marked the Gabrielino's western border, although the language dialect spoken there differed somewhat from that which was spoken throughout the rest of the basin. The northeast limit of their territory was marked by the Santa Susana, San Gabriel, and San Bernardino mountain ranges. Their southeast border was near San Juan Capistrano, approximately at Aliso Creek.

Gabrielino society emphasized a harmonious relationship with the natural environment. That is not to say that the relationship was a passive one. The Gabrielinos, like many other Indian peoples, were keen observers of natural phenomena. Even as outside forces rendered many of their traditional practices obsolete, their innovative social adaptation allowed for new and better use of local resources.

The specific location of and distance between Gabrielino villages was largely determined by environment because they grew out of economic activities that followed the natural availability and distribution of food and raw material. Each village was located near areas of good hunting and fishing. Most were located near adequate supplies of acorns, seeds, and other plant foods. Depending upon the particular foods most available, individual villages relied most on hunting, fishing, and gathering plant foods.

Seacoast villages, particularly those along the sheltered coast from Santa Monica Bay to San Pedro, appear to have been more technologically sophisticated than many of the inland villages. For offshore fishing, these coastal people built wooden plank canoes caulked with asphalt. Many of these vessels could hold more than a dozen men at one time. Bone barbs, shell fish hooks, nets with sinkers, and spears were also manufactured and used for ocean catch. Sea animals used as food included porpoise, California sea lion, harbor fur seal, Guadalupe fur seal, shark, ray, sea bass, shell fish, and even whale. Villages along the more exposed coast from San Pedro to present Newport Beach were unable to enjoy so extensive a fishing industry. Hence, they had a less complex material culture and, relying heavily on shell fish gathered along the shore, a less varied food supply.

Villages further inland specialized in hunting or gathering and often engaged in both activities. Animals regularly hunted included deer, rabbit, squirrel, various birds, lizards, even insects. In the flat prairie plains, the em-

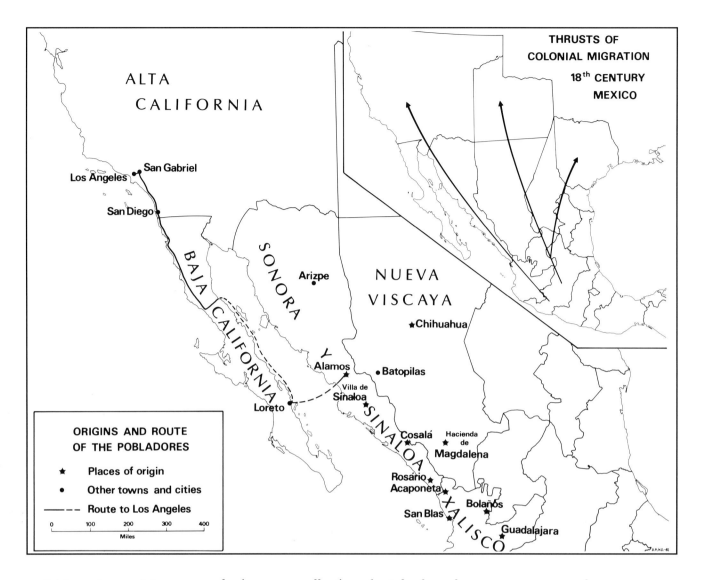

ALTA CALIFORNIA

Los Angeles • San Gabriel
San Diego •

BAJA CALIFORNIA

Loreto •

SONORA

Arizpe •

Alamos ★
Villa de Sinaloa ★

SINALOA Y

Cosalá ★

Rosario ★
Acaponeta ★
San Blas •

JALISCO

NUEVA VISCAYA

Chihuahua ★
Batopilas •

Hacienda de Magdalena ★

Bolaños ★

Guadalajara ★

THRUSTS OF COLONIAL MIGRATION
18th CENTURY MEXICO

ORIGINS AND ROUTE OF THE POBLADORES

★ Places of origin

• Other towns and cities

– – – Route to Los Angeles

0   100   200   300   400
Miles

Origins and route of the founders of Los Angeles. The group of 42 included Indians, blacks, and mestizos from northern Mexico and one Spaniard.

phasis was on collecting plant foods such as acorns, sage seeds, yucca roots, pinon nuts, and tunas (cactus fruits). But even in these villages, small animals and birds associated with marsh areas were hunted.

Hunting equipment was generally made of bone, wood, and hide. Spears, bow and arrows, dart throwers, darts, knives, scrappers, and arrow shaft straighteners were everyday tools among the Gabrielinos. Stone grinders, bedrock mortars, pestles, manos, and basket hopper mortars were manufactured and used to process acorns and other plant foods. Baskets made of various plant fibers were so carefully constructed and so tightly woven that they could hold water and serve as kettles for boiling food.

Gabrielino villages were politically autonomous units, although several small villages would sometimes ally themselves under the leadership of a larger, dominant one. Socially, these villages were organized into groups, or clans, based upon descent from a common (apparently male) ancestor. Village chiefs, who came from the oldest or most prestigious descent line, enjoyed ritual as well as administrative authority over their people. Their names were typically a modified form of the village name and their position within the community was one of lifelong responsibility and privilege. As important to each village as its chief, was its shaman, whose religious power derived from spiritual visions induced with ritual drugs.[20]

Gabrielino religion was highly developed, and the tribe's ritual life ultimately influenced many neighboring Indian peoples. The Luiseños, the Serranos, and the Kameyaays—all of whom lived to the southeast of the Gabrielinos—were deeply affected by the Gabrielino's worship of *Chingichngish* or *Qua-o-ar*, who had made the world and placed it on the shoulders of seven giants. Also associated with the worship of Chingichngish was the worship of the sun and moon. Religious symbols included the eagle, crow, owl, raven, and porpoise.

Ceremonies were elaborate and conducted by the older men of each village at *Yuva-r* (sacred enclosures or shrines), which were constructed of woven reed walls wrapped around a framework of poles and built in the shape of an oval. These shrines were extravagantly decorated with inlaid or engraved carvings and emblems as well as other ritual objects made of wood, bone, shell, and stone. Within each of these enclosures were representations of Chingichngish and, sometimes, other deities. Sand painting, a sophisticated art form, also played an important role in Gabrielino ritual.

Despite their lack of overall political organization, and except for periodic conflict among their own villages and occasional war with neighboring peoples, the Gabrielinos enjoyed peaceful relations among themselves and with outsiders. Villages traded freely, both internally and with neighboring

Presidial soldier of Monterey and wife. 1786. The Mexican settler population of Alta California was composed primarily of vaqueros and presidio soldiers and their families.
(Courtesy of the Bancroft Library)

Indian groups. In fact, a chain of exchange between groups made long distance trade with Indians throughout the Southwest an integral part of the Gabrielino's economic life.

Via the Colorado River tribes, the Gabrielinos traded steatite (soapstone) utensils, bowls, ornaments, and pipes, as well as sea shell beads, jewelry, and otter skins to Indians as far away as central Arizona and, remarkably, even to the New Mexican Pueblo tribes. Their manufacturing center for steatite items was the Channel Islands, where they found their source of soapstone —a resource upon which they based a large part of their trade economy. In exchange for these items, the Gabrielinos received obsidian, deer, and other animal skins, large quantities of food, and, possibly, pottery goods from distant Indian trade allies.

In addition to material goods, the Gabrielinos exported and imported religious beliefs and ritual practices. By the time Spanish-Mexican settlers arrived in California, the cult of Chingichngish had spread to other peoples of Southern California. From the east, specifically from Native Americans of the Colorado, the Gabrielinos had received the use of Jimson weed as a ritual herb for the stimulation of visions. The full extent of this spiritual trade network is not known. In the 1920s, however, anthropologist William Duncan Strong gathered evidence to suggest that intricate systems of ceremonial exchange linked several Southern California peoples to the traditions of the Cahuillas:

> Besides the . . . organization based on actual participation in the same ceremonies, and marked by the exchange of *Witcu* (long strings of shell money) between the united groups, there seems to have been a looser form of union which was discontinued many years ago and may now only be reconstructed with great difficulty. It was customary . . . for all the clans north of Palm Springs irrespective of linguistic differences, on hearing of death in another clan, to send one string of shell money to the leader of that clan. This smaller string of money was called by the Palm Springs Cahuilla, *napanaa*. Thus there would seem to have existed a looser ceremonial union between all the Cahuilla, Serrano, Luiseno, and Gabrielino clans who inhabited the territory from the San Gorgonio Pass west to the Pacific Ocean.[21]

NEIGHBORING TRIBES

Surrounding the Gabrielinos were other tribal/linguistic groups, each of which played an important part in the history of Los Angeles. On the northeast, from Malibu north to present-day Ventura and Santa Barbara counties, were the Chumash, a people skilled in building plank boats and fishing. To the southwest, across the channel, the Santa Catalina and San Nicolas islands were inhabited by people who spoke a dialect of the Gabrielino language. They, too, were skilled in fishing, in working the soapstone of the islands into utensils, and in manufacturing boats, and clam shell jewelry.[22]

North of the San Fernando Valley were the Tataviam, who appear to have been heavily influenced by their Chumash and Gabrielino neighbors. In 1769, this group was estimated to have had a population of 1,000 spread over about 20 villages. To the northeast of the Gabrielinos, occupying the area east of the crests of the San Gabriel and San Bernardino mountains, were the Serrano. In 1769, the population of this tribe was estimated to be between 1,500 and 2,500.[23]

Southeast, in present Riverside County, were the Cahuilla. Like the Gabrielinos, these people were linguistic members of the Cupan subgroup of

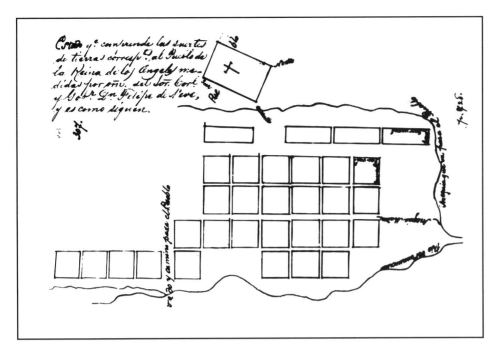

1786 town plan depicting the house lots, fields, and common pastures of Los Angeles.

(Courtesy of the Bancroft Library)

the Takic family of the Uto-Aztecan language. In 1769, the Cahuilla had an estimated population of 7,000 to 10,000 spread throughout 50 villages. They were primarily hunters and gatherers but there is some evidence to suggest that they also engaged in farming practices involving corn, beans, and squash. They probably learned these skills from the Yuman peoples of the Colorado River area, who were agriculturalists.[24]

The Luiseños, and the Juaneños—names derived respectively from mission San Luis Rey de Francia and San Juan Capistrano—lived to the south and southeast in what is now Orange County. The Juaneños were actually a subdivision of the Luiseños, and both tribes spoke a language related to the Gabrielino. It is estimated that, in 1769, they had a population of 4,000 to 10,000 scattered throughout 50 villages. The material culture of the Luiseños was similar to the Gabrielinos, and their spiritual life was greatly influenced by the cult of Chingichngish. Unlike the Gabrielinos, the Luiseños had relatively little sexual division of labor. Women hunted and fished, and men were permitted to gather and process plant foods.[25]

Significant to the history of Los Angeles were several other Native American peoples who did not border on the territory of the Gabrielinos. Among these tribes were the Cupeño, whose estimated 1769 population was 500. In keeping with their numbers, the Cupeño's territory was relatively small and surrounded by the Cahuilla.

A larger group of people, the Kameyaay, lived in what are now San Diego and Imperial counties, and in northern Baja California. Previously known as Diegueños, after Mission San Diego de Acalá, and now called Tipai Ipai by some anthropologists, the Kameyaay (the name now preferred by a majority of this tribal group) spoke a dialect of the Yuman language and were the first Native Americans in Alta California affected by colonization and missionization. In 1769, they had an estimated population of 4,000 to 8,000.

The more distant Yumans of the Colorado River were also of historical importance to the Los Angeles area, as were the even more distant Utes of the Great Basin, who acted as long-distance traders and occasionally raided neighboring villages.[26]

Town plan of Los Angeles.
1793.

(Courtesy of the Bancroft Library)

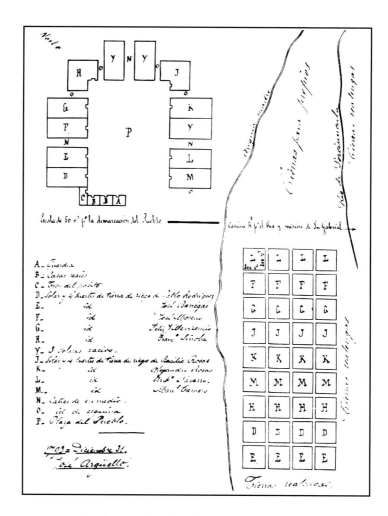

BEFORE COLONIZATION

When the first Spanish explorers arrived in California, they did not step into a political or cultural vacuum. Contrary to conventional myths, a thriving social community existed in what is now the Southern California area. The sweeping basin had known continuous human habitation for perhaps 100,000 years. Over thousands of years, it had hosted various Indian peoples who had learned to trade over great distances, exchange complex religious rituals, and coexist harmoniously with their environment.

With a few exceptions, later Spanish-Mexican settlements, ranchos, towns, and cities were built on the very sites once occupied by prehistoric and historic Indian villages and camps. The new settlers took not only the land but sometimes the very names as well. Gabrielino words, such as *Kawenga* (Cahuenga), literally "the place of the mountain," and *Asukangna* (Azusa), "his grandmother," survive to this day. Chumash words, like *Maliwu* (Malibu) and *Simj* (Simi) were also incorporated. And the Tataviam influence remains in words such as *Kamulos* (Camulos) and *Kastic* (Castic).

Clearly, the roots of Mexican Los Angeles extend to the area's most ancient and earliest inhabitants. The social fabric of the future metropolis was overlaid and grafted upon a cultural and political network created and nurtured by Native Americans. The Gabrielinos and other tribes may be considered the true founders of Los Angeles. Their lives and societies helped create the circumstances that led to the racial and cultural unfolding from which Mexican Los Angeles would eventually emerge.

The Mission San Gabriel Archangel, founded in 1771, was the oldest and most important mission in the Los Angeles area and a base camp for the original settlers.

(Courtesy of Seaver Center for Western History Research, Natural History Museum of Los Angeles County)

NOTES

1. For more information on the geologic and tectonic history of the Los Angeles region see Don L. Anderson, "The San Andreas Fault," *Scientific American* (1971). See also Michael Donley, et. al., eds., "Recent Tectonic Evolution of Southern California," *Atlas of California* (Culver City, 1979), p. 117.

2. For more information on the geography of the Los Angeles region see Howard J. Nelson and William V. Clark, "The Physical Setting and Natural Hazards," *Los Angeles: The Metropolitan Experience* (Cambridge, Massachusetts, 1979), pp. 7-20. See also Jonathan Garnst, "A Geographical Study of the Los Angeles Region of Southern California," (Ph.D. dissertation, University of Edinburgh, 1931).

3. Nelson, op. cit.

4. Vincent Ostrom, "The Los Angeles Water Supply," *Water and Politics* (Los Angeles, 1953), pp. 3-26. Also Clark W. Eliot and Donald F. Griffin, "Waterlines—Key to Development of Metropolitan Los Angeles," (Los Angeles, 1946); Nelson, "The Physical Setting," *Los Angeles: The Metropolitan Experience*, pp. 7-20.

5. Anthony F. Turhollow, "From Shore Protection to Flood Control," *A History of the Los Angeles District, U.S. Army Corps of Engineers, 1898-1965* (Los Angeles, 1975), pp. 144-237. J. W. Reagan, *Research, Los Angeles County Flood Control, 1814-15*, 2 vols., (Los Angeles, 1915). See also Richard Bigger, *Flood Control in Metropolitan Los Angeles* (Berkeley, 1959).

6. Harry P. Bailey, *The Climate of Southern California*, California Natural History Guides No. 17, (Berkeley, 1966). George F. Carter, "Man, Time, Change in the Far Southwest," special supplement to *Annals of the Association of American Geographers* 49 (3, pt. 2, September 1959): 8-31.

7. Homer Aschmann, "The Evolution of a Wild Landscape and its Persistence in Southern California," *Annals of the Association of American Geographers*, (September 1959): 34-57.

8. J. N. Bowman, "The Names of the Los Angeles and San Gabriel Rivers," *Southern California Quarterly* 29 (2, Summer 1947). Also Hubert Howe Bancroft, "Local Annals—Santa Barbara District, 1821-1830," *History of California*, 7 vols., (San Francisco, 1885), 2:563, footnote 8.

9. For expert discussion of the debate on the antiquity of man in the Americas with reference to the Southwest, see Carter, op. cit. See also Luther Cressman, "The Wanderers," *Prehistory of the Far West: Homes of Vanished Peoples* (Salt Lake City, 1977), pp. 57-76. For a more speculative treatment see Jeffrey Goodman, *American Genesis* (New York, 1981).

10. Cressman, op. cit., Goodman, op. cit.

11. Rainer Berger, "Advances and Results in Radiocarbon Dating: Early Man in America," *World Archeology*, 7 (No. 2, 1957): 174-84. Also Jose L. Lorenzo, "Early Man in Research in the American Hemisphere," in A. L. Bryan, ed., *Early Man in America* (Edmonton, 1978).

12. Ibid.

13. Goodman, op. cit.

14. Berger, op. cit., Lorenzo, op. cit.

15. Edwin Francis Walker, "A Stratified Site at Malaga Cove," *Five Prehistoric Archeological Sites in Los Angeles County* (Los Angeles, 1951), pp. 27-68.

16. Hudson, op. cit.

17. Ibid.

18. Carter, op. cit.

19. Bernice Eastman Johnston, *California's Gabrielino Indians* (Los Angeles, 1962), pp. 1-15. Also Lowell John Bean and Charles R. Smith, "Gabrielino," in Robert T. Heizer, ed., *Handbook of North American Indians: California* (Washington, D.C., 1978), 8:538-49.

20. Johnston, op. cit.

21. William Duncan Strong, *Aboriginal Society in Southern California* (Berkeley, 1929), p. 98.

22. Campbell Grant, "Chumash: Introduction," in Heizer, *Handbook* 8:505-508. Also Johnston, op. cit., pp. 6-12.

23. Chester King and Thomas Blackburn, "Tataviam," in Heizer, *Handbook* 8:535-537.

24. Lowell John Bean, "Cahuilla," in Heizer, *Handbook* 8:575-587.

25. Lowell John Bean and Florence C. Shipek, "Luiseño," in Heizer *Handbook* 8:550-563. Also Johnston, op. cit., 37-74.

26. Katherine Luomala, "Tipai and Ipai," in Heizer, *Handbook* 8:592-609.

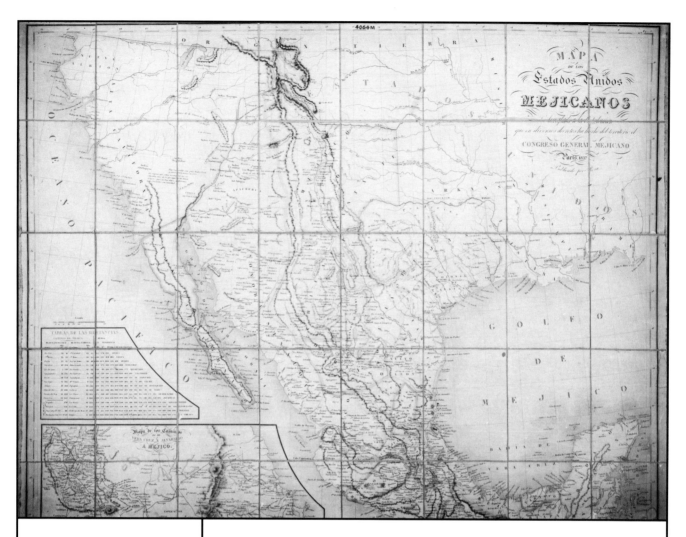

The United States of Mexico, 1837, showing the territorial boundaries established by the Mexican congress. In Alta California Mexican authority actually extended only a hundred miles from the Pacific coast. The central valley was beyond the effective control of Mexican authorities and a refuge for Indians who had resisted conversion.

(Courtesy of the Bancroft Library)

Decree of the Mexican government establishing Los Angeles as the capital of Alta California. 1836.

(Courtesy of Los Angeles County Museum of Natural History)

El Exmo. Sr. Presidente interino de los Estados-Unidos Mexicanos se ha servido dirigirme el decreto que sigue.

„El Presidente interino de los Estados-Unidos Mexicanos, á los habitantes de la República, sabed: Que el Congreso general ha decretado lo siguiente.

„Se erige en ciudad el pueblo de los Angeles de la Alta California, y será para lo sucesivo la Capital de este Territorio =Basilio Arrillaga, diputado presidente.=Antonio Pacheco Leal, presidente del Senado.=Demetrio del Castillo, diputado secretario.=Manuel Miranda, senador secretario.”

Por tanto, mando se imprima, publique, circule, y se le dé el debido cumplimiento. Palacio del Gobierno federal en México, á 23 de Mayo de 1835. =Miguel Barragán.=A D. José Maria Gutierrez de Estrada.”

Y lo comunico á V. para su inteligencia y fines consiguientes.

Dios y libertad. México 23 de Mayo de 1835.

Gutierrez Estrada.

CHAPTER TWO

Early Exploration and the Founding
of Los Angeles

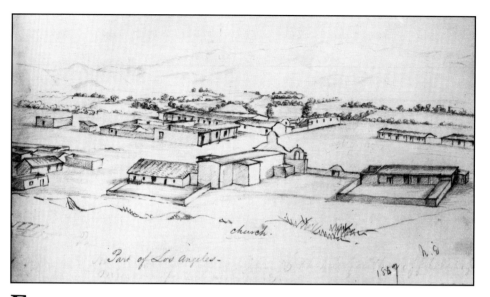

View of the Placita of Los Angeles looking north from Olvera Street. 1847.

(Courtesy of Huntington Library, San Marino, California)

Early Spanish exploration of California marked the beginning of a new period in the history of the Los Angeles basin. From Spain's political perspective, lands throughout Southern California were chiefly symbols of the Crown's influence in the New World. In this light, the settlement of el Pueblo de La Reina de Los Angeles was only one part of an overall colonization strategy. It would also prove to be Spain's last major advance in North America.

Since the initial conquest of central Mexico in the 1520s and despite temporary setbacks and intermittent pauses, military officers and individual settlers had concentrated their energies northward. Enticed by the possibility of better land, richer resources, and further geographic hegemony, these men and women made colonization a reality. Thus, in a broad sense, the city's founding came as a natural extension of Nueva España's (colonial Mexico's) northward expansion.

Directly in the path of this move to the north stood thousands of indigenous people. Their lands were lost and their lives sacrificed in the name of Christ and country. Yet beneath the surface of racial brutality and cultural genocide that typified the colonial period, new and complex relationships were slowly shifting ethnic identification.

Mestizaje—the gradual intermixing of Indian, European, and African people—had already changed the cultural face of early colonial Mexico. Far from simple acculturation to a new language or country, mestizaje was the fundamental transformation of all these peoples into a single and distinct cultural entity. And, as a social phenomenon, it would form the basis of California's ethnic future.

The years between the initial landings of Spanish ships on the coast of Baja and the formal founding of Los Angeles were brutal ones, especially for the Native Americans of Southern California. They were also among the most determinant years in the history of the city and its Mexican community.

EARLY EXPLORATION

The history of Los Angeles would be incomplete without a basic knowledge of Europe's territorial explorations along the Pacific Coast. It would likewise be incomplete without a sense of the society from which the city's first settlers

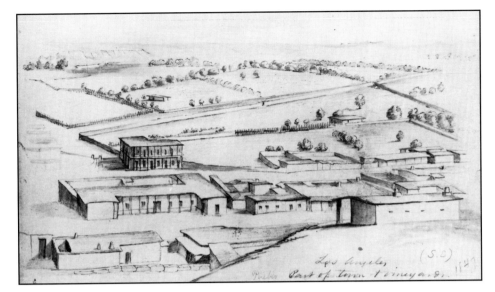

View to the south of the Placita. 1847. The José Antonio Carillo adobe is to the right center, below the two story adobe which housed the offices of Pio Pico, the last Mexican governor.

(Courtesy of Huntington Library, San Marino, California)

were recruited. Colonization of the Mexican northwest began when Hernán Cortés first explored the waters of the Pacific Ocean and the Gulf of California. Then, when the conquests of Niño de Guzmán subjugated Michoacan and Jalisco to the Spanish Crown, the City of San Miguel de Culiacán was founded and the occupation of Sinaloa began.

In 1533, Cortés sent a second sea expedition into the area now called the Peninsula of Baja California. His men returned with tales of what they thought was an island, and the region was named Santa Cruz. It was not until 1539, when the Cortés-sponsored voyage of Francisco de Ulloa sailed to the head of the Gulf of California, that Spanish officials realized that the area was not an island but a peninsula jutting out into the Pacific. The first Europeans to reach what is now the State of California may well have arrived in 1540. It was in that year that Hernando de Alarcón, in command of a support ship of the Coronado expedition, ascended the Colorado River. At the same time, his associate, Melchor Díaz, marched along the Colorado River in present Arizona and probably crossed into California near what is today Blythe.[1]

The first group of Spaniards to reach the Los Angeles region sailed under the command of Portugese-born Captain Juan Rodríguez de Cabrillo. Sent in the service of the Viceroy of Nueva España from the port of Natividad in present Jalisco, this expedition was sent to locate the fabled strait of Anian, a reputed northwest passage from the Atlantic to the Pacific Ocean. Sailing up the west coast of Baja California, Rodríguez de Cabrillo entered the waters off present California on September 28, 1542. On that day, his ships reached a sheltered bay which he called San Miguel. Today, we call it San Diego Bay.[2]

The following month, the expedition reached Catalina Island, where it stopped briefly before sailing to the coasts of the San Pedro and Santa Monica bays. Just off the Los Angeles coastline, Rodríguez de Cabrillo observed smoke rising from the shore and, unaware of the people who lived there, named the bay (probably at San Pedro) the Bay of Smokes. Cabrillo and his crew were the first Spaniards to make contact with Indian people of the Los Angeles area. Anchored off Catalina Island, the explorers were suddenly confronted by a contingent of armed Indians who appeared more than willing to resist their unexpected guests. The Spaniards, however, were able to convince their leery hosts of only peaceful intentions. They exchanged trade goods for food before sailing north.[3]

LOS ANGELES AREA
LAND GRANTS:
RANCHOS AND
PUEBLO LANDS,
1781–1848

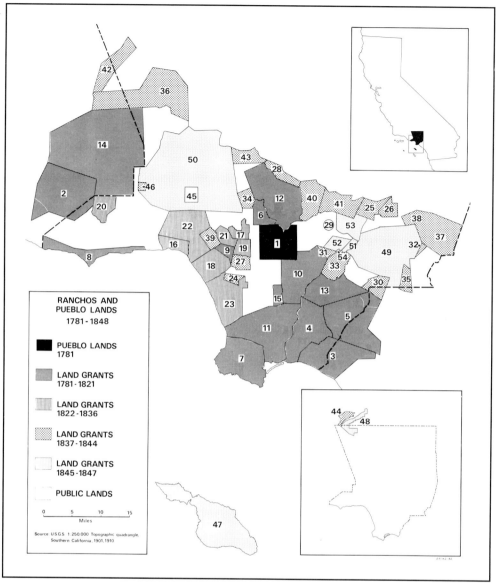

RANCHOS AND
PUEBLO LANDS
1781 - 1848

PUEBLO LANDS
1781

LAND GRANTS
1781 - 1821

LAND GRANTS
1822 - 1836

LAND GRANTS
1837 - 1844

LAND GRANTS
1845 - 1847

PUBLIC LANDS

0   5   10   15
         Miles

Source: U.S.G.S. 1:250,000 Topographic quadrangle,
Southern California, 1901, 1910

*Not Shown on Map: Land
Grants in District/Prefecture
of Los Angeles, Now Within
Adjoining Counties*

	NAME OF LAND GRANT	SIZE IN ACRES	YEAR ESTABLISHED	GRANTEE
I. Granted from 1781–1821:	1. El Pueblo de la Reina de Los Angeles	4 Sq. Leagues, 17,172	1781	Pueblo.
	2. El Conejo	48,672	1802–03	Ygnacio Rodriguez, José Poblanco
	3. Los Alamitos	28,027	1784	José Manuel Nieto
	4. Los Cerritos	27,054	1784	José Manuel Nieto
	5. Los Coyotes	48,806	1784	José Manual Nieto
	6. Los Felis	6,647	1796	José Vicente Feliz
	7. Los Palos Verdes	13,629	1821	José Dolores Sepulveda
	8. Topanga Malibu Sequit	13,316	1804	José Bartolome Tapia
	9. Ricon de Los Bueyes	3,128	1821	Francisco and Secundino Higuera
	10. San Antonio	29,513	1810	Antonio María Lugo
	11. San Pedro	43,119	1784	Juan José Dominguez
	12. San Rafael	36,403	1784	José María Verdugo
	13. Santa Gertrudes	17,602	1784	José Manuel Nieto
	14. Simi	113,009	1795	Patricio, Miguel and Javier Pico Francisco
II. Granted from 1822–1834:	15. Tajuata	3,560	1820	Anastasio Avila
	16. Boca de Santa Mónica	5,657	1828	Ysidro Reyes, Francisco Márquez
	17. La Brea	4,439	1828	Antonio Rocha
	18. La Ballona	13,920	1822	Felipe and Tomás Talamantes, Agustin and Ygnacio Machado
	19. Las Cienegas	4,439	1823	Francisco Avila
	20. Las Vigenes	8,885	1822	Miguel Ortega
	21. San Antonio or Rodeo de las Aguas	4,449	1831	María Rita Valdez de Villa
	22. San Vicente y Santa Mónica	30,260	1828	Francisco Sepulveda
	23. Sausal Redondo	22,459	1822	Antonio Ignacio Avila

	NAME OF LAND GRANT	SIZE IN ACRES	YEAR ESTABLISHED	GRANTEE
III. Granted from 1835-1844:	24. Aguaje de la Centinela	2,219	1844	Ignacio Machado
	25. Azusa (Duarte)	6,596	1841	Andres Duarte
	26. Azusa (Dalton)	4,431	1837	Ignacio Palomares, Ricardo Vejar
	27. Ciénega o Paso de la Tijera	4,481	1843	Vicente Sanchez
	28. La Cañada	5,832	1842	José Del Carmen Lugo
	29. Huerta de Cuati	128	1838	Victoria Reid
	30. La Habra	6,699	1839	Mariano R. Roldan
	31. La Merced	2,364		Maria Casilda Soto
	32. Los Nogales	1,004	1840	José de la Cruz Linares, María de Jesus Garcia
	33. Paso de Bartolo	8,885	1835	Juan Crispin Perez
	34. Providencia	4,064	1843	Vicente de la Ossa
	35. Rincon de la Brea	4,453	1841	Gil Ybarra
	36. San Francisco	48,612	1839	Antonio Del Valle
	37. San José	22,340	1837	Ignacio Palomares
	38. San José (Addition to)	4,431		
	39. San José de Buenos Aires	4,439	1840	Maximo Alanis
	40. San Pascual	13,694	1843	Manuel Garfias
	41. Santa Anita	13,319	1841	Hugo Reid
	42. Temescal	3,560	1843	Francisco Lopez
	43. Tujunga	6,661	1840	Pedro and Francisco Lopez
IV. Granted from 1845-1847:	44. Los Alamos y Agua Caliente	26,626	1846	Francisco Lopez
	45. El Encino	4,461	1845	Vicente de la Ossa, Ramon, Roque and Francisco
	46. El Escorpion	1,110	1845	Odan and Manuel
	47. Isla de Santa Catalina	45,820		Juan María Covarrubias
	48. La Liebre	17,341	1846	José María Flores
	49. La Puente	48,791	1845	John Rowland, William Workman
	50. Ex-Mission San Fernando	116,858	1846	Eulogio de Celis
	51. Potrero de Felipe Lugo	2,042		Felipe Lugo
	52. Potrero Grande	4,432		Juan Matias Sanchez
	53. San Francisquito	8,894	1845	Henry Dalton
	54. Portrero Chico	83		Antonio Valenzuela, Juan Alvitre
ORANGE COUNTY				
I. Granted from 1781-1821:	55. Santiago de Santa Ana	78,941	1809	Antonio Yorba
II. Granted from 1822-1836:	56. Cañon o Cañada de Santa Ana	13,329	1834	Bernardo Yorba
	57. Las Bolsas	33,460	1834	Catarina Ruiz de Nieto
III. Granted from 1837-1844:	58. San Juan Cajón de Santa Ana	35,971	1837	Juan Pacifico Ontiveros
	59. La Bolsa Chica	8,107	1841	Joaquin Ruiz
	60. Trabuco	22,184	1841	Santiago Arguello
	61. Cañada de los Alisos	10,669	1842	José Serrano
	62. Niguel	13,316	1842	Juan Avila
	63. San Joaquin	48,803	1842	José Sepulveda
IV. Granted from 1845-1847:	64. Lomas De Santiago	47,227	1846	Teodosio Yorba
	65. Mission Viejo	46,433	1845	Agustin Olvera
	66. Potreros de San Juan	1,168	1845	John Forester
	67. Boca de la Playa	6,607	1846	Emigido Vejar
SAN BERNARDINO COUNTY				
IV. Granted from 1837-1844:	68. Cucamonga	13,045	1839	Tiburcio Tapia
	69. Muscupiabe	30,145	1839	Juan Bandini
	70. Santa Ana del Chino	22,234	1841	Antonio María Lugo and Isaac Williams
	71. San Bernardino	35,509	1842	José del Carmen Lugo
RIVERSIDE COUNTY				
II. Granted from 1822-1836:	72. Temecula	26,609	1835	José Antonio Estudillo
III. Granted from 1837-1844:	73. Jurupa	33,819	1838	Juan Bandini
	74. El Rincon	4,431	1839	Juan Bandini
	75. San Jacinto Viejo	35,503	1842	José Antonio Estudillo
	76. San Jacinto y San Gorgonio	4,440	1843	Santiago Johnson
	77. La Laguna	13,339	1844	Abel Stearns
	78. Pauba	26,598	1844	Vicente Moraga and Luis Arenas
IV. Granted from 1845-1847:	79. La Sierra	17,774	1846	José Sepulveda
	80. La Sierra	17,787	1846	Bernardo Yorba
	81. Santa Rosa	47,787	1846	Juan Moreno
	82. Sobrante de San Jacinto	48,847	1846	María del Rosario Estudillo de Aguirre
	83. San Jacinto Nuevo y Potrero	48,861	1846	Miguel Pedroreña
KERN COUNTY				
III. Granted from 1837-1844:	84. San Emido	17,710	1842	José Antonio Dominguez
	85. Castac	22,178	1843	José María Covarrubias
	86. El Tejon	97,617	1843	José Antonio Aguirre and Ygnacio del Valle
	87. Los Alamos y Agua	26,626	1843	Pedro C. Carrillo (claim rejected) Francisco Lopez (claim approved)

The next known European visit to the Los Angeles area took place in 1602, when a Spanish expedition led by merchant explorer Sebastián Vizcaino sailed along the Pacific coast in search of safe harbors. At the time, continuous raids by English and Dutch pirates on the Manila galleon made protection of the coastline a military necessity. Ports along the coasts of Mexico and South America were continually threatened and several cargos of precious Asian trade goods had been captured. Vizcaino's assignment was to locate ports from which the Spanish might police their ships and safeguard their trade cargos.

Like Rodríguez de Cabrillo, Vizcaino anchored off Catalina Island. Unlike his predecessor, Vizcaino enjoyed an immediately friendly reception. He and his crew were greeted by Indians who offered them a feast of sardines and fruit and who expressed an interest in trading their goods for European materials. Reports of this expedition describe the people of Catalina as intelligent, attractive, and skilled in fishing and manufacturing utensils and tools. In fact, these reports were so encouraging that, for a brief period after the expedition, Spanish authorities considered colonizing the Alta California coast. But these plans were soon aborted when thoughts turned to the difficulty of supplying remote settlements and to the possibility of piracy by foreign marauders.[4]

It was not until Visitador General José de Gálvez visited Nueva España from 1765 to 1771 that the colonization of Alta California was again given serious consideration. Gálvez, a royal bureaucrat charged with reforming Nueva España's fiscal administration, initiated a thorough reorganization. Part of his program involved expanding and developing the northern frontier provinces of the Viceroyalty. His "Bourbon reforms" also called for the creation of a Comandancia General of the Provincias Internas, by which northern frontier provinces could be systematically defended by a single, unified military command.

Gálvez recommended the colonization of Alta California and urged its diligent defense. He claimed that such an expansion program would prove a long-term investment which would ultimately increase revenues for the Viceroyalty of Nueva España.[5] Although Gálvez did not specifically point to the area's strategic importance vis-á-vis Russian explorations of Alaska or warn against mounting competition from England in the Pacific Northwest, both issues were of concern to Spanish officials, who wanted to secure their country's dominance in western North America. Alta California's potential importance as a middle ground for future trade with Asia also spurred official interest in the Gálvez recommendations. Less significant in terms of military rationale, but of tremendous value in ideological justification for colonization, was the desire of the Franciscan order to open a new missionary province in the upper California area.

In 1768, when the Spanish Ambassador to Russia reported that the Russians were planning to occupy the area around California's Monterey Bay, the King of Spain immediately acted to initiate all of the reform measures. Gálvez himself took charge of preliminary preparations for the early California expedition and by mid-year sailed to Baja California. From central Mexico on the west coast and from Loretto in the south, men and months-worth of supplies were dispatched to San Blas, where ships were being readied to support a land expedition for the following year.

Gálvez wanted the occupation of Alta California to be carried out by a joint land and sea expedition and, so, he authorized the preparation of two land and sea components. The objectives of this two-tiered 1769 expedition were, first, to rediscover and occupy the port of Monterey that had originally been discovered by Vizcaino in 1602 and, second, to establish missions and presidios there and at San Diego. To lead this military enterprise, Gálvez selected the newly appointed governor of Baja California, Lieutenant Colonel Gaspar de Portola, and the recently arrived Franciscan head of a former Jesuit mission at Baja, Father Junípero Serra. Portola was to be the military commander and civil governor of the Californias. Serra was to be the father president of all new missions in the region.[6]

Although both men were considered greenhorns, they were supported by veteran military and naval officers. Their ships, the San Carlos and the San Antonio, were commanded respectively by the experienced Pacific sea captains Vicente Vila and Juan Pérez. Born in Mexico and considered an accomplished veteran of the Baja California frontier presidios, Captain Fernando de Rivera y Moncada was to command the land column of rugged presidial troops called *soldados de cuero* (leather jackets) after the thick uniforms they wore as protection against arrows. Twelve years later, Rivera y Moncada was to play a primary role in the founding of Los Angeles.

Included in the expedition, and under the command of Lieutenant Pedro Fages, were 25 soldiers from the newly arrived Spanish regiment, Voluntarios de Cataluña, a small contingent of Franciscan missionaries, a dozen artisans, and about 60 christianized Baja California Indians.

After many difficulties, including bitter disputes between Portola and Serra, the expedition accomplished its two primary objectives: to occupy the Port of Monterey and establish Franciscan missions there and in San Diego. It was during the course of long marches by land from San Diego to the vicinity of Monterey that the Los Angeles area was first examined in some detail. Father Juan Crespi, a Franciscan who accompanied Portola on the march to resettle Monterey, described the area through which they journeyed as a promising area for future occupation. In his written narrative reporting the progress of the expedition, Crespi wrote:

> *Wednesday, August 2, 1769.* We set out from the valley [the San Gabriel Valley] in the morning and followed the same plain in a westerly direction. After traveling about a league and a half through a pass between low hills, we entered a very spacious valley [the Los Angeles Basin], well grown with cotton woods and alders, among which ran a beautiful river from the north-north-west, and then, doubling the point of a steep hill, it went on afterwards to the south [later site of the Pueblo]. Toward the north-northeast there is another river bed [the Arroyo Seco] which forms a spacious watercourse, but we found it dry. This bed unites with that of the river giving a clear indication of great floods in the rainy season, for we saw that it has many trunks of trees on the banks. We halted not very far from the river which we named the Porciuncula [the Los Angeles River]. Here we felt three consecutive earthquakes in the afternoon and in the night. We must have traveled about three leagues today. This plain where the river runs is very extensive. It has good land for planting all kinds of grain and seeds, and the most suitable site for a mission, for it has all the requisites for a large settlement. As soon as we arrived about eight heathen from a good village came out to visit us; they live in this delightful place among the trees on the river [probably Yangna]. They presented us with some baskets of pinole made from seeds of sage and other grasses. Their chief brought some strings of beads made of shells, and they threw us three handfuls of them. Some of the old men were smoking pipes well made of baked clay and they puffed at three mouthfuls of smoke. We gave them a little tobacco and glass beads, and they went away well pleased.

> *Thursday, August 3, 1769.* At half past six we left the camp and forded the Porciuncula River, which runs down the valley, flowing through it from the

These Diegueños, as other Indians, adopted aspects of Mexican culture, language, religion, and dress and many intermarried and assimilated into the Mexican population. 1851.

(Courtesy of UCLA Research Library)

Yuman Indians.

(Courtesy of UCLA Research Library)

mountains to the plain. After crossing the river we entered a large vineyard of wild grapes and an infinity of rosebushes in full bloom, all the soil is black and loamy, and is capable of producing every kind of grain and fruit which may be planted. We went west, and continually over good land well covered with grass. After traveling about half a league we came to the village of this region, the people of which, on seeing us, came out into the road. As they drew near us they began to howl like wolves; they greeted us and wished to give us seeds, but as we had nothing at hand in which to carry them we did not accept them. Seeing this they threw some handfuls of them on the ground and the rest in the air. We traveled over another plain for three hours, during which we must have gone as many leagues. In the same plain we came across a grove of very large alders, high and thick, from which flows a stream of water about a buey in depth. The banks were grassy and covered with fragrant herbs and watercress. The water flowed afterwards in a deep channel toward the southeast. All the land that we saw this morning seemed admirable to us. We pitched camp near the water. This afternoon we felt new earthquakes, the continuation of which astonishes us. We judge that in the mountains that run to the west in front of us there are some volcanoes, for there are many signs on the road that stretches between the Porciuncula River and the Spring of the Alders, for the explorers saw some large marshes of a certain substance like pitch; they were boiling and bubbling, and the pitch came out mixed with an abundance of water. They noticed that the water runs to one side and the pitch to the other, and there is such an abundance of it that would serve to caulk many ships. This place where we stopped is called the spring of the alders of San Estevan.

Friday, August 4, 1769. At half past six in the morning we set out from the camp, following the plain to the northwest. At a quarter of a league we came to a little valley between some small hills and continued over plains of level land, very black and with much pasturage. After two hours travel, during which we must have covered about two leagues, we stopped at the watering place, which consists of two little springs that rise at the foot of a higher mesa. From each of the two springs runs a small stream of water which is soon absorbed; they are both full of watercress and innumerable bushes of castillian roses. We made camp near the springs, where we found a good village of very friendly and docile Indians, who as soon as we arrived, came to visit us, bringing their present of baskets of sage and other seeds, small round nuts with a hard shell, and large and very sweet acorns. They made me a present of some strings of beads with white and red shells which resemble coral, though not very fine; we reciprocated with glass beads. I understood that they were asking us if we were going to stay, and I said that we were going farther on. I called this place San Gregorio, but to the soldiers the spot is known as the springs of El Berrendo, because they caught a deer alive there, it having a leg broken the preceding afternoon by a shot fired by one of the volunteer soldiers, who could not overtake it. The water is in a hollow surrounded by low hills not far from the sea.[7]

INITIAL MOVES

The potential of the Los Angeles region as a promising site for future missions and ultimately as a major town was readily noted by Father Crespi and his superiors. Between 1769 and 1770, while the presidios of Monterey and San Diego as well as the missions of San Diego and San Carlos de Borromeo de Carmelo were being founded, civil and religious authorities planned for the settlement of a chain of missions along the Alta California coast. Their plans called for at least one mission in the Los Angeles area.

By this time, the mission was a well-established institution in most Spanish colonies and was viewed even by civil authorities as an important element of frontier settlement. While the primary rationale for the mission system was salvation of heathen souls, Franciscan-run frontier centers also served more earthly objectives: they effectively concentrated and contained potentially hostile Indian people in an environment of social indoctrination and acculturation. What's more, they allowed for the formation, training and control of a relatively large Indian labor force capable of producing foodstuffs, materials, and finished products for official purposes. From the perspective of colonial administrators, the ultimate goal of missionization was the incorporation of Indians into colonial society and, ultimately, the conversion of the missions into civil towns.[8]

For their part, Indians saw the missions as places where they could practice adapted religious ceremonies and social activities and work toward the special grace and everlasting life that Christianity promised. Many tribes also sought the opportunity to acquire new material goods (such as iron tools), agricultural skills, regular meals, and new food stuffs (such as tortillas, beans, fruit, and candies).

When priestly persuasion and material enticements failed to attract willing converts, the threat or actual use of military coercion forced many Indian villages to relocate. This *congregación y reducción* (congregation and reduction) policy forcibly confined hundreds of California Indians at missions or other locations where they could be most easily controlled. Although information records are sketchy, there is some evidence to suggest that troops forcibly moved Los Angeles area villages to mission San Gabriel. As described many years later by ranchero Hugo Reid:

So taking an Indian as guide, part of the soldiers or servants proceeded on expeditions after converts. On one occasion they went as far as the present Rancho del Chino, where they tied and whipped every man, woman and child in the lodge, and drove part of them back with them. On the road they did the same with those of the lodge at San Jose. On arriving home the men were instructed to throw their bows and arrows at the feet of the Priest, and make due submission. The infants were then baptized, as were also all children under eight years of age; the former were left with their mothers, the latter kept apart from all communications with their parents. The consequence was, first the women consented to the rite and received it, for the love they bore their offspring; and finally the males gave way for the purpose of enjoying once more, the society of wife and family. Marriage was then performed, and so this contaminated race, in their own sight and that of their kindred, became followers of Christ.[9]

First founded in September 1771, Mission San Gabriel was moved to its present location in 1774.[10] By the end of the decade, California's Franciscan missionaries, along with their soldier guards, had successfully relocated a population of several hundred Indians to the site. Under the auspices of their Franciscan padres, these *neophytes* (converts)—as Indians living at the missions were called to distinguish them from their *gentile* (unconverted) kinsmen —followed a strict schedule of work and religious indoctrination. As a result, and in spite of occasional violent outbreaks, Mission San Gabriel soon became the most productive mission in Alta California. With a 1774 yield of 2,000 bushels of maize, only Mission San Luis Rey could boast as productive a congregation.[11]

Although Indian missions were an essential component of Spanish colonization, Nueva España reflected its New World power in other institutions as well. *Presidios* (military forts), *pueblos* (civilian towns), and *Real de Minas* (mining districts) all played vital roles in the northward expansion of colonial Mexico. The presence, absence, relative importance, and specific characteristics of these institutional forms varied from region to region according to actual situations. As was the case with missionization, the motivation for each of these settlements was unique. Rumors of mineral wealth and, sometimes, its actual discovery spurred many settlements, as did the need to expand markets for livestock grazing land and agricultural production. And, as always, concern for the strategic defense of the Spanish Empire against hostile European powers pushed the frontier further north into California.

By the late 1770s, the northern region of Mexico was a land marked by a combination of these small settlements. In fact, continual colonization had by then created three major north-south regions: Texas, Tamaulipas, Coahuila, and Nuevo Leon; New Mexico, Chihuahua, and Durango; Alta California, Baja California, Sonora, and Sinaloa. In all of these regions, the southernmost provinces had been settled first and served as bases from which groups moved north in search of a better life.

Essential to the ultimate founding of Los Angeles were the provinces of Sinaloa (first colonized in the 1530s) and Sonora (initially settled in the 1620s). Unified in 1733 as the Gobernación de Sonora y Sinaloa, these two areas contained several historic subregions. Among them were the *Chiametla*, including the towns of Rosario and Matzatlán; *Culiacán*, around the city of Culiacán —the present capital of the State of Sinaloa; *Sinaloa*, incorporating the towns of El Fuerte, Alamos, and Sinaloa; *Ostimuri* including the geographical area between the Mayo and Yaqui rivers; and *Sonora*, encompassing most of present Sonora and the Pimeria Alta (now the southern part of Arizona).[12]

Most settlers of Alta California came from Sonora or Sinaloa. So it is not surprising that, even into the nineteenth century, Californians referred to these Mexican states as *la madre patria* (motherland). Nor is it hard to understand why the basic social and cultural patterns of Los Angeles mirrored the place from which its early inhabitants had come. Many of these *pobladores* (settlers) were, in part, the descendants of Sinaloa Indians who had culturally assimilated and ethnically intermixed into the provinces' growing Spanish-speaking mestizo society. In short, they were a mixed population that was continually amalgamating itself into a community of central Mexican Indians, Europeans, and Africans who had settled in the region.

By 1769, when settlement of Alta California began in earnest, Sinaloa had long since ceased to be considered a frontier area. Sonora, however, was still characterized by a large and only partially subjugated Indian population that frequently raided small camps. The Apache, who had only recently been forced west of New Mexico by the Comanches, were a constant threat to settlements throughout the province and effectively rendered the Sonora frontier, the *tierra adentro* (back country), a *tierra de guerra* (land of warfare), where presidial troops, miners, and isolated settlers regularly clashed with defiant Indian raiders.

Nevertheless, Sonora as well as Sinaloa had developed certain social and economic stratifications. Both regions reflected this divison in the widening gap between the small group of provincial elite (wealthy mineowners, landowners, merchants, and officials) and the already burgeoning lower classes. In Sinaloa, especially, the chances for economic and social advancement were limited. During this period Sinaloa was considered a *despoblado* (a depopulated area). In modern terms, it would be called an "economically depressed region." For *jornaleros* (agricultural laborers) and *labradores* (small farmers, miners, and artisans), the wild frontier had ceased to be a land of expanding opportunity. In fact, the ownership of even a small farm was beyond the reach of the working classes.[13]

In contrast to these areas of concentrated poverty, the *frontera* (frontier) offered limitless possibility. To those willing to work hard, Sonora and the northern settlement promised high wages and the chance to own or, at least, to use land. For many young men, enlistment in a company of presidial soldiers meant a regular salary and, perhaps, a future promotion to corporal or sergeant. Moreover, it meant the possibility of a small land grant upon retirement. Of course, the risks were correspondingly great, as was the reluctance of people to leave their birthplace. But these were the hard choices that faced the settlers of Alta California and Los Angeles, recruited as they were from among the laboring class of western Mexico.

THE FOUNDING OF LOS ANGELES

Initial plans for the founding of San José, Los Angeles, and Santa Barbara, including their actual location sites, were made by Felipe de Neve, governor of the Californias and colonel in the Spanish army. A European Spaniard, de Neve was the third governor of Baja and Alta California but the first to reside in Monterey.[14]

Highly respected for his administrative skill, de Neve was recognized by his superiors (Viceroy Bucareli and the commandant general of the Interior Provinces, Teodoro de la Croix) as an exceptional military man and a shrewd politician. So when he approached the viceroy to suggest a new agricultural settlement in northern Baja California, he was immediately ordered to exchange military posts with his lieutenant governor, the veteran Fernando de Rivera y Moncada. In 1777, de Neve transferred to Monterey and Rivera y Moncada left for Loreto in Baja California. Viceroy Bucareli told de Neve to identify possible sites for his proposed agricultural settlements—a task the governor was more than willing to undertake. In the course of his duties, he selected the future sites of San José, Los Angeles, and Santa Barbara. His recommendation was that they be settled as two civil pueblos and one new presidio.

In November 1777, de Neve acted on his own initiative to found the first civil settlement in Alta California, San José de Guadalupe. This action was retroactively approved by both the viceroy and commandant general. In planning the new settlements, de Neve was able to draw from more than two centuries worth of successful and failed colonization efforts and from a large body of existing colonial law. Furthermore, because his superiors so trusted in his ability, de Neve was able to write the specific regulations to govern his Alta California settlement sites. In fact, the viceroy ordered him to draft suggestions for a new set of laws that might ultimately govern all of California.

It was this set of suggestions (with slight modification and some additions) that was adopted in October 1781 as the new "Reglamento y instrucción para el gobierno de la provincia de Californias." All of this is to say that de Neve enjoyed the right to directly control the early California pueblos and, consequently, was able to tailor them specifically after his own political sensibilities. Those sensibilities would prove to have a long-lasting influence in the area. This one man's work formed the foundation of subsequent regulations governing the operation of civil settlements and the granting of land to the region's founding pobladores.[15]

In December 1779, Viceroy Bucareli and Commandant General de la Croix officially approved de Neve's proposal for the founding of Los Angeles and Santa Barbara. On December 27, 1779, La Croix wrote to Don Fernando de Rivera y Moncada, instructing him to take charge of the recruitment of colonists for both settlements. Rivera y Moncada's orders called for him to proceed directly to Arizpe, capital of the Internal Provinces, where he would meet with the commandant general to discuss the details of his assignment. Meanwhile, de Neve received orders to prepare for arrival of settlers and new presidial recruits.

The Vaquero.

At their meeting in Arizpe, La Croix told Rivera y Moncada to recruit 24 settlers and their families. Also needed were 59 presidial recruits, 25 of whom would fill posts being vacated in Sonora by soldiers sent to Alta California, and 34 of whom were to serve in the new Alta California presidios. Rivera y Moncada was to purchase nearly 1,000 head of livestock, including remounts for the military troops and livestock to be given to each settler. To help him carry out the task, he was assigned several veteran officers (a number of non-commissioned officers and 25 veteran soldiers). He was also instructed to draw upon the treasury of the Internal Provinces at Alamos for all necessary funds.[16]

At this meeting, the commandant general warned the lieutenant governor that his task might be made more difficult by widespread rumors concerning the conditions of service in Alta California. La Croix made it clear that he was not to exaggerate the benefits of the northern military post or promise potential settlers more than they might realistically hope to receive. Rivera y Moncada was to be precise and detailed in explaining both the benefits and liabilities of a new life in Alta California.

He was also informed of the desired—in fact, required—qualifications for pobladores and soldiers. All pobladores were to be men and heads of families. They were to be experienced farmers or agricultural laborers skilled in farming techniques and irrigation. In the words of La Croix, "La cabeza o padre de cada familia ha de ser hombre de campo, labrador de ejercicio, sano, robusto, y sin conocido vicio o defecto. . . ." ("the father or head of each family must be a man of the field, a hard working farmer, sane, robust, and without known vices or defects. . . .").[17] Soldiers also were to be married men and were to meet all the standards imposed on pobladores. Moreover, they were to possess enough strength and endurance to meet the extra hardships of service on the frontera.

The Patron
(Courtesy of the Bancroft Library)

The battle of San Pasqual
(1846) during the Mexican-
United States war. The
Mexican militia, composed of
eighty vaqueros and rancheros,
vanquished 160 United States
cavalrymen in the bloodiest
battle in California history.
Mexican forces were
commanded by Don Andres
Pico.

(Courtesy of the Bancroft Library)

Lassoing the steer

(Courtesy of the Bancroft Library)

Several skilled artisans—all of whom met the strict qualifications—were recruited. Among them, there was one mason; a carpenter who could make *yugos* (yokes), *arados* (ploughs), *rodadas* (cart wheels), and *carretas* (carts); and a blacksmith skilled in making *rejas* (ploughshares), *azadones* (pickaxes), *hachas* (axes), and *barras* (crowbars).

Once in Alta California, each poblador was to receive a house lot, two *suertes* (fields) of irrigable land and two suertes of dry land. Furthermore, each was to have use of common pueblo lands which were to be set aside for grazing and storage of raw materials, such as firewood. From the date of enlistment, each man was to receive ten pesos a month plus regular rations for himself and his family for a full three-year period. All were entitled to tools, clothing, and a substantial number of livestock—including two cows, two oxen, two ewes, two goats, two horses, three mares, and one mule. The three-year salary, livestock, and land were to be considered a loan payable in agricultural produce and due within ten years. For their part, all settlers were to remain in Alta California for at least ten years, working their farm or practicing their skilled trade.[18]

Even with these inducements, which at the time were impressive, Captain Rivera y Moncada found it difficult to recruit the specified number of willing settlers. Alta California was far away, even further than the frontiers of Sonora and Sinaloa. Furthermore, there was only one direct land route into the area and that was across the Sonora Desert—through the Colorado River and over the Mojave Desert. Opened by Colonel Juan Bautista de Anza in 1777, this route was considered too strenuous for small children and thus discouraged many potential pobladores.

There were other problems. Even to the inhabitants of the frontier, a move to Alta California seemed impetuous. Communication in the area was extremely complicated and irregular, even for top military officials. Most people feared that once they had settled so far north, they would be cut off from virtually all relations with the outside world and would probably never return to the lower province. And, to add more fuel to a fire of reticence, there were widespread rumors (in part true) that soldiers already stationed in Alta California were not receiving the full amount of their promised pay.

It was against all these odds that, in 1780, Captain Rivera y Moncada began looking for potential settlers. Traveling south, toward the lower provinces, he learned that the number of settlers from Sonora and other internal provinces were to be kept to a minimum because these settlements were themselves underpopulated frontier areas from which previous expeditions had already drawn too many recruits. Instead, his instructions called for recruits from the *tierra de afuera* ("the land beyond"), the better-settled provinces of central Mexico. The captain was ordered to go well beyond the boundary of the Provincias Internas and, if necessary, to enlist pobladores and military recruits from as far away as the city of Guadalajara.[19]

Visiting the towns of Alamos, Villa de Fuerte, Villa de Sinaloa and Culiacán, Rivera y Moncada managed to gather together 45 soldiers and seven settlers by August 1, 1780. By December, he had traveled through southern Sinaloa—including Mazatlán and the mining town of Rosario in the Chiametla—and had recruited the desired number of soldiers. But he still could claim only 14 settlers, two of whom deserted before the expedition ever left the area.

Far short of their anticipated quota, he and his superiors decided against any further recruitment effort. Concerned about the cost of continuing to feed the waiting expedition members, they chose to proceed with the long march north toward Alta California.[20]

The entire expedition of settlers, soldiers, livestock, and supplies was assembled at Alamos, where Rivera y Moncada divided it into two smaller groups. The first contingent of all 12 pobladores and their families along with an escort of 17 soldiers was handed over to *Alfaréz* (Ensign) José de Zúñiga and Alfaréz Ramón Laso de la Vega. The group left on February 2, 1781 and headed for the coast, where they were met by *lanchas* (launches) that sailed them to Loreto. From there, they were to march overland to the presidio at San Diego and then on to San Gabriel.

The second group, commanded by Captain Rivera y Moncada himself, remained at Alamos until April. It included 42 soldiers, their families, and a large herd of nearly 1,000 horses, cattle, mules, goats, sheep, and other livestock. Because they were taking so many animals with them, these recruits were ordered to follow the arduous overland route opened by Juan Bautista de Anza.[21]

OF STRENGTH AND COURAGE

In terms of economic background, the 23 adults and 21 children who made up this first expedition were representative of the laboring class majority popula-

Rodeo at the Mission San Gabriel. *(Courtesy of California State Library)*

Secularization decree of the Alta California missions. 1833. Established to centralize, convert and assimilate local Indians, the missions were secularized in the 19th century after a period of intense political debate.

(Courtesy of Seaver Center for Western History Research, Natural History Museum of Los Angeles County)

MINISTERIO DE JUSTICIA

Y

NEGOCIOS ECLESIASTICOS.

El Exmo. Sr. Vice-Presidente de los Estados-Unidos Mexicanos se ha servido dirigirme el decreto que sigue.

„El Vice-Presidente de los Estados-Unidos Mexicanos, en ejercicio del Supremo Poder Ejecutivo, á los habitantes de la República, sabed: Que el Congreso general ha decretado lo siguiente.

Art. 1.º „El Gobierno procederá á secularizar las misiones de la Alta y Baja California.

2.º En cada una de las dichas misiones se establecerá una Parroquia servida por un Párroco del clero secular, con la dotacion de dos mil hasta dos mil y quinientos pesos anuales á juicio del Gobierno.

3.º Estos Curas párrocos no cobrarán ni percibirán derecho alguno en razon de casamientos, bautismos, entierros, ni bajo otra cualquiera denominacion. En cuanto á derechos de pompa, podrán percibir los que se espresen terminantemente en el Arancel que se formará con este objeto á la mayor brevedad por el Reverendo Obispo de aquella Diócesis, y aprobará el Supremo Gobierno.

4.º Se destinan para Parroquias las iglesias que han servido en cada mision, con los vasos sagrados, ornamentos y demás enseres que hoy tiene cada una, y además las piezas anexas á la misma iglesia que á juicio del Gobierno estime necesarias para el mas decente uso de la misma Parroquia.

5.º Para cada Parroquia, el Gobierno mandará construir un campo santo fuera de la poblacion.

6.º Se asignan quinientos pesos anuales para dotacion del culto y sirvientes de cada Parroquia.

7.º De los edificios pertenecientes á cada mision, se destinará el mas á propósito para la habitacion del Cura, agregándole terreno que no pase de doscientas varas en cuadro, y los restantes se adjudicarán especialmente para casa de Ayuntamiento, escuelas de primeras letras, establecimientos públicos, y talleres.

8.º Para proveer pronta y eficazmente á las necesidades espirituales de ambas Californias, se establece en la Capital de la Alta un Vicario foraneo que estienda su jurisdiccion á los dos Territorios; y el Reverendo Diocesano le conferirá las facultades correspondientes, con toda la amplitud que ser pueda.

9.º Por dotacion de esta Vicaría se asignarán tres mil pesos, siendo de la obligacion del Vicario todo su despacho, sin exijir bajo ningun título ni pretesto, ni aun para el papel, derecho alguno.

10. Si por cualquier motivo sirviere el Cura párroco de la Capital ó de otra Parroquia de aquellos Distritos esta Vicaría, se le abonarán mil quinientos pesos anuales á mas de la dotacion de su Curato.

11. No podrá introducirse costumbre alguna que precise á los habitantes de las Californias á hacer oblaciones por piadosas que sean,

aunque se digan necesarias; y ni el tiempo ni la voluntad de los mismos ciudadanos puede darles fuerza y virtud alguna.

12. El Gobierno cuidará eficazmente de que el Reverendo Diocesano concurra por su parte á llenar los objetos de esta ley.

13. Nombrados que sean los nuevos Párrocos, les proporcionará el Supremo Gobierno gratuitamente su trasporte por mar con sus familias, y además para su viage por tierra podrá dar á cada uno de cuatrocientos á ochocientos pesos, segun la distancia y la familia que lleve.

14. El Gobierno costeará el trasporte á los religiosos misioneros que vuelvan, y para que lo hagan cómodo por tierra hasta su colegio ó convento, podrá dar á cada uno de doscientos á trescientos pesos, y á su juicio lo que fuere necesario para que salgan de la República los que no han jurado la independencia.

15. El Supremo Gobierno llenará los gastos comprendidos en esta ley, de los productos de las fincas, capitales y rentas que se reconocen actualmente por fondo piadoso de misiones de Californias — Manuel R. Veramendi, presidente de la Cámara de Diputados.—J. M. Troncoso, presidente senador.—Ignacio Alvarado, diputado secretario.—Antonio Pacheco Leal, senador secretario."

Por tanto, mando se imprima, publique, circule, y se le dé el debido cumplimiento. Palacio del Gobierno federal en México á 17 de Agosto de 1833.— *Valentin Gomez Farías.*—Al Secretario del despacho de Justicia y Negocios eclesiásticos."

Y lo comunico á V. para su inteligencia y fines consiguientes. Dios y libertad, México 17 de Agosto de 1833.

Por ausencia del Exmo. Sr. Secretario del Despacho,

Joaquin de Iturbide.

---

tion of Mexico's northwestern frontier provinces. Contrary to historical narratives that depict these founding settlers of Los Angeles as inept colonists, the men and women who left that February in 1781 for Alta California were, with only one exception, *hombres y mujeres de ejercicio* (hard working men and women). The single exception was a European Spaniard, José de Velesco y Lara, who was a bigamist and fugitive from the law.

Most of Los Angeles' founding settlers were experienced farmers, laborers, or mine workers. Two are known to have been artisans: one a *sastre* (tailor) and the other an *armador* (gunsmith). Later *padrones* (census records), however, would suggest that several members of the expedition had some artisan skills, listing among the group a mason and a carpenter.

Ethnically, the group was reflective of Sonora and Sinaloa, the two areas from which most of the recruits had come. Eight of the 23 adults were Indian. Ten were of African descent, two being *negros* (blacks) and eight being mulattos. Records show, however that one of the black settlers, Luis Quintero, was actually of mixed ancestry. His father had been a black slave and his mother was an Indian from Alamos. Only one recruit had been born in Spain but a second was listed as an *español americano* (someone of Spanish descent born in Mexico). One settler was *mestizo* (a person of mixed Spanish and Indian descent). One was a *coyota* (a term for someone of either mestizo and Indian background or of mulatto and Indian descent). One person was a *chino* (literally "Chinese," this term sometimes meant a person of mixed black and Indian descent). This individual, Antonio Miranda Rodríguez, was probably Filipino because he had been born in Manila, the capital of the then Spanish colony of the Philippines.[22] Out of the expedition's 21 children, 19 were of racially mixed descent. The other two were full-blooded Indians.

In short, the background of these founding pobladores reflects the dynamic reality of ethnic mixture that was resulting from colonization. Throughout Nueva España, and especially in California, a new racial and cultural group was coming into existence. And from that group, a dominant mestizo majority would soon emerge to shape the destiny of Los Angeles.

Actual accounts of the founding of Los Angeles have always varied. In recent years, new and sometimes even conflicting information has been added on to records of those early years of the pueblo's existence. For example, most nineteenth and twentieth century accounts state that the city was founded on September 4, 1781, with Governor Felipe de Neve and a soldier escort in attendance. It was also long assumed that the entire expedition arrived at Mission San Gabriel several weeks before and that a formal ceremony and mass were held at the site on that particular date. The latest evidence shows that each of these assumptions was incorrect.

Particularly important in correcting the errors is research from Dr. Harry Kelsey of the Los Angeles County Museum of Natural History. According to Dr. Kelsey, Governor De Neve first approached Gabrielino Indians living in Yangna and Yabit in early 1781. His aim was to ensure peaceful and perhaps even friendly relations between the tribe and the settlement's new inhabitants. In the spring of that year, De Neve arranged for three dozen Gabrielinos to be baptized and personally stood as *padrino* (godfather) for 12 Indian converts. He further sponsored the baptism and remarriage of a Gabrielino couple who were remarried, Felipe and Phelipa de Neve. According to Kelsey, the governor was probably grooming the couple to serve as a nucleus for a series of Christian Indian settlements that he wanted to establish throughout the area. Because he was replaced the following year by Pedro de Fages, these plans were never realized.[23]

Woman grinding corn on a metate.

It also appears that not all of the expedition settlers left Alamos on February 2, 1781. At least three of them left several days later and probably joined their fellow pobladores on the coast prior to leaving for Baja California. Historians have also learned that after their arrival in Baja, many of the settlers developed smallpox and were unable to travel. On March 12, 1781, Alfaréz Laso de la Vega escorted, by ship, the healthier members of the expedition up the coast of the Gulf of California to Bahia de San Luis. From there, he marched them overland to San Diego and then San Gabriel.

Alfaréz Zúñiga followed later with all the others, except for Antonio Miranda Rodríguez and his daughter, who were still too ill to travel. These two remained in Loretto and although Miranda Rodríguez's land was held for him, he and his daughter never settled in Los Angeles. When he finally arrived in Alta California, authorities learned that he was a skilled gunsmith and he was reassigned to the presidio at Santa Barbara in 1782.

The people traveling with Alfaréz Laso de la Vega arrived at Mission San Gabriel Arcángel on June 9, 1781. The group included Antonio Mesa and three other families whose names were not recorded. It appears that all these families, or at least the men from each of them, started working and living in the pueblo site even before the end of June 1781. The second group of settlers arrived in mid-July. Among this group were José de Velesco y Lara, Luis Quintero, and their families, who probably joined the others at the camp.

The Fiesta depicting the Mexican period.

(Courtesy of Seaver Center for Western History Research, Natural History Museum of Los Angeles County)

The last group of pobladores to recover from smallpox arrived at San Gabriel under the command of Alfaréz Zúñiga on August 18, 1781. This last contingent included Manual Camero and Basilio Rosas and their families. Because of fear that they might still spread infection, this entire group was quarantined about two miles south of the mission. But by the end of the month, most—if not all—of the settlers and their families were living and working at the site of the pueblo. It appears that Governor De Neve had already ordered the marking off of house lots and agricultural fields outside the town site. In a letter to Teodoro de la Croix, dated October 29, 1781, De Neve reported:

> ". . . That having arrived at this Mission on August 18, the lieutenant José Zúñiga provided that the recruits, pobladores, and families which he brought under his charge, should camp at a distance of one league (from the mission) because of the fact that some children among the party had but recently recovered from the smallpox. From (their camp) they went to establish themselves on the ground where they are founding the pueblo of Los Angeles, and now having finished the Zanja madre are continuing with building their houses and also corrals for their stock. The latter has not as yet been distributed because they are concentrating their efforts on finishing the pueblo and when it is completed, they begin to plow the fields for the sowing of the wheat. That to this pueblo there arrived but eleven pobladores, and of these eight alone (are) of any use."[24]

The actual number of Los Angeles founders may also have been somewhat larger than once assumed. A military escort composed of four soldiers and their families probably accompanied the pobladores to the pueblo site and may have been among the original residents of the community. Included in this escort were Vicente Feliz, acting corporal and known resident of Los Angeles as of 1785. A veteran of the De Anza expedition in 1776, Feliz had been accompanied by his wife, but she died in childbirth before reaching Alta California, leaving him with an infant son. He and a command of three other veteran soldiers were already in Alta California by the time the expedition parties arrived. These men were privates Roque Jacinto de Cota, Antonio Cota, and Francisco Salvador Lugo, father of the later prominent ranchero, Don Antonio María Lugo.[25]

Another point of controversy concerns the original name of Los Angeles. The full name has been variously cited as "El Pueblo de Nuestra Señora la Reina de Los Angeles de Porciuncula" and/or "El Pueblo de Nuestra Señora la Reina de Los Angeles." However, letters and reports from Governor De Neve, Commandant General La Croix, and Viceroy Bucareli all refer to "El Pueblo de La Reina de Los Angeles." So the phrase, *Nuestra Señora* and the early name of the Los Angeles river, the *Porciuncula* (named after the site of a church in Italy beloved by Saint Francis of Asisi, founder of the Franciscan order), were never part of the pueblo's official or popular names.[26]

As far as can be determined from existing information, the September 4, 1781, foundation date of El Pueblo de la Reina de Los Angeles was fairly arbitrary. Although it is definitely the establishment date indicated by Governor De Neve in all legal documents and community reports, there is no evidence to suggest that any formal ceremony (secular or religious) took place on September 4th. Nor is there proof that the governor, clergy, or a military escort were present in the pueblo on that date. In hindsight, it seems reasonable to suppose that military men and their families were actually at the

Dancing on the veranda.

(Courtesy of Seaver Center for Western History Research, Natural History Museum of Los Angeles County)

site weeks or months before this date because later documentation refers to Feliz and other officers as long-term, permanent residents of the pueblo.

MORE THAN A PUEBLO

Impressive as these expeditions were, and despite their historic significance to the Los Angeles area, the small pueblo that was to settle deep in the heart of the basin would remain surrounded by an overwhelming majority of Indians for many years. The social and cultural adjustments that still lay before these people as of 1781 would slowly yet radically transform them all. Over time, these adjustments would flower into the ethnic intricacies that remain a part of the city to this day.

The founders of Los Angeles, the second civilian settlement in Alta California, displayed an unerring determination to settle the area. A strange and fascinating clarity of purpose shines through the bold actions of many early Californians. From Felipe de Neve, who conceived the initial plans for transporting political and social structures from colonial Mexico into Alta California; to Fernando de Rivera y Moncada, who struggled against almost insurmountable odds to recruit qualified settlers from among the Spanish empire's outposts; to the many individual pobladores, who chose to gamble on the journey north, Southern California was infused with the lifeblood of men and women who made settlement a reality.

It is equally true that this Spanish/Mexican sense of mission caused many officials to blind themselves to the consequences of their actions. Inarguably, their fervent sense of duty led to the brutal enslavement of thousands of Indian peoples throughout California.

Without ceremony, the founders of Los Angeles simply put out their roots and began building a new life for themselves and their children out of three-years' rations and a lack of better options. In the end, their remote links to Spain were gone. They were alone in a strange land. The nature of what they created is the result of tremendously complex relationships between race, ethnicity, and culture.

NOTES

1. Charles E. Chapman, *A History of California: The Spanish Period* (New York, 1921), pp. 43-69.

2. Herbert E. Bolton, *Spanish Exploration in the Southwest, 1542-1706* (New York, 1916).

3. Ibid.

4. Michael Mathes, *Viscaino and Spanish Expansion in the Pacific Ocean, 1580-1630* (San Francisco, 1968). Also Bolton, op. cit., and Chapman, op. cit. pp. 133-34.

5. Chapman, op. cit., pp. 207-231.

6. Ibid., pp. 216-231. Herbert E. Bolton, translator, *Fray Juan Crespi, Missionary Explorer on the Pacific Coast, 1769-1774* (Berkeley, 1927). Ray Brades, translator, *The Costano Narrative of the Portola Expedition* (Newhall, 1970). Herbert H. Bolton, ed., *Fray Francisco Palou. Historical Memoirs of New California* (Berkeley, 1926).

7. Bolton, *Fray Juan Crespi*, pp. 146-150.

8. For accounts of the Jesuit Missions of Sonora and Sinaloa see William Eugene Shiels, "Gonzalo de Tapia (1561-1594), Jesuit Pioneer in New Spain," in *Greater America: Essays in Honor of Herbert Eugene Bolton* (Berkeley, 1945). Also John Francis Banon, "Pioneer Jesuit Missionaries on the Pacific Slope of New Spain," in *Greater America*, pp. 181-197. And Edward H. Spicer, *Cycles of Conquest* (Tucson, 1962)

9. Robert T. Heizer, ed., *The Indians of Los Angeles County: Hugo Reid's Letters of 1852* (Los Angeles, 1968), pp. 75-76.

10. Thomas Workman Temple II, *The Foundings of Mission San Gabriel* (Los Angeles, 1977). Fr. Zephyrin Engelhardt, *San Gabriel Mission and the Beginnings of Los Angeles* (San Gabriel, California, 1927). Fr. Francis J. Weber, "Mission San Gabriel's Bicentennial," *Southern California Quarterly*, 53 (No. 3, 1971).

11. Bancroft, *History of California*, vol. 1.

12. Luis Navarro Garcia, *Sonora y Sinaloa en el Siglo XVII* (Seville, 1967). Also Oakah L. Jones Jr., *Los Paisanos: Spanish Settlers on the Northern Frontier of New Spain*, and Ignaz Pfefferkorn, *Sonora: A Description of the Province*.

13. Navarro Garcia, op. cit; Jones, op. cit.

14. Edwin A. Beilharz, *Felipe de Neve: First Governor of California* (San Francisco, 1971). Also Lindley Bynum, "Governor Felipe de Neve - Chronological Notes," *Southern California Quarterly*, 15 (September 1931): 57-62. Lindley Bynum, "Four Reports by Neve, 1777-1779," *Southern California Quarterly*, 15 (September 1931). Also Thomas Workman Temple II, "Se fundaron un Pueblo de Españoles - The Founding of Los Angeles," *Southern California Quarterly* 15 (September 1931).

15. Edwin A. Beilharz, "Reglamento," in *Felipe de Neve*, p. 85-96. Also John Everett Johnson, translator, *Regulations for Governing the Provinces of Californias* (San Francisco, 1929).

16. Workman Temple II, "Se Fundaron un Pueblo." Harry Kelsey, "A New Look at the Founding of Old Los Angeles," *California Historical Quarterly* 55 (No. 4, Winter 1977).

17. Teodoro de Croix to Captain Fernando de Rivera y Moncada, Instructions for the Recruital of Soldiers and Settlers for California—Expedition of 1781, Provincias Internas, Tomo 122, Archivo General. In *Southern California Quarterly*, 15 (September 1931): 192.

18. Ibid., pp. 189-201.

19. Ibid., p. 191.

20. Workman Temple II, "Se Fundaron un Pueblo."

21. Kelsey, "A New Look."

22. William Mason, curator of history at the Los Angeles County Museum of Natural History, has examined a document in the Archivo General de la Nación, Mexico, which records Antonio Miranda Rodríguez's birthplace as Manila, the Philippines.

23. Kelsey, "A New Look."

24. Neve to the Comandante General, October 29, 1781, "Bancroft Library Transcripts of Documents Pertaining to the Foundation of Los Angeles," *Southern California Quarterly*, 15 (September 1931): 144ff.

25. Workman Temple II, "Se Fundaron un Pueblo."

26. Kelsey, "A New Look." Also Theodore E. Treutlein, "Los Angeles, California: The Question of the City's Original Spanish Name," *Southern California Quarterly*, 55 (Spring 1977): 1-7.

In 1877 the officers of the Sociedad Patriotica de Juarez, the most important Mexican civic organization in Los Angeles, posed for this photograph. On the right is Narciso Botello, president of the society and prominent businessman. Botello had served as an official of the Mexican government prior to 1848 and as an officer in the war of 1846–1848.

(Courtesy of Seaver Center for Western History Research, Natural History Museum of Los Angeles County)

CHAPTER THREE

Early Los Angeles and a People Transformed

Well into the early 1800s, Los Angeles settlers were still relative newcomers to the basin. Their cultural background and technological expertise set them apart from the neighboring Indian people who were indigenous to the area. At the same time, these early Los Angeles residents were entirely unlike the European authorities who, at every turn, proclaimed political and cultural sovereignty over colonial lives. In contrast to history's mythical conquistadores and their hacienda sons and daughters, the real founders of Los Angeles were linked to Spain by few blood lines and even fewer emotional ties. They were, essentially, a people fully transformed—an embodiment of many different races and overlapping cultures.

As a concrete manifestation of racial and cultural genesis, the founding of Los Angeles can be viewed as a true beginning. More than a mere extension of European imperialism, Los Angeles was a city of people who had evolved beyond the traditional ethnic categories of their day. Certainly, their small pueblo was the prelude to a complex political system and the progenitor of what is today an urban metropolis. Even more significant, it was a symbolic departure from political and cultural affiliations that had been rendered meaningless by a complex system of racial and cultural fusion.

PUTTING OUT ROOTS

By June 1781, the first settlers had reached their new pueblo community, but Captain Rivera y Moncada and his contingent of presidial recruits had traveled only as far as the Colorado River. With their families and the livestock they were transporting to Los Angeles, the men stopped to rest at two mission settlements that had been recently established among the Yuma Indians. After several days, the captain sent most of his command on to San Gabriel, while keeping about a dozen soldiers with him at the rest site so that the animals would have another few days to recoup their energies. Rivera y Moncada and all his men were killed at their posts when a group of Yuma Indians rose up against them. Their entire herd was slaughtered. The women and children chosen to stay behind were taken captive, as clear evidence of a Yuma victory.

It is generally assumed that the Yuma Indians revolted because they were angry over the abuse of their natural resources and because they felt a desperate need to establish political autonomy in the region. Their lands had been trampled and their crops destroyed by usurping settlers and their hungry herds. In fact, it is quite possible that the colonists' 1,000 livestock had managed to devour all the vegetation upon which the Yuma were depending for the coming winter. If so, then the immediate cause of the revolt may have been their rage over the possibility of impending starvation. In any case, the incident forced Mexican authorities to close the De Anza trail, the one direct overland route to Alta California. Thereafter, only large and well-armed parties that were able to brave the Colorado River route could reach the Los Angeles basin.

News of the bloodshed sent shock waves through the northern frontier. Not only did it terrify pueblo settlers, it meant the temporary loss of valuable livestock. Unable to count on deliveries from the southern provinces, settlers in Los Angeles and San José had to depend fully on their own ability to meet immediate material needs. From an official vantage point, the Yuma revolt triggered serious concern that the two new pueblos would have to somehow produce enough surplus agriculture to feed the nearby presidios. But perhaps worst of all, the revolt raised fears that other Indian groups would attack

without warning and lead to a blood-soaked and unpredictably violent frontier.

Soon after the settlement of El Pueblo de La Reina de Los Angeles, the Presidio de Santa Bárbara was founded and formally established on April 21, 1781.[1] During its first decades of growth and development, Los Angeles remained intimately bound to this military post, as well as to the Presidio of San Diego. Soldiers stationed at both camps were linked to the early pobladores by family ties that stretched back to northwestern Mexico. These ties were only strengthened as officers began retiring from the presidios and settling with their relatives in Los Angeles.

The influence of presidial society was also reflected in the new community's social structure. Since there had been so few officers in the original troops of Alta California, sergeants and corporals began to constitute a local elite. As these men married young women of Los Angeles, a notion of "prominent family" emerged and a sense of social status seasoned the pueblo's emerging ambience.

On a political level, the new civilian settlement and the Los Angeles basin as a whole were jurisdictionally divided between the commandants of Presidios Santa Bárbara and San Diego. The Los Angeles pueblo came under the administrative authority of Presidio Santa Bárbara and Acting Corporal José Vicente Feliz was appointed to serve as on-site representative for the fort's military commander. Economic relations between the pueblo and the presidios also developed as surplus crops were sold to the garrison.

Los Angeles had equally close (if occasionally less amicable) relations with the nearby Mission San Gabriel Arcángel and, after its founding in 1797, with Mission San Fernando Rey de España. Because the Franciscan priests felt that secular influence on the area's Indian population threatened conversion, feelings between the settlers and the missionaries were often strained and sometimes even antagonistic. In some ways, clerical concern was legitimate: many Indians were more attracted to the enticements of town than to the discipline of mission life. Conflicts also developed over the use of regional

The architectural skyline of Los Angeles in 1857 reflects Mexican, Anglo American and European influence.

(Courtesy of Seaver Center for Western History Research, Natural History Museum of Los Angeles County)

Distribution of Mexicans in Los Angeles. 1884. With the influx of United States settlers to Los Angeles, the Mexican population dwindled to 19%, and was increasingly segregated into the area around the placita along with Chinese, Italians and Indians.

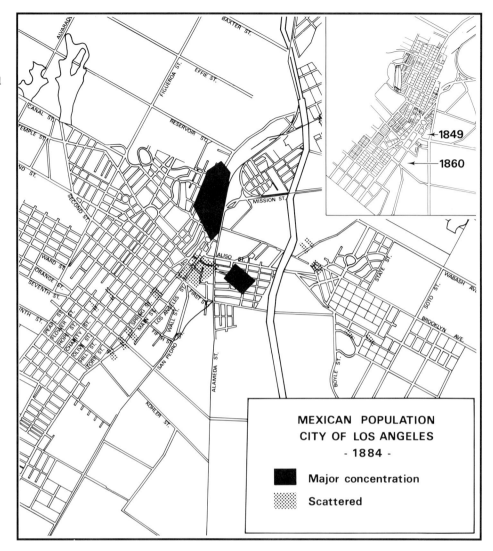

MEXICAN POPULATION
CITY OF LOS ANGELES
- 1884 -

■ Major concentration

▒ Scattered

natural resources. The priests claimed that their holy mission and their roles as the special guardians of Indian property gave them first rights to the land itself and to its limited water supply.

It is important to understand that the chasm between religious and secular interests in Alta California ran much deeper than any specific altercation between Los Angeles residents and the clergy of Mission San Gabriel. Although the priests often expressed disgust over the conduct of individual settlers, Franciscan authorities were far more concerned over the actions and policies of the province's political officials. Prior to his death, Rivera y Moncada had been strongly criticized by the Franciscans for what they said was his obsessive insistence on civilian settlement. Well into the 1790s, De Neve and Governor Pedro de Fages confronted constant pressure from zealous missionaries who quite naturally, but erroneously, assumed that the primary purpose of colonization was the Christian conversion of California Indians. In reality, colonial authorities viewed the missions merely as means to their own strategic end. Franciscan concerns were taken into account, but only after the presidios and pueblos had been considered and assured of all necessary support.

Moreover, colonial officials viewed the missions as transitional institutions. Certain that Indians could be absorbed into Spanish-speaking society, these officials planned to eventually transform the Franciscan settlements into civil towns, each with its own secular parish. So, as missionaries tried to nurture Indian dependence on the Kingdom of God, Nueva España worked to limit the dynamics between priests and their mission congregations.

Significant as all of these institutionalized relations were, the pobladores' single most important relationship—aside from ties to relatives stationed at the presidios—was with the Indian tribes of Southern California. This was especially true when the pueblo was very young. At that time, the Gabrielinos of Yangna and other surrounding villages were an overwhelming majority of the basin's population. In fact, the settlers themselves, the Franciscan missionaries and the soldiers at San Gabriel were the only non-Indian inhabitants of the area.

The full extent of Mexican-Indian relations has never been adequately examined, and the information that does exist looks almost exclusively at settlers' often exploitive use of Indian labor. Equally important aspects of the relationship, such as intermarriage and cultural exchange, have been virtually ignored. In large measure, this oversight is the result of an ethnocentric perspective that fails to acknowledge the intricate racial and cultural mixtures that characterized colonial society in Alta California.

The first few years of the community's existence were dominated by hard work. After all, the settlers were establishing their pueblo literally from the ground up. A major portion of time was devoted to maintaining and expanding the region's irrigation network, the zanja. Also important were constructing temporary and then permanent housing, erecting a chapel and a town building, as well as cultivating, irrigating, harvesting crops, and caring for livestock.

The pueblo's irrigation canal system clearly represents the settlers' ability to creatively interact with their environment. By Spanish and Mexican law, the zanja was an irrigation network owned, built, maintained, and operated by the community. It was designed and constructed to move water by the flow of gravity from the Los Angeles River to the pueblo. The main canal, *zanja madre*, was constructed on high ground, about two miles north of the pueblo. From there, opposite present day Elysian Park, the zanja was dug southwest, between the town and the fields. To divert water into the canal, a dam of willow poles and wickerwork was built where the zanja penetrated the river. Farmers also built smaller ditches that could tap the main ditch and irrigate all parts of their cultivated fields.[2]

The construction and maintenance of the zanja was a major and continuous community task. Although its operation was primarily a responsibility of the pueblo's public officials, every head of household was required to contribute a certain amount of time to its upkeep. Given the semi-arid climate of the Los Angeles basin, the zanja determined the successful cultivation of crops upon which the pueblo depended. Fortunately, most of the pobladores had come from a similiar climate, and were fairly well-skilled in the use of irrigation techniques. Indeed, the eventual growth of the community into a major agricultural settlement was the direct result of that skill, creatively applied to a new environment.[3]

The first shelters built by pobladores were *jacales* (huts). Their wickerwork walls were constructed around a framework of poles and covered with dried mud. These temporary homes, all of which had been roofed with tiles, were gradually replaced by more substantial adobe dwellings. By the end of 1784, only three years after the pueblo's founding, it was reported that Los Angeles consisted entirely of adobe homes, a small public building, and an

Andres Pico (1810-1876), a wealthy ranchero and brother of Governor Pio Pico. Andres Pico was third in command of Mexican forces in the Mexican-United States War. Under United States rule he became a member of the state constitutional committee, a state senator and general of the California State militia.

(Courtesy of Seaver Center for Western History Research, Natural History Museum of Los Angeles County)

adobe chapel still under construction. It was probably at this time that residents adopted the practice of waterproofing their roofs with *brea* (tar) that was brought by *carretas* (carts) from the La Brea tar pits west of town. Thus, adobe brick buildings—an architectural form that would become classically associated with the city in later years—were commonplace long before the arrival of Anglo settlers.[4]

The pobladores devoted most of their time to cultivating crops and tending to livestock. The later activity was to form the basis of immense herds of cattle and horses that even now remain identified with California's Mexican national period. Farming practices followed patterns learned in Sinaloa. Once a year, the land was tilled with a heavy wooden iron-pointed plow, usually drawn by oxen. If a blacksmith's iron point was not available, an oak point was used. Seed was sown by hand, and the entire family participated in the planting. The most important crops included *maiz* (corn), *frijol* (beans), barley, and wheat. Other vegetables and fruits probably grown in small quantities include *chiles* (chili peppers), *calabazas* (squash), *cilantro* (coriander), and melons.[5]

In any agricultural society, work cycles follow the seasons. Early Los Angeles was certainly such a society. Planting was done in the spring and harvesting from May through September. Although this meant that summer was the most grueling time of the year, when harvest time finally came, so did full community involvement. Men, women, children, Mexicans, Indians—all participated in the annual ritual. Thrashing was done by men who used *garrotes* (sticks) to beat the grain, and winnowing was done by women who tossed the grain in *boteas* (wooden bowls) to separate the seed. The produce was then stored for the winter in *trojes* (granaries), most likely built of adobe. As in all agricultural societies, the end of harvesting marked a period of fiestas and celebrations.

FAMILY PORTRAITS OF EARLY LOS ANGELES

As the small pueblo grew and as its economy developed, life in the settlement changed. There was a degree of initial population turnover as some people left the community and newcomers arrived and settled down. With regard to the early inhabitants of Los Angeles, biographical information exists primarily about adult males. Less information is available about women, who were usually thought of in relation to their fathers or husbands.[6]

From among the founding settlers, three families left the pueblo by 1782. Contrary to some accounts, only one person was ordered to leave the settlement. José Velesco de Lara, who had joined the settlers to avoid possible legal prosecution, confessed to Father Junípero Serra that, by mistake, he had remarried when he heard a false rumor that his first wife had died. Judged a bigamist by local authorities, de Lara was ordered to return to Nayarit.

Two other families left on their own accord. Antonio Mesa and his wife apparently became disillusioned with Alta California. After requesting permission to leave the province, the Mesa family returned to Sonora in 1782. Finally, Luis Quintero moved to the Presidio of Santa Barbara, most probably because he wanted to be near his three daughters, all of whom had married soldiers stationed at the garrison.

The remaining eight original settler families appear to have been hard working people who completed the terms of their enlistment and received title to their land in 1786. In several cases, they even achieved positions of honor and responsibility in the new province. Among the most successful was José Vanegas, an Indian from Real de Bolaños, Durango. A man of varied abilities, Vanegas was appointed the first *alcalde* (mayor) of Los Angeles in 1788. He served in that position until 1789, and was appointed to a second term in 1796. Then, in 1801 following the death of his wife, Máxima Aguilar, Vanegas moved to Mission San Luis Rey. There he became *mayordomo* (foreman) for the missionaries. This was a position of great responsibility, particularly because San Luis Rey was one of the two most productive Alta California missions. Only the mission of San Gabriel was as important to the Alta California mission system.

During his 20-year residence in Los Angeles, Vanegas was considered a successful farmer. Apparently he also worked as a skilled artisan because the *padron* (census) of 1790 lists him as a *zapatero* (shoemaker). His son, Cosme Damién, also left Los Angeles to serve as a presidial soldier at Santa Barbara. In 1833, he was granted Rancho Carpintería.

Pablo Rodríguez, an Indian from Real de Santa Rosa, Durango, and his wife, María Rosalía Noriega, lived in Los Angeles for 15 years. After they moved to Mission San Diego in 1796, Rodríguez advanced in status and eventually became mayordomo. He later served in the same capacity at Mission San Luis Rey, where he died in 1817.

José Moreno, a mulatto who was among the original founders of Los Angeles, was a fairly successful farmer. He was among the first *regidores* (councilmen) appointed to the city in 1789.[7] His wife, María Guadalupe Pérez, was the longest lived of the original residents. She died in 1860, having lived through the Colonial, Mexican National, and United States periods of the pueblo's history. Her granddaughter, Catarina Morena, married Don Andrés Pico (brother of Pio Pico), Mexican commander at the battle of San Pasqual and a California state senator in the early United States period.

Manuel Camero, also a mulatto, was a farmer who served as *regidor* in 1789. He died in Los Angeles in 1819. Basilio Rosas was an Indian from Hacienda de Magdalena, Durango. He, too, was a farmer and, according to the padron of 1790, served as a community *albañil* (mason or maker of adobe bricks). José Antonio Navarro, a mestizo from Rosario, Sinaloa, was a farmer and was listed as a *sastre* (tailor) in the 1790 census. Felix Villavicencio, a criollo from Chihuahua, was also a farmer for several years. Later, however, he became a *vaquero* (cowboy) and took charge of the pueblo's herd of cattle. Finally, the briefest biographies of all the founders are those of Alejandro Rosas and his wife Juana Rodríguez. After living as farmers in the pueblo for seven years, they died within a month of each other in December 1788, and January 1789.

As word of Los Angeles spread south toward the lower Mexican provinces, more settlers came to the pueblo in search of a better life. José Sinova arrived in 1785 and was granted the same status and land as the original pobladores. Sinova was listed in the 1790 census as a *herrero* (blacksmith) and, so, must have been a most welcomed addition to the community. He was appointed the second mayor of the pueblo in 1789. Cornelio Avila arrived with his family in 1783 and in less than a decade was reported to have owned some of the cattle tended by Felix Villavicencio.[8] The Avila family became well-known and highly-respected members of the pueblo, especially after Cornelio's sons gained official positions within local government. One of them, Francisco, was the mayor of Los Angeles from 1810 until 1811. He also built the Avila adobe—the oldest house still standing in the city—in 1818, which re-

Guadalupe Aguilar dressed as 'Liberty' for the September 16th celebration of Mexican independence. 1887.

(Courtesy of Seaver Center for Western History Research, Natural History Museum of Los Angeles County)

mains as a testament to the quality of the adobe craft. His brother, Anastasio Avila, served as mayor from 1820 until 1821.

Given the dynamic interplay between early Los Angeles and nearby presidio settlements, it is not surprising to learn that several military men figured decisively in the history of the basin area. Most prominent among them was acting Corporal José Vicente Feliz. In command of the pueblo's original military escort, Feliz was the community's chief public official from 1791 until 1795. Also appointed the town's *comisionado* (commissioner), Feliz was the top representative for the commander of the Santa Barbara presidio. Other men to hold this position were Ignacio Olvera (1794 until 1795), Francisco Javier Alvarado (1795 to 1796), Guillermo Olvera (1810 to 1817), Juan Ortega (1817 to 1821), and Anastasio Carrillo (1821 to 1823).

Several other presidial soldiers settled in Los Angeles. Among them were José María Verdugo, Manuel Nieto, Juan José Domínguez, Felipe Talamantes, and Mateo Rubio—all veterans of the San Diego garrison.[9] José María Verdugo, who would later become a prominent ranchero, was a former corporal and had commanded the *escolta* (escort) at the mission of San Gabriel. Mateo Rubio, born in Flanders, was the first non-Spanish-Mexican settler in Los Angeles. His name "Rubio" means "light complexioned." He was probably given the name because of his fair skin and light hair. Mariano Verdugo was a former sergeant at the Monterey garrison who retired to Los Angeles in 1787. Guillermo Soto, a veteran of the Santa Barbara presidio, arrived in Los Angeles two years later.

The best known presidial veterans were those who received regional grazing permits. These legal documents granted their holders a right to use a specific tract of land for grazing purposes. Actual title to the tract had to be petitioned for after the land had been improved and occupied for several years. In effect, grazing permits established what would become the first private ranchos in the Los Angeles area.

The first such permit, issued in 1775, granted Manuel Butrón and his wife 140 varas of land in the Carmel Valley. The next permits were issued in 1784 to three retiring veterans of the San Diego Presidial Company: Juan José Domínguez, José María Verdugo, and Manuel Pérez Nieto. Each of these men were natives of La Villa de Sinaloa and had served in Baja California before being sent to the northern province. All three had arrived in Alta California in 1769 with the Portola-Serra expedition, immediately under the command of Mexican-born Captain Fernando Rivera Moncada.[10]

It appears that Corporal Juan José Domínguez was the first among them to petition and be granted a grazing permit in the Los Angeles area. Assisted by two fellow retirees, Felipe Talamantes and Mateo Rubío—both of whom later received their own land—Domínguez moved his cattle and possessions from San Diego to an area now know as Dominguez Hills. Upon arrival, Rancho San Pedro was built. Near a spring of fresh water, the three men constructed a two-room adobe house as well as other buildings and corrals. Initially, only Talamantes stayed on to work for Domínguez, but veteran Manuel Gutíerrez (a European Spaniard and mayor of Los Angeles from 1822 until 1823) was hired later. Both these men are mentioned in various records as Domínguez's *mayordomos*.

By 1805, the stock of Rancho San Pedro was reported to number "3,000 mares, 1,000 fillies, 1,000 colts, 700 cows, 600 heifers, and 26 bulls." At about the same time, and on the same rancho, nearly 2,000 acres of grain were being cultivated along the San Gabriel River.[11]

Corporal José María Verdugo was the next petitioner to be granted a grazing permit. In 1784, while still in command of the guard at the mission of San Gabriel, Verdugo was granted a permit for what became Rancho San Rafael. His grant included use of over 36,000 acres in the present cities of Glendale and Burbank. Also in 1784, Manuel Pérez Nieto petitioned for and was granted the "place called La Zanja" and Rancho Los Nietos was established. This rancho would eventually include over 130,000 acres and would be divided into five separate ranchos during the Mexican period: Santa Gertrudis, Los Coyotes, Los Alamitos, Los Cerritos, and Las Bolsas.[12]

Grazing permits were not again granted in the Los Angeles area until the 1790s. When they were approved, they went to Francisco Reyes; to Javier Patricio, and Miguel Pico; and to José Vicente Feliz. Francisco Reyes, mayor of Los Angeles from 1793 until 1795, was granted a permit for Rancho Encino (land that was actually used to graze the entire pueblo's livestock). In 1797, the territory was transferred to Franciscan missionaries who used it as the site of a new mission, San Fernando Rey de España. And in 1796, Feliz was rewarded for his many contributions to Los Angeles with a grant to Rancho Los Feliz, which included much of present day Silverlake and Griffith Park.[13]

Other grazing permits of the Spanish colonial period included El Portezuelo, granted in 1802 to Mariano de la Luz Verdugo; El Conejo, granted in 1804 to José Polanco; Topanga Malibu, granted in 1804 to José Bartolomé Tapia; San Antonio, granted in 1810 to Antonio María Lugo; La Tajauta, granted in 1820 to Anastasio Avila; and Santiago de Santa Ana, granted sometime in the early 1800s to José Antonio Yorba. Additional ranchos probably occupied by the beginning of 1822 included Las Virgenes, owned by Miguel Ortega; Sausal Redondo, by Antonio Ygnacio Avila; Rincón de los Bueyes, by

The Pico House, built in 1869 by Pio Pico, was the largest and most elegant hotel in Los Angeles for many years.

(Courtesy of Seaver Center for Western History Research, Natural History Museum of Los Angeles County)

Map of East Los Angeles.
1873. Until the 1870s East Los
Angeles was a sparsely
populated farmland. By 1873,
however, the middle class
suburb of Boyle Heights had
intruded on the pastoral area,
laying the basis for urban East
Los Angeles.

*(Courtesy of Seaver Center for Western
History Research, Natural History
Museum of Los Angeles County)*

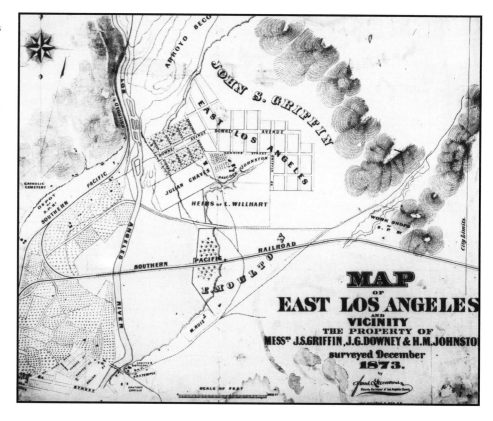

View of Los Angeles. 1871.

(Courtesy of the Bancroft Library)

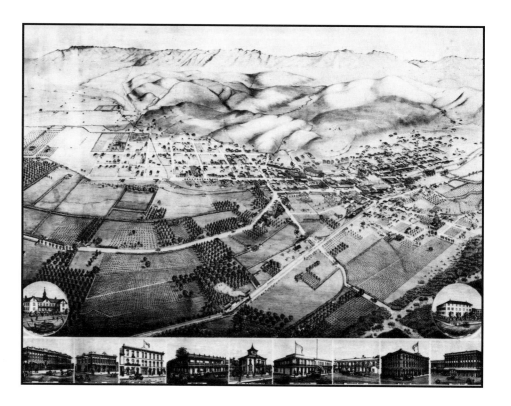

Bernardo Higuera; San José de Buenos Aires, by Máximo Alanís; and Rodeo de las Aguas, by María Rita Valdez.[14]

Contrary to popular myth and Hollywood movie extravaganzas depicting early Los Angeles as a city of sprawling haciendas, most pobladores struggled hard just to maintain small farms. By definition, haciendas were large, economically diversified estates that employed a huge labor force. Although particular size and specific economic activities varied from region to region, haciendas usually combined agriculture, grazing, and other production.

Depending upon geographic limitations, climatic conditions, the availability of labor, and the opportunity to realize impressive profits from the production of commerical commodities, some haciendas did develop in the north during the colonial period. They were, however, few in number. Certainly, Alta California offered long-term potential for such estates, but it was decades before the region was anything that might remotely resemble American motion picture fantasy.[15]

Even by 1822, Alta California ranchos were still in the embryonic stage of their development. In fact, it was not until the secularization of the missions in 1833 that opportunities for export of hides and tallow increased enough to warrant commercially-oriented ranchos. Even then, it took the most industrious families many years of careful breeding to stock their land with cattle and horses, to develop a sizeable labor pool, and to begin producing a surplus that could be sold for profit. Development of a labor force became more and more difficult as coastal Indians were forced onto mission settlements or died of contagious diseases. As fewer gentiles were available to work the fields, competition for the services of those who remained pitted a growing number of farmers and rancheros against one another.

Tiburcio Vasquez. The son of a Santa Clara county ranchero, Vasquez became a guerilla or social bandit who took up arms to resist Anglo American occupation. Vasquez was captured and executed in 1877.

(Courtesy of Seaver Center for Western History Research, Natural History Museum of Los Angeles County)

MESTIZAJE: CULTURAL METAMORPHOSIS

Probably the least understood and most controversial aspect of Los Angeles history concerns the ethnic origins of the city's original settlers. While it has been acknowledged that the 11 founding families were a racially mixed group of mulattos, Indios, and mestizos, many historians have attempted to prove that these first settlers were culturally atypical of later pueblo residents and presidial soldiers. In fact, the opposite is true: they were typical both of later settlers to the area and of colonial Mexico's northwest coastal provinces.

Controversy over the ethnicity of these *Californios* (Mexican inhabitants of eighteenth and nineteen century California) stems not from any real historical data but from a fundamental limitation in the traditional Anglo-American perspective. Operating from an assumption of racial purity and polarization which classifies people in only one of a given number of mutually exclusive racial groups, most nineteenth century Anglo-Americans failed to understand an ethnic reality that they were unprepared to accept as normal.

Even today, racial attitudes are reflected in romantic myths of a culturally insular Spanish southwest, where European trailblazers maintained a racial identity separate from California Indians and colonial Mexicans. Even more frustrating is the fact that a small minority of the real pobladores' descendants contribute to the myth. Choosing mainstream social acceptance over a claim to their true ancestry, they perpetuate the fantasy of a California founding Spanish elite.

For nearly 200 years, this myth has distorted the historical reality of this country's Mexican community by attributing its achievements to a group of

View of Los Angeles looking
west from Brooklyn Heights.
1877.

*(Courtesy of I. N. Phelps Stokes
Collection, New York Public Library)*

Spaniards that never existed. Social interaction, itself, has been molded largely
out of a contrived effort to nurture the myth. As a result, many Anglo-Americans still consider it polite to use the term "Spanish" instead of "Mexican." For
years, restaurants catering to an Anglo-American clientele advertised Mexican
food as "Spanish" cuisine. And many New Mexicans still refer to themselves as
Spanish Americans when speaking English while calling themselves *mexicanos*
(Mexicans) when speaking Spanish in their own community.

Examination of colonial population statistics quickly dispels any notion
that Europeans were in a majority among Alta California's founding families.
In fact, a Mexican census conducted in 1793 found that there were only 32
European Spaniards in the entire region, of whom all but four were Franciscan
missionaries.[16] There were 435 *españoles americanos* (people of Spanish descent born in Mexico), 183 mulattos (or people of partial African descent),
and 418 *castas* (racially mixed persons of Indian, African, or European descent who today would simply be called mestizo). Finally, the census listed
3,234 indios (Indians)—and this figure counts only those tribal members who
had settled in Franciscan missions.

Moreover, the actual number of Europeans was probably a lot smaller
than the 1793 census would suggest because a designation of "español" or "criollo" was frequently given to people of mixed racial descent if they possessed a
certain level of personal prestige, official position, or relative wealth within
pueblo society. In short, anyone who offered the town essential skills (e.g., a
blacksmith), military rank (e.g., a corporal or even a private in the presidial
troops), or prosperity by local standards (e.g., a successful ranchero) would
most likely be considered and counted as "español"—regardless of actual
ethnic background. Also, a racially mixed person with a light complexion was
usually considered an "español" simply because of physical appearance in a
predominantly dark-complexioned population.

The 1793 census indicates that a much larger portion of the population
was of African descent than has often been assumed. Mulattos, mestizos, and

other persons of mixed caste were not a rarity in Los Angeles, Sonora, Sinaloa, or colonial Mexico as a whole. For instance, while there were only 139 European Spaniards living in Sinaloa in 1793, there were 18,394 españoles americanos, 15,780 mulattos, 2,671 persons of mixed caste, and 18,780 Indians permanently settled in the province.[17] Sonora's ethnic composition was equally mixed, although there were fewer mulattos and more Indios recorded to be living in the area. All of this is simply to say that the Los Angeles pobladores were not an ethnic or cultural aberration in their own time. Rather, they were a representative cross-section of the laboring class population of Mexico's northern provinces.

Particularly during the early years, few, if any, color barriers limited acceptable social relationships in the small pueblo. Mexican children played freely with Indian children and adults from the settlement interacted with their Indian neighbors on an almost daily basis. As a way of trying to preserve even the most minimal cultural distinctions, Governor Pedro de Fages once issued orders to regulate the number of Indians allowed in the pueblo at any given time and to prohibit those who did come from staying overnight.

So extensive was contact between Indians and settlers that several Franciscan missionaries at Mission San Gabriel complained about the bad influence that settlers might have on neophytes still easily distracted from their catechism. The priests were equally concerned about the impact that close cultural contact might have on settlement residents. In 1814, the priests at San Gabriel described the *vecinos* (inhabitants of Los Angeles) as speaking the Indian language better than Spanish:

> ". . . with regard to the people of the other classes (the Los Angeles settlers) it seems that they have the same origin as those of Mexico; for the first settlers came from Sonora, Sinaloa, and Nueva Vizcaya provinces. Some of them, nevertheless, have another origin for having mixed, now Spaniards, now other castes, with Indian women of this peninsula (California). . . . Those (Indians) who deal more with the people of the other classes, especially with the settlers, commonly speak the Indian idiom also, and even better and more fluently than their own language which is the Spanish."[18]

The first marriages between Los Angeles pobladores and California Indians took place in 1784 and 1785, when the two sons of Basilio Rosas, Carlos and Máximo, married María Antonia and María Dolores from the Gabrielino *rancherías* (villages) of Jajamobit and Yangna.[19] Even more commonplace than mixed marriage, however, were children born of casual relationships between the two peoples. For the most part, these youngsters were readily incorporated into the pueblo's growing population of *gente de razón*. In essence, they served as the physical embodiment of mestizaje—a gradual process of intermixing that was transforming cultural elements from all the California peoples to form a wholly new ethnic identity.

Work was one of the most important catalysts for mestizaje. It regularly brought Indians, Europeans, and mixed persons together, exposing each to the others' cultures. Through work, all California residents learned to speak Spanish and so found a common form of social communication that allowed people of different ethnic origins but of relatively similar social status to enjoy a wide variety of relationships.

None of this is to suggest that Alta California was utterly without racial bias. Prejudice did operate in Spanish-Mexican society. But as a direct result of the caste system of the colonial period, it must be carefully distinguished from the Anglo-American racial system, wherein races are qualitatively ca-

Mexican family visiting their Gabrielino relatives. 1870s.

tegorized regardless of social status. Mexican and Latin American societies of the 1800s were characterized by a class caste system within which skin color was simply one variable of social prestige. Along with wealth, education, and occupation, skin color affected an individual's position within the community.[20]

European physical characteristics were considered more attractive than those of darker people. They were not viewed, however, as the sole or even primary determinant of social status. On the far northern frontier, skin color was particularly irrelevant because a large portion of the community was dark complexioned. Instead, economic and social contributions to the town formed the basis of early Californian prestige. So, it was not an accident that the first mayor of El Pueblo de La Reina de Los Angeles, José Vanegas, was an Indian from Durango. When contrasted with his keen pioneer sensibilities and well-honed frontier skills, Vanegas' complexion seemed of little consequence.

Nonetheless, throughout colonial Mexico and its northern provinces, cultural superiority remained an issue separate and apart from racial attitudes. On this level, Mexican settlers felt unequivocally "better" than their Indian neighbors. To their way of thinking, their profession of Christianity, varied material possessions, agricultural skills, horsemanship, and animal expertise all set them levels above the Native Americans with whom they lived and worked.

Thus, relations between the settlers and the Alta California Indians were marked by social inequality, economic exploitation, and cultural imperialism. Clearly, the settlers viewed Indians as human beings with souls, legal rights, and important contributions to make to the community. Nevertheless, they manifested at every turn a firm conviction that Indians should recognize a superior culture when they saw one. And in so doing, adopt Christianity, the

Spanish language, and the Mexican world view. The goal of such adaptation was obvious: full incorporation into the colonial Mexican social system.

When such social incorporation occurred, it was generally at the bottom of the social hierarchy, in the ranks of day laborers on the pueblo. And although many Indians sought a role in the Spanish-speaking pueblo, others refused all moves toward cultural transformation. To avoid what they perceived to be economic, military, social, and cultural usurpment, some Indian groups actually left the coastal areas of Alta California for new villages, where they might live free of the unbending colonial will.[21]

GROWING PAINS

The period between 1781 and Mexico's formal break with Spain in 1821 constituted a time of dramatic change in Alta California. The small Los Angeles pueblo was growing into a full-fledged town and was fast becoming an important agricultural center in Spain's colonial empire. Mexico's entire northern frontier was coming into its own and suddenly was viewed by ambitious officials as a special gem for the crown's expanding treasure trove.

In the beginning, a monotonous daily routine governed pueblo life. Simple existence meant hard work and long months without diversion. For the city's founding fathers, the spectacular and sensational were daydreams given vague contour by memories of life to the south, where there might have been time for frivolity. Nevertheless, important events did occur between 1781 and 1822. Most significant was the fulfillment of the pueblo's primary objective, to become a self-supporting agricultural community.

Los Angeles began to take on the essence of a permanent settlement. Grazing permits were approved. A government effort to foster weaving and sheep raising was initiated. As stipulated in the original agreement between settler recruits and the Mexican government, land titles were officially transferred to individual settlers. Pueblo farms had begun to produce surplus grain that was sold to Santa Barbara. In 1788, a local municipal government was appointed. By 1820, the city's population had grown to 650 *gente de razón*, marking it the largest town in Alta California as well as the economic and cultural center of the most important agricultural-ranching area in the northern province.[22]

Occasional rumors of Indian raids still plagued the area. In 1785, a planned revolt against the mission of San Gabriel Arcángel was uncovered. Led by a 17-year-old prophetess, Toypurina, Indian rebels were plotting to seize the mission and kill everyone stationed there. However, a neophyte betrayed their plans to the corporal of the guard, José María Verdugo, and the rebels were suppressed before the ambush could occur. Still, fear mounted within the settlement and colonial authorities were pushed to send a supply of guns, powder, and ammunition from the presidio at Santa Barbara—simply to quell anxiety.[23]

Without question, the most important event of the 1780s was the formal transfer of land title to all those pobladores who had fulfilled the terms of their enlistment contract. On September 4, 1787, Alfarez José Arguello was ordered to Los Angeles by Governor De Fages to put the settlers in official possession of their house lots and fields. Ceremonies were held on September 18, with Acting Corporal José Vicente Feliz and Private Roque de Cota present as witnesses.

In 1790, a formal census was conducted because Mexican officials wanted to know how many *gente de razón* were living in the pueblo and surrounding area. They found that, since 1781, the city's population had tripled to 131 permanent residents. It is quite likely that the actual population increase was even greater, since the census did not include two dozen young men who had joined the army and were stationed at nearby presidios.

Although census figures reveal that the ratio of men to women was about equal (67 men and 64 women), the 1790 count listed occupations only for adult males. Twelve were categorized as small farmers, five as shoemakers, and one each as a weaver, blacksmith, mason, tailor, and servant. In a few instances, these skills were full-time occupations. For the most part, however, pueblo men also cultivated their own plot of land.[24]

No occupations were listed for women, but their work contributions were essential to the community's survival. They worked in the fields, prepared food, maintained homes, and, in many cases, assisted their husbands in performing skilled trades. Children above the age of five were also expected to take responsibility for a share of the workload. Feeding chickens and keeping track of pigs and goats were only a few of the household chores handed over to youngsters.[25]

Aside from *gente de razón*, the pueblo's workforce also included a variable but significant number of Indian laborers. During the colonial period, they were primarily non-mission Indians who seasonally worked for pobladores who could afford to pay their hire. Converted Indians might have sought these jobs if they had been allowed to leave the missions. But with rare exception, neophytes were kept separate and apart from secular life by Franciscan missionaries.[26]

Indians were first attracted to the pueblo's fields and later to its ranchos by human curiosity. Intrigued by the colonial strangers and their unfamiliar way of life, many came simply to get a look at the pobladores and to examine their buildings, animals, crops, and irrigation canals. Other obvious attractions included new technology, metal tools, home decorations, and new foods—all of which the gentiles planned to acquire through trade.

Long accustomed to exchange networks, the Indians saw trade with the new settlers as a logical extension of traditional practices. By securing a positive relationship with the small pueblo, they felt confident that they could acquire trade goods, technology, and foodstuffs even while they kept themselves independent of the Catholic missionaries who so zealously sought their souls rather than their raw materials. For their part, the settlers welcomed trade with surrounding Indian people because such exchange brought them desirable deer skins, herbs, and fresh game meat. Indian labor was also sought by the small community still struggling to bring its land under cultivation.

By 1790, the size of pueblo-owned herds had increased to a recorded total of 1,096 horses, 39 mares, 4 burros, and 528 sheep. Agricultural production had produced a crop of 1,848 fanegas of maize, 340 fanegas of kidney beans, and 9 fanegas each of lentils and garbanzos.[27] The number of houses and other buildings in the pueblo had reached about 30 and the settlement itself was reportedly enclosed by an adobe wall.[28]

According to the 1790 census, the second largest population center in Alta California was Mission San Gabriel Arcángel. Records indicate that 1,037 neophytes and 4 *gente de razón* made the mission site their permanent residence. It is interesting to note that the mission's Indian population was constantly growing—largely due to continued and often forced relocation of

tribal villages. But the turnover rate was staggeringly high due to death from epidemic disease. Between 1780 and 1790, a total of 1,267 Indians were baptized at the mission; 1,124 were buried there, after succumbing to infections against which they had no immunity.

In addition to their mission work, the Franciscans served the pueblo of Los Angeles, which did not have its own pastor until the 1830s. While the priests occasionally traveled to the settlement, individual families were forced to travel to the mission for mass and other spiritual needs. As the settlers began to press for regular visits from the priests and as they demanded more and more attention from the missionaries, Franciscan resentments toward the pueblo festered and the priests grew increasingly outspoken about the town's use of natural resources and its recruitment of Indian labor.[29]

A CHRONOLOGY

In August 1796, Governor Diego de Borica acted to encourage the growth of sheep herding and a weaving industry in the Los Angeles area. Specifically, he distributed 200 free sheep to every household that did not have any of their own. But the campaign fell far short of its lofty objectives. While the number of sheep increased, herding of the animals permanently remained a secondary economic activity. On a more positive note, however, Governor Borica also ordered that land be given free to those families that had none, on the simple condition that they cultivate the tract.[30]

The year 1796 witnessed the city's largest harvest yet, with a total production of 7,800 fanegas of grain. But the following year's drought dropped the total to only 2,700 fanegas.[31] Also in 1796, weaver Manuel Arellanes was appointed mayor, and Mission San Fernando Rey de España was founded on what had previously been the rancho of Francisco Reyes. This latter develop-

Francisco Ramirez, best known as editor of *El Clamor Publico*, published in Los Angeles during the 1850s. Nineteen years old when he started the newspaper, Ramirez championed the rights of the Mexican community. He later served as postmaster before taking over the editorship of *La Cronica* in 1872.

(Courtesy of Seaver Center for Western History Research, Natural History Museum of Los Angeles County)

Office of *La Cronica* newspaper, the major Spanish language newspaper of Los Angeles from 1872 to 1892.

(Courtesy of Seaver Center for Western History Research, Natural History Museum of Los Angeles County)

ment may have further alienated the pobladores from their Franciscan priests because it meant that community grazing lands were lost to clerical powers on the frontier.

From 1798 to 1799, Guillermo Soto, a retired veteran, served as mayor of Los Angeles. The main achievement of his term was the construction of a town *juzado* (jail). In 1799, Francisco Serrano became mayor and was replaced the following year by Joaquin Higuera.[32]

The harvest of 1800 was a good one: 4,600 fanegas, mainly of maize. In fact, the pueblo was by then confident enough to contract with San Blas and Nayarit, agreeing to supply these settlements with 3,400 fanegas of grain each year at $1.66 per fanega.[33]

As a result of heavy rain, the Los Angeles River flooded and overflowed its banks in 1801, probably causing considerable damage to town buildings. Between 1800 and 1810, the Los Angeles *gente de razón* population increased only slightly—from 315 to 365 persons. But like earlier census figures, these numbers do not include as many as 50 pueblo men who served in the presidial garrisons. The number of horses and cattle declined through the year 1816, partly because there was a drought and partly because herds of excess animals were intentionally slaughtered.[34]

Los Angeles was growing up on another level as it was coming into regular contact with people outside its own immediate community. In fact, by 1800, Alta California was regularly visited by foreign ships, most of which were United States and Russian owned vessels illegally engaged in otter hunting and trade. Although such activity was strictly prohibited by Spanish law,

Antonio F. Coronel and wife at their home. 1870s.

(Courtesy of Seaver Center for Western History Research, Natural History Museum of Los Angeles County)

there were few coastal patrol ships and there was little that colonial officials could do to stop it.

Los Angeles did not offer these trade renegades an easily accessible natural harbor, but the smugglers nevertheless made inroads toward the pueblo. Contraband trade goods were frequently landed at secluded beaches on Catalina Island, Santa Monica, and San Pedro bays. Assisting in these clandestine efforts were a few members of the community. Local resident and later ranchero Máximo Alanis, for example, had a well-established reputation as an accomplice to more than one foreign sea captain. But the most experienced intermediaries in the distribution of smuggled goods were Franciscan missionaries who, after all, controlled the largest share of Alta California's hide production.

Following the outbreak of Mexico's revolt against Spain in 1810, presidios, missions, and pueblos were cut off from virtually all legally supplied trade goods. Had it not been for contraband, the entire population of Alta California might have faced insurmountable difficulty in meeting supply needs. Increasingly, government officials were forced (or bribed) into permitting the illegal trade simply because it was the one practical way of acquiring desperately needed supplies. Smuggling became nothing short of an accepted part of life in Los Angeles. In fact, in 1805, five years before the war of independence began, one foreign smuggler, William Shaler, became the first United States citizen to visit Los Angeles—apparently after landing an illegal cargo at Santa Catalina Island.[35]

The years 1805 and 1806 were bad ones in terms of local agriculture. In 1805, swarms of deadly locusts devastated the pueblo's crops of corn, beans, and peas.[36] Farmers were left with barely enough for themselves, let alone surplus merchandise. Los Angeles continued to be a center for the recruitment of young soldiers and, in 1805, 18 men from the pueblo joined the San Diego presidial company.[37] In December 1806, neighboring Mission San Fernando celebrated the consecration of its new adobe church, complete with a tile roof.

By 1808, the impact of the French Revolution and Napoleonic wars was felt even as far west as Alta California. Rumors of war and increased foreign threats kept Los Angeles pobladores on constant alert. Then, in August, an Indian from the central valley arrived at Mission San Fernando with an unknown flag he claimed had been relayed "through ten tribes from an unknown captain, who wanted to know if there were priests and settlers west of the Sierra." In an atmosphere of such high-pitched political anxiety, the incident took on unrealistic significance. The flag was forwarded to Monterey, where it was ultimately identified as an English flag. But the story behind its presence in California remained a mystery.[38]

In late 1808, the entire Spanish Empire—including Mexico and Alta California—was thrown into an unprecedented political crisis. News spread that Napoleon Bonaparte had deposed the Spanish royal family and had declared his own brother Joseph the new King of Spain.

In 1809, Francisco Javier Alvarado was again appointed commissioner and Guillermo Soto served as mayor of Los Angeles. Alvarado's reports for that year point to a rise in public drunkenness and gambling, as well as to his frequent use of stocks to publicly punish offenders.

In early 1810, the community became embroiled in two separate battles with Franciscan Fathers Zalvidea and Dumetz of Mission San Gabriel. First, the missionaries had built a dam on the Los Angeles River above the *zanja* intake, which obstructed the pueblo's water supply. Eventually, both sides

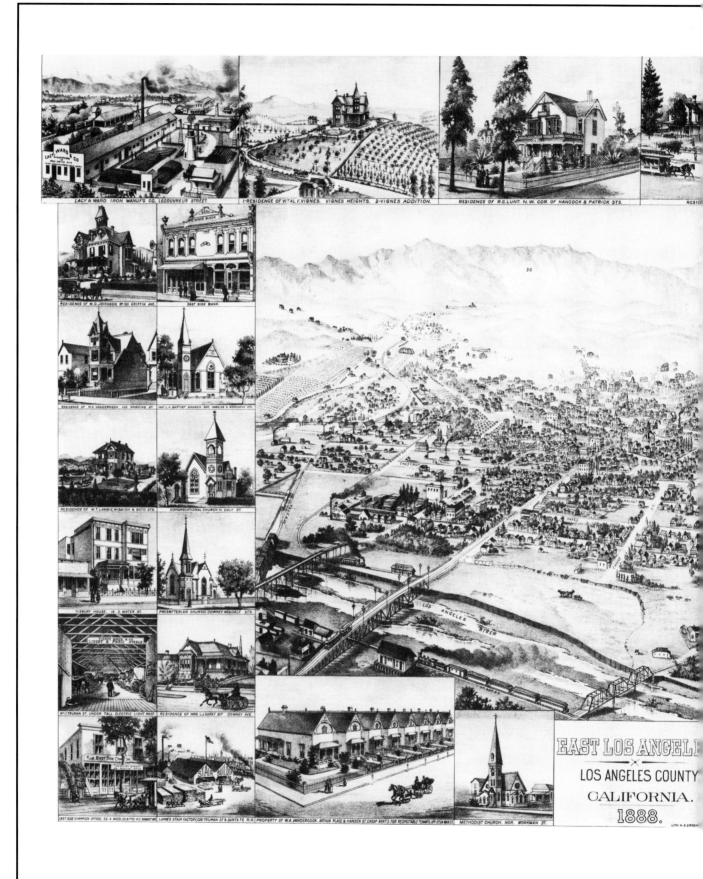

LACY & WARD IRON MANUF'G CO. LECOUVREUR STREET.

1-RESIDENCE OF VITAL F. VIGNES. VIGNES HEIGHTS. 2-VIGNES ADDITION.

RESIDENCE OF R.G. LUNT. N.W. COR. OF HANCOCK & PATRICK STS.

RESID

RESIDENCE OF M.D. JOHNSON Nº 165 GRIFFIN AVE.

EAST SIDE BANK.

RESIDENCE OF W.A. VANDERCOOK. 223 HAWKINS ST.

EAST L.A. BAPTIST CHURCH. COR. HAWKINS & WORKMAN STS.

RESIDENCE OF W.T. LAMBIE. MISSION & SOTO STS.

CONGREGATIONAL CHURCH. N. DALY ST.

TISBURY HOUSE. 19 S. WATER ST.

PRESBYTERIAN CHURCH. DOWNEY AV. & DALY STS.

Nº 11 TRUMAN ST. UNDER TALL ELECTRIC LIGHT MAST.

RESIDENCE OF MRS. L.J. GAREY 917 DOWNEY AVE.

EAST SIDE CHAMPION OFFICE. ED A. WEED. ED & PRO. 412 DOWNEY AVE.

LAMB'S STAIR FACTORY. COR. TRUMAN ST & SANTA FE R.R.

PROPERTY OF W.A. VANDERCOOK. ARTHUR PLACE & HANSEN ST. CHEAP RENTS FOR RESPECTABLE TENANTS OFF 27½ N MAIN ST.

METHODIST CHURCH. NOR. WORKMAN ST.

EAST LOS ANGELES
LOS ANGELES COUNTY
CALIFORNIA.
1888.

LITH. H.S. CROCKER

By 1888 the Los Angeles real estate boom and an influx of European immigrants had transformed East Los Angeles into a suburban enclave.

(Courtesy of Seaver Center for Western History Research, Natural History Museum of Los Angeles County)

appealed their case to the governor at Monterey. He ruled that if it could be proven that the settlers were really being injured, then the priests would have to remove the dam.

The second conflict concerned a pueblo complaint that the priests had twice refused to come to Los Angeles to administer the last rites to local residents. In lengthy correspondence with the governor and the father president of Alta California missions, Fathers Zalvidea and Dumetz argued in their own defense that there were only two of them to attend to the needs of over 1,000 neophytes, several hundred of whom were regularly ill, and that it took them half a day to visit and return from Los Angeles. To solve the problem, they suggested that a separate parish be established in Los Angeles and that a priest be sent to look after the spiritual needs of the pueblo's growing community. The people of Los Angeles also felt the need for a parish of their own. Frustrated by the nine-mile trip to Mission San Gabriel, they applied to the father president for a permit to begin constructing a church.

In November 1810, officials heard about a neophyte plan to attack Mission San Gabriel. Along with a group of Mohave raiders, the Indian converts evidently intended to attack and destroy not only the mission but the nearby secular settlement as well. Over 400 men were mobilized, many of them Mohave warriors who had long displayed their hostility toward the settlers and missionaries by stealing pueblo livestock and other goods.

Upon word of the impending attack, troops were ordered to the mission site. Alfarez Gabriel Moraga commanded an outfit from the north and Sergeant José María Pico (father of the future governor, Pio Pico) led a group of soldiers from the San Diego presidio. A company of militia was also mobilized

Baseball team of Mexicans and Anglos. 1870s.

(Courtesy of Huntington Library, San Marino, California)

from among the Los Angeles settlers. Under the command of Commissioned Sergeant Guillermo Cota, all the men met at San Gabriel. By December 31, 1810, they had captured 21 rebel neophytes and 12 gentiles for complicity in the planned revolt. The captured rebels were imprisoned at the Santa Barbara presidio and assigned to hard labor.

Alta California was becoming increasingly isolated as the result of the Mexican War of Independence. Spanish colonial authorities were no longer able to send supply ships from San Blas. Los Angeles settlers increasingly were left to fend for themselves in what was still a new environment. Officially, news of the revolution was suppressed by colonial authorities and Franciscan missionaries who were given strict orders to keep information from provincial soldiers, settlers, and Indians. Nevertheless, rumors of war—and whispers about the revolutionary principles of Hidalgo and Morelos—managed to reach Alta California. Quite likely, these rumors contributed to the growing dissatisfaction among presidial troops. Although hard work characterized military service in the area, troops went practically without pay for most of the decade. Revolutionary ideals may well have spurred a spirit of independence among the inhabitants of Southern California.

A fairly large earthquake shook most of Southern California in 1812, but it caused only minor damage in Los Angeles. The following year, the Flora, a naval ship from Peru, visited the Alta California coast on the lookout for foreign vessels. Observing that Los Angeles was utterly without coastal defenses, the Flora's captain Noe left several small cannon in the care of artillery veteran Bartolomé Tapia, grantee of rancho Topanga Malibu, and ordered him to see to their upkeep and their command in the event of an attack.

Pio Pico (1801–1894), the last Mexican governor of Alta California. 1880s.

(Courtesy of California Historical Society)

East Los Angeles in the 1880s as seen from the site of what is now Elysian Park. In the center is the Los Angeles river. The country road to the left is now Brooklyn Avenue.

(Courtesy of Huntington Library, San Marino, California)

Russian otter hunters and Yankee smugglers were becoming increasingly active along the California coast. In September 1815, local authorities captured Russian captain Taranoff, his English or Yankee supercargo, and several Aleut Indian otter hunters. All these prisoners were sent to Monterey but were eventually exchanged with the Russians. The pueblo's first public school was funded for 1817-1818 and was run by retired presidial soldier Máximo Piña. Lack of financial resources, however, forced the school to close after just one year.

Throughout 1818, Los Angeles lived under the very real threat of a foreign naval raid. Privateer Captain Hippolyte Bouchard, a Frenchman with letters of marquee from the revolutionary government of Buenos Aires, had already raided parts of the Alta California coast. He had landed at Monterey, stealing anything that was of value and burning everything else. Clearly on the defensive, Los Angeles commissioner Juan Ortega mobilized the available adult males as a militia force to repel a possible landing. Assisted by Bartolomé Tapia and armed with the cannon left by Captain Noe, Ortega posted men on hills overlooking the coastline, including present day Baldwin Hills. A water spring, *Agua de Centinela* (Water of the Sentinels), flowed through these hills and the street we now call Centinela serves as an everyday reminder of the early Los Angeles lookout. Fortunately for Los Angeles residents, Bouchard left Alta California before he reached the pueblo. Disappointed by a lack of valuable plunder and met with the furious resistance of people who had no option but to fight, Bouchard returned to the sea with little to show for his efforts.

TOWARD INDEPENDENCE

In general, the years between 1800 and 1820 were poor ones for Los Angeles agriculture and livestock, largely because of continued drought and pestilence. This falloff in production must have meant hardship for the 650 *gente de razón* and 200 Indians who lived in the pueblo. In fact, hard times throughout the entire basin may have been responsible for the increase in Indian raids toward the end of the 1820s. For example, in March 1820 a raiding

Views of the Mexican community in the 1880s. In the 1880s Mexicans were increasingly segregated into central Los Angeles around the placita which Anglos erroneously called "Sonoratown."

(Courtesy of the Bancroft Library)

party of hostile Kamayaay or Diegueño Indians made their way as far as Los Angeles but were driven off by a militia force led by regidor Antonio Ygnacio Avila. The group was subsequently commended by Governor Sola for having killed the raiding party's leader in hand-to-hand combat.

By the beginning of the 1820s, agricultural conditions in Alta California had begun to improve. Before long, production equalled and then surpassed earlier levels. Fundamental political changes were also impacting on the pueblo. In early 1821, a coup d'etat occurred within the colonial Mexican army and, in February, Mexico declared its independence from Spain. By August, the nation had declared itself an Empire and in 1823 it became a republic.

Another chapter in Los Angeles was about to unfold.

View of the Mexican community from San Fernando Street. 1880s. *(Courtesy of the Bancroft Library)*

NOTES

1. Edwin A. Beilharz, "Reglamento," *Felipe de Neve: First Governor of California* (San Francisco, 1971), pp. 110–120.

2. Harry Kelsey, "A New Look at the Founding of Old Los Angeles," *California Historical Quarterly* 55 (No. 4, Winter 1970): 326–39.

3. Vincent Ostrom, "The Los Angeles Water Supply," *Water and Politics* (Los Angeles, 1953), pp. 3–26.

4. Hubert Howe Bancroft. *History of California*, 1: 346.

5. Hubert Howe Bancroft. *California Pastoral* (San Francisco, 1886), p. 357.

6. For further information on women in Mexican Alta California, see J. N. Bowman, "Prominent Women in Provincial California," *Southern California Quarterly* 39 (No. 2, June 1957). Also Gloria E. Miranda, "Gente de Razón Marriage Patterns in Spanish and Mexican California: A Case Study of Santa Barbara and Los Angeles," *Southern California Quarterly* 63 (No. 1. Spring 1981). Also Cynthia Orozco, "Nineteenth Century Mexican Women in Southern California: Work, Social Life, and Intermarriage," unpublished paper, 1982. The best general description of the original Los Angeles pobladores is found in William Mason, "The Founding Forty-four," *Westways*, July 1976.

7. Bancroft. *History of California* 1:660–661, footnote 34.

8. Marie Northrop, (trs.) "Padron (Census) of Los Angeles: 1790," *Southern California Quarterly* 41 (No. 2, June 1959): 181–82; Hubert Howe Bancroft. "California Pioneer Register," *History of California* 1:461.

9. Bancroft. *California Pastoral*. op. cit. Also William M. Mason, "Fages' Code of Conduct Toward Indians, 1787," *Journal of California Anthropology*, 2 (No. 1, Summer 1975): 90–100.

10. W. W. Robinson. *Land in California*, (Berkeley, 1948), pp. 46–67.

11. Robert Cameron Gillingham. *The Rancho San Pedro* (Los Angeles, 1961) p. 87.

12. Robinson, op. cit., pp. 47–48.

13. Ibid., pp. 45–48.

14. Ibid.

15. Colin M. Maclachlan and Jaime E. Rodriguez, *The Forging of the Cosmic Race: A Reinterpretation of Colonial Mexico* (Berkeley, 1980), pp. 55–57. Also George McCutchen McBride. *The Land Systems of Mexico* (New York, 1923). Also Enrique Florescano. *Haciendas, latifundios y plantaciones en America Latina.* (Mexico, 1975).

16. Gonzalo Aguirre Beltran. *La población negra de Mexico, 1519–1810*, p. 228.

17. Ibid.

18. Fr. Zephyrin Engelhardt. *San Gabriel Mission and the Beginnings of Los Angeles* (San Gabriel, 1927), pg. 97. Also Maynard Geiger (ed.) "Reply of Mission San Gabriel to the Questionnaire of the Spanish Government in 1812 Concern the Native Culture of the California Mission Indians," *Southern California Historical Quarterly* 53 (No. 3, September 1971): 235.

19. Mason, op. cit., p. 95.

20. For further information on the Mexican caste class system of the colonial period, see Machlan and Rodriguez, op. cit., pp. 196–228. Also Ralph Beals, "Indian-Mestizo-White Relations in Spanish America," *Race Relations in World Perspective* (Honolulu, 1955). Also Nicolas Leon, *Las Castas de México Colonial o Nueva España* (Mexico D.F., 1924). Also J. I. Israel. *Race, Class and Politics in Colonial Mexico, 1610–1670* (Oxford, England, 1975). Also L. N. McAlister, "Social Structure and Social Change in New Spain," *Hispanic American Historical Review* 43 (1963): 708–14.

21. Mason, op. cit., pp. 90-100. Also, for a summary of statistical analysis of mestizaje between Mexicans and California Indians, see Sherburne F. Cook. *The Population of the California Indians 1796-1970* (Berkeley, 1976), pp. 152-174. Concerning intermixture among the Indians of Southern California from 1769-1970, Cook notes "In region 5 are the survivors of the southern missions, almost exclusively San Fernando, San Gabriel, San Juan Capistrano, San Luis Rey, San Diego. . . . Despite some irregularity in the points, it is clear that in the decades 1828-1847 their degree of Indian blood had already decreased to a mean of 70 or 80 percent. In this feature they resemble the group from the northern missions, although the dilution of the Indian component was not as great. It is therefore also evident that a great deal of intermarriage with non-Indians (almost entirely Mexicans) had taken place between the foundation of the missions and the entrance of the Americans in the 1840's.

"From the 1840's onward the mean degree of blood (degree of Indian vis-á-vis non-Indian descent) continued to decline, but at a consistent rate (b equals -0.571) as late as the Roll of 1928, at which time the mean degree of blood had fallen below 30 percent. Here, as in the northern mission area, interracial fusion has gone ahead rapidly. In the majority of cases the non-Indian element is Mexican, but since 1928 there has been an increase in crossings with other ethnic components, such as Puerto Rican, Filipino, and Negro." pp. 162-163. Thus, according to Cook's analysis not only was intermixture proceeding rapidly during the colonial and Mexican National periods, but since 1848, Mexicans have continued to be the largest single group intermixing with Native Southern California Indians.

22. Howard J. Nelson, "The Two Pueblos of Los Angeles: Agricultural Village and Embryo Town," *Southern California Quarterly*.

23. Thomas Workman Temple II, "Toypurina the Witch and the Indian Uprising at San Gabriel," *The Masterkey* 32 (No. 4, July-August 1968): 136-52.

24. Northrop, op. cit.

25. Hubert Howe Bancroft. *California Pastoral* p. 357.

26. Mason, op. cit., pp. 90-100. Also George Harwood Phillips, "Indians in Los Angeles, 1781-1875: Economic Integration, Social Disintegration," *Pacific Historical Review* 49 (No. 3, August 1980):427-51. Also William D. Estrada, "Indian Resistence and Accommodation in the California Missions and Mexican Society, 1769 to 1848: A Case Study of Mission San Gabriel Archangel and El Pueblo de Los Angeles," pp. 3-23, unpublished paper, 1980.

27. Alejandro Malaspina, "General Summary showing . . . the new establishments in Upper California . . . to the end of 1790." Also Donald C. Cutter. *Malaspina in California* (San Francisco, 1980), p. 82 ff.

28. Bancroft. *History of California* 1:460-61.

29. Bancroft. *History of California* 2:112

30. Bancroft. *History of California*. 1:620-22.

31. Ibid., pp. 660.

32. Ibid., pp. 661.

33. Ibid., pp. 661, footnote 34.

34. Ibid. Also Bancroft. *History of California* 2:111.

35. Ibid., pp. 22-23.

36. Ibid., p. 111.

37. Ibid., p. 101.

38. Ibid., pp. 85-86.

The Los Angeles City Market on Central Avenue. 1900.

(Courtesy of Seaver Center for Western History Research, Natural History Museum of Los Angeles County)

CHAPTER FOUR

The Mexican National Years:
Growth, Prosperity, and Conflict

It took over a year for news of Independence to reach the pobladores of Alta California. Finally, in March 1822, more than a year after the official Plan of Igüala and more than six months after the Manifesto of Igüala, Governor Joaquín Sola learned that his government had formally declared itself free from the Spanish crown and had established its own Mexican Empire.[1]

The following month, a junta composed of Governor Sola, the presidial commanders of San Diego and Santa Bárbara and the father president of the Franciscan missions met at Monterey and agreed to acknowledge Alta California's acceptance of Mexican Independence. At this same time, the junta affirmed California's new status as a territory of the Mexican nation. Appropriately, it was spring—a time of new beginnings and promises of growth. It ushered in the Mexican national period, a 26-year span of exhilarating self-determination and community pride.

CONSOLIDATION AND PROSPERITY

The War of Independence exacted a high cost from the pobladores. Essential Spanish supply ships no longer stopped in the area to deliver cloth, manufactured goods, and tools. Concomitantly, the area had experienced several years of poor crops, depleted herds, drought, pests, and the periodic incursions of foreign privateers, smugglers, and hunters. Added to the repercussions of war, these pressures made the final years of the colonial period a test of perseverance and struggle for people still living in a foreign environment.

But in 1821, the settlers saw a turnabout. The drought came to an end, the pests were contained, and the harvest was the largest reaped thus far by the small town's farmers. The number of pueblo cattle and livestock began to increase rapidly. After so many years of travail, Angelinos saw the possibility of recovery and prosperity. And by early 1822, they found themselves poised on the verge of historic change on several fronts.

Shortly after learning of Independence, Alta California held its first election. In early May of 1822, a group of provincial electors were voted into office. It was their job to select the territory's *diputado* (deputy)—someone to formally represent the region in Mexico's new Congress. Ranchero José Palomares was elected as the provincial elector of Los Angeles and together with associates from other settlements, he helped select Governor Sola as the *diputado* for all of California.[2]

To ensure the North's political alliance, the Mexican Empire sent a special *Canonigo* (canon), Commissioner Vincente Fernández, to inspect the area. On September 26, 1822, Fernández arrived at Monterey, where public ceremonies were held to welcome him. Throughout the territory, Spanish flags were replaced with Mexican flags as a reflection of budding loyalty to a new government. But more than cosmetic changes resulted from the Fernández visit. Under his direction, governmental reorganization began. Local authorities were given more administrative power and a system of representative government was established on the territorial level. A *diputación* (legislature) was formed and, by law, its members were to be selected by regular local elections.[3] In turn, this body elected a *diputado* to the Congress in Mexico City.

Then, in 1823, another political change in Mexico City sent ripples up toward Los Angeles. Emperor Agustín Iturbide was deposed and Mexico established itself as a republic. As a direct result, citizen participation in the political process expanded. For Los Angeles residents, this meant increased involvement in territorial decisions. It also meant the challenge of sorting through shifting alliances and conflicting ideologies.

Antonio Coronel demonstrating a Mexican dance for author/ photographer Charles Lummis. Coronel actively supported educational and cultural programs, was a member of the Los Angeles Board of Education, part owner of *La Cronica* and supporter of the Los Angeles County Museum.

(Courtesy of Seaver Center for Western History Research, Natural History Museum of Los Angeles County)

Demographically, the 1820s marked the last decade of an Indian majority in the area. By 1820, 650 *gente de razón* had settled in the pueblo and its surrounding ranchos. Significantly, the number of Indians living in the area at that time was not recorded. But early California historian, Hubert Howe Bancroft, has stated that the basin's Indian population varied a great deal throughout the entire decade.[4]

In any event, it is certain that during the national period California's coastal population began making its way toward a Mexican majority. The drop in Indian population can be traced, first and foremost, to the forced concentration of many tribes at Missions San Gabriel and San Fernando where indigenous death rates far exceeded the birth rate. But other factors also come into play. For one thing, racially mixed children were so readily absorbed into Mexican society that their Indian identification was easily lost in the process of acclimating to pueblo life. And many fugitive Indians, in an effort to escape mission life, fled the region altogether and moved to distant interior areas of the basin and beyond.

In 1830, the Mexican population of the Los Angeles district totaled 1,180 persons. Of that number, 770 lived in the pueblo itself, 230 lived on surrounding ranchos, and 160 lived at Missions San Gabriel and San Fernando. The Indian population in 1830 was 2,479 persons, 300 in the pueblo or on the ranchos, and 2,179 at the missions.[5] According to the padron of 1836, the population had increased to 1,675 *gente de razón* and 2,553 Indians, of whom 427 Indians lived in the pueblo or on the ranchos. Secularization of the missions would soon result in the dispersion of hundreds of neophytes from San Gabriel and San Fernando.[6] The majority of these people moved to the pueblo or onto a rancho where they could find work. Some assimilated into the Mexican population through intermarriage, and, as the offspring of more casual liaisons, others found their way into pueblo society. A few left the Los Angeles area completely because they feared cultural assimilation and economic exploitation.

During the 1820s, the number of ranchos increased only a bit, mostly because few additional land grants were authorized. Although many of the existing grants underwent considerable growth in terms of livestock and human habitation, the missions remained the largest commercial producers of the period. It is true that emerging secular interests were enjoying increased herds and the growth of a legal export trade of hides and tallow. Nevertheless, when compared to the missions and their enormous land claims, even the most successful farms appear less than impressive.

Territory alone did not account for the missions' economic dominance throughout the 1820s and early 1830s. More important still, the Franciscans controlled a huge neophyte labor force. Ironically, however, it was the size of that labor force that as much doomed the missions as buoyed them. Despite the Franciscans' enormous land base, the Church failed to reap substantial profits because it had to feed and care for so many neophytes. Each mission demanded a tremendous level of production simply to survive. Analogous to present-day prisons, missions needed all that they produced just to support their own Indian labor pools and maintain their actual settlement sites. If some surplus was left over, it was inevitably taken by the territorial government (in the form of loans which never got repaid) for the support of local presidios.

Perhaps for this very reason, the scale of mission production was substantial. The mission of San Gabriel, for example, was reported to have owned and operated the following ranchos in 1828: "La Puente, Santa Ana (different from the private rancho Santa Ana), Jurupa, San Bernardino, San Timoteo, San Gorgonio, plus four sitios on the Rio San Gabriel and the lands between San Rafael and Los Angeles."[7] It also owned a large water-powered mill and a small coastal trading vessel. Most of the *gente de razón* on the mission lands at this time were employees, members of the soldier guard, or renters of agricultural or grazing land.

Although the relationship between Angelinos and mission priests was sometimes marked by controversy and resentment, constructive cooperation also characterized their dealings with one another. For instance, they worked together to build a small parish church in Los Angeles. Completed in 1823, it was constructed by neophyte labor supplied by the missions and with special contributions solicited by the Franciscans' father president.[8]

Three caballeros at a Los Angeles fiesta. 1890.

(Courtesy of Seaver Center for Western History Research, Natural History Museum of Los Angeles County)

Another major construction project involved the rebuilding of the irrigation canals. Throughout 1821 and 1822, all heads of household were required either to contribute their personal labor to the project or to provide a substitute to perform the work for them. For the two years that it took to complete necessary repairs, the *zanja* project limited the time, energy, and local funds available for other pueblo ventures (especially the new church). But dam reconstruction was considered so essential to the economic well-being of the settlement and its surrounding areas that even visitors to the town were sometimes compelled to contribute their labor. Pio Pico, who would serve as the last Mexican governor of Alta California in the 1840s, once wrote that on a journey to Los Angeles, "I was ordered by Alcalde Avila, an ignorant fellow who ruled 'a la fuerza de machete', to go to work with the citizens on the new aqueduct, but being on horseback and armed with a musket, I escaped the task."[9]

Political muscle of another sort was flexed in early 1823, when the Los Angeles *ayuntamiento* (town council) came into conflict with military authorities from Santa Bárbara. The council flatly refused to recognize the authority of Guillermo Cota who was appointed commissioner of Los Angeles by the commandant of the Santa Bárbara presidio. The townspeople realized that by having judicial control over the pueblo's veterans, his power would supersede civil authority. After weeks of debate, the military gained the upper hand and, the following year, Cota became mayor of Los Angeles.[10] The town council had lost an important strategic move and, although it did succeed in appointing a new school master in 1823, its stature was minimized by the Cota incident.

At least according to records, 1823 was an important and busy year for Los Angeles. Among other notable events, it included the town's first formal livestock count. It was reported that there were 10,623 cattle, 2,851 horses and mules, 96 asses, and 468 sheep in Los Angeles and environs. By 1830, the numbers had grown to 42,903 cattle, 3,057 horses and mules, and 2,469 sheep.[11]

As a result of Mexican laws which opened the California coast to foreign merchant ships, the 1820s and 30s also saw an increase in legal and illegal

The Del Valle family and friends entertain themselves at Rancho Camulos. 1890s

(Courtesy of Seaver Center for Western History Research, Natural History Museum of Los Angeles County)

Mexican musicians. 1890s.

(Courtesy of Huntington Library, San Marino, California)

commerce. Vessels that docked legally declared their cargoes at Monterey, where they paid custom duties and were then allowed to trade in various pueblos along the coast. In Los Angeles, these ships generally anchored off the coast behind the Palos Verdes peninsula at San Pedro. Not all foreign traders wanted to comply with legal mandate. After all, traders knew that substantially more impressive (if less honorable) profits could be made by systematically evading all custom duty. Before long, large-scale smuggling had skyrocketed.

Various levels of political conflict dot the historical record during the early Mexican period. In 1825, for example, Commissioner Cota wrote to the military commander at Santa Bárbara to say that he planned on filling

Los Angeles' military recruitment quota from among the "large number of vagrants in the town." It may be that the commissioner's way of punishing the political opposition was to induct their relatives into the military.[12]

In April 1825, it reached the governor in Monterey that Los Angeles had publicly declared its refusal to recognize any military authority outside its own community. It was also reported that some citizens were refusing to pay their taxes.[13] José María Avila was mayor at this time. According to historian Bancroft, Avila had ordered a private citizen to copy public documents. When the innocent citizen refused, the mayor had him put in irons. Such brazen abuse of the public trust did not bode well for Avila. His popularity plummeted, and he was suspended from office that October.

Still, much more than public policy was changing course in 1825. The Los Angeles River overflowed and it caused massive flooding throughout the entire basin. Until that time, the river had flowed into a series of *cienegas* (marshes) that extended in the general direction of present-day Washington Boulevard to the Ballona Creek on Santa Monica Bay. After the flood, the River jumped its old channel, united with the channel of the San Gabriel River and, in the process, created a new waterway that flowed right through the middle of the small pueblo. The settlement was badly flooded and people were forced to take temporary refuge on high ground.[14] The change in drainage patterns also caused the spread of mustard weeds in the south bay area and the formation of new marshes in and around Rancho San Pedro. Unfortunately, the new weeds grew as high as a vaquero on horseback and, so, made poor grazing for the ranchers' herds. To make matters worse, during the fall of 1827, a major earthquake struck the pueblo.

In 1826, a group of trappers from the United States arrived at Mission San Gabriel. Led by famed mountaineer Jedediah Smith, these men are considered to be the first U.S. citizens to arrive by land in Alta California. Their visit caused something of a sensation but it also renewed fears of foreign interest in California.[15]

As early as the mid-1820s, there were several foreigners living in the area. One of them, Joseph Chapman, had deserted from the crew of privateer Brouchard. A skilled artisan, Chapman helped build the plaza church and later worked for the Franciscans at Mission San Gabriel. There he was put in charge of the construction of *El Molino Viejo* (the old mill) and a small coastal ship owned by the mission.

The late 1820s again brought drought to Los Angeles as well as continuous political conflict within municipal government. Guillermo Cota served as mayor from 1827 to 1828. José Antonio Carrillo was next, serving from 1828 to 1829.[16] But when he was accused of opening the mail of Father President Sánchez—supposedly with the aim of implicating him in various smuggling activities—Carrillo was reprimanded by Governor José María Echeandía. It was reported that, by the end of the decade, the pueblo had a public school with an enrollment of 61 students and regular classes were also conducted at the missions. According to Franciscan records, 20 students were enrolled at San Fernando and 8 attended school at San Gabriel.

It had been a decade of both struggle and success. Government and nature had determined much of what it took from and brought to the pueblo's farm families. But as the growing pains of the 1820s gave way to the greater prosperity and political sophistication of the 1830s, Los Angeles residents moved toward what may be considered the most dynamic decade of the Mexican period.

Mexican longshoremen on the deck of the Scottish sailing ship, the *Lucaipara*, docked at the Santa Monica Long Wharf. 1900.

(Courtesy of Ernest Marquez Collection)

POLITICS IN THE MEXICAN PERIOD

Throughout the 1830s, Los Angeles enjoyed nothing short of spectacular economic growth. This is best reflected in the great expansion of a burgeoning cattle industry and in increased trade with foreigners. It was also during this period that Los Angeles began to compete with Monterey for the political and military leadership of Alta California. What's more, mission lands were secularized in 1833. More than any other single event of the decade, secularization thrust Alta California into a new flurry of economic, political, and cultural transition. The number of ranchos increased and the middle Mexican national period witnessed the ascension of a provincial elite based on political office and possession of ex-mission lands.

Economically, the decade was a remarkable highpoint in the history of early California, particularly in terms of the cattle industry. For instance, in 1834, the receptor of customs duties at San Pedro estimated that 5,000 hides had been exported from the territory. Other, less official accounts, suggest that production may have been even higher. At least one foreign visitor claimed that the year's exports totaled 10,000 hides, 2,500 centals of tallows, and several cargoes of soap.[17]

This sudden burst of economic activity did not result solely from hard work. The success of California's cattle industry as well as the dramatic increase in hide, tallow, and soap exports were all directly related to the secularization of mission lands after 1836. Suddenly, enormous tracts of land once held by the Church were within secular control, and government authorities were again able to grant large land permits to deserving Angelinos. Within a few years, the promise of lucrative private industry in California began to unfold.

All of these developments left their mark on the region's body politic. Economic, military, and civic decisions—each in their own way—wore the stamp of a political maneuver. By the force of circumstance, Mexican Los Angeles learned to balance lofty ideology with harsh political reality.

All too often, historical texts depict Alta California as a wild land where senseless revolution and "bombastic rhetoric" ruled the day. In reality, the politics of the period—like the politics of any nation at any time—were concerned with resolving the most pressing issues of the day. As in all political process, the nobility of social principle was weighed against the complexity of political reality. And at every turn, local authorities tried to make decisions that were consistent with a political system that had been established by Mexican officials thousands of miles away.

Most histories of this period contrast Mexican California with U.S. politics. But, in fact, they fail to place their respective principles and practices alongside each other for a fair comparison and contrast. The corrupt practices of a few Californios are contrasted to the idealized policies of U.S. political theory. And in the process, inflated fantasies of American honor make California's desperate attempts to retain autonomy look like a senseless string of frontier violence.

Essential to the understanding of California politics is a single, overriding reality: the region's governmental process was an experiment in the operation of a large-scale republic. Alta California, like all of the Mexican Republic, was formulated to offer citizens a representative government based

Mexican workers constructing the Pacific Electric Railroad line. Mexican workers formed a major part of the labor force in the construction and maintenance of the Pacific Electric Railroad Line, by 1900 the largest suburban transportation system in the world.

(Courtesy of Huntington Library, San Marino, California)

upon the notions of equality for all citizens before the law, the election of public officials, and the promotion of the public good. Within this framework, two political options emerged. On the one hand, Mexico could opt for a centralized form of government with distinct states or departments individually organized under a uniform system of laws, and overseen by the national government. On the other, it could choose a federal system, which would provide greater regional autonomy to each state.

From 1824 to 1836, the United States of Mexico was organized as a federal republic in which all states enjoyed considerable administrative freedom. Then, in 1836, a coup d'état initiated by President Santa Ana abolished the Federal Constitution and instituted a centralized system of government under which the states became departments. Thereafter, these departments were administered by a central government that either appointed governors or confirmed their election.[18]

Only within the context of this overall political dichotomy can Alta California politics be scrutinized. From the perspective of territory residents, the issue of centralism versus federalism was primarily a question of whether the governor and other major officials would be locally elected citizens or outsiders appointed by Mexico's president. Just as they stood divided on myriad other issues of their day, Angelino politicians disagreed over which political approach would be best for the northern province. Moreover, California politicians were known to change their position on the federalism versus centralism question, usually to align and re-align themselves with the faction that Mexico City considered the "legitimate" regional authority.[19]

Aside from coping with political principles that essentially had been dictated by distant forces, Alta Californios were faced with an array of their own special concerns. Most important of these was the tug-of-war that existed between *arribeños* (northern Californios) and *abajeños* (southern Californios). In bitter competition, they fought for control of the territory's governorship, diputación, customs house revenues, and military authority. In the end, hard fact decided the issue. Two-thirds of the Mexican population lived in southern Alta California, and Los Angeles was that region's demographic center. With these two facts to bolster their cause, many Angelinos grew increasingly convinced that Los Angeles, rather than Monterey, should be the capital of Alta California. Only because Monterey had been the capital for so long, and be-

Mexican workers baling hay in the San Gabriel Valley. 1890s. Mexican agricultural workers played a primary role in the development of southern California's fruit, vegetable and grain industries.

(Courtesy of Seaver Center for Western History Research, Natural History Museum of Los Angeles County)

cause northern California had possession of the territory's official records, was the formal transfer of government so late in coming. But finally, the inevitable happened. In 1836, Los Angeles was named the capital of Mexico's northern border. In reality, the capital did not actually move until 1845.[20]

Closely related to the north-south rivalry was the tendency of northern leaders to seek political autonomy from Mexico. Upper Alta California, with its smaller population base and elite political tradition, was inclined to view Mexico with more detachment. But the southern pueblos, with their geographical proximity and historical bloodline to Sonora and Sinaloa, attached a greater importance to Mexico. In short, Angelinos and other southern Californians displayed a stronger political loyalty to the motherland, and that loyalty won them the favor of officials in Mexico City.

Another major political issue of the Mexican period was secularization of the missions. Theoretically, the purpose of secularization was to convert each mission into a civil pueblo and to give Indian residents all the same rights as Mexican citizens. Officials promised that the lands and property of the missions would be evenly divided between the neophytes, on the condition that any excess lands be granted to other, non-mission citizens. Throughout the transition, missions-becoming-pueblos were to be run by administrators or commissioners appointed by the government.

Theory aside, the push for secularization was sheer economics. On a purely pragmatic level, the region's 21 Franciscan missions constituted the single largest block of productive grazing and agricultural land in Alta California. Without question, the priests possessed the territory's largest herds of livestock and controlled its major properties of value. In essence, the group that controlled the missions directed the destiny of Alta California. With such impressive gains at stake, the issue of secularization and debate over its speedy implementation preoccupied every political faction in the region.

When the missions were finally transferred to the public domain, appointments as mission administrators became treasured political plums. By carefully ensuring that a share of ex-mission property be reserved for themselves, dozens of politicians and militarymen used their official positions to grow rich. Thus, by 1840, the incestuous relationship between government administrators and land grantees had bred a truly affluent local elite.[21]

Only one political reality can compare to secularization, in terms of its importance to California history during the Mexican period. And that is the haunting political reality of foreign takeover. Even beyond secularization, the threat of invasion by the United States loomed over the entire region. With a few exceptions, the leaders and the people of Alta California opposed foreign designs on the territory and wanted to remain part of the Mexican nation. Unfortunately, a serious political crisis was in the making: the United States clearly intended to acquire the territory.

Just prior to the ebb of Mexican power, Angelinos enjoyed a period of robust political activity. Following the 1830s, Los Angeles and its politicians played a central role in the life of Alta California. Between its economic influence and the sophistication of its leading residents, the region became the dominant political force of the middle and late Mexican period. The Los Angeles area was no longer under the administrative control of Santa Bárbara. It was the center of its *districto* (district).

During the 1830s and 40s, the form of district government underwent various changes which reflected changes in Mexico's central government. Originally, the pueblo's chief public official was the *alcalde* (mayor). This officer was assisted by two *regidores* (councilmembers), a *procurador síndico* (public attorney), a secretary, and a treasurer. But after 1836, when Mexico adopted a centralized form of government, the country's states and territories became *departamentos* (departments). The Department of Alta California was divided into two *prefecturas* (prefectures), one of which was in Los Angeles. The *alcalde* system was abolished and replaced by two *jueces de paz* (judges of the peace). The *regidores* and other officers remained.[22]

Under the new department system, the governor became the *jefe político* (political chief) and the *diputación* was called the *junta departamental*. There were various other officials who functioned under both systems. Among them, the *jueces del campo*, judges who held jurisdiction over disputes involving cattle and grazing rights. Then, in 1845, this position was abolished and the post of mayor was restored to handle these matters.[23]

Among the most politically active Angelinos of the Mexican period were men whose names still live in California history. Cities, beaches, streets, and landmarks bear their names. José Antonio Carrillo was a member of Alta California's most politically powerful family and he became one of his pueblo's most astute politicians. Both he and his father had risen from the ranks to become captain and presidial commanders. One of his brothers, Anastasio, was commissioner of Los Angeles from 1818 to 1821. His other brother, Carlos, was Alta California's representative to the Mexican Congress from 1831 to 1832 and was later appointed governor of the territory. José Antonio Carrillo himself often served as a member of the *diputación* and held several other offices, including that of mayor. Perhaps most significant, he was a brother-in-law of Pio and Andrés Pico and allied himself with them on most issues.[24]

Pio Pico is, of course, the best-known politician of the Mexican period. Although he is associated with both Los Angeles and San Diego, he was not actually a resident of the city until 1840. Born at Mission San Gabriel, Pico was the son of the sergeant of the guard, José María Pico. He served as San Diego's deputy in the *diputación*, where he became known as the most vocal spokesman for Southern California in its continuous political rivalry with the North. A protegee of San Diego politician Juan Bandini, Pico first gained notice in 1818 when he proposed that the capital be moved from Monterey to Los Angeles.[25] Among his many claims to fame, Pico was an extremely wealthy man. Presumably, he acquired much of his fortune while serving as administrator of the territory's richest mission, San Luis Rey. His term of governorship, which began in 1845, distinguishes Pico as the last Mexican governor of Alta California.

Pico's younger brother, Andrés, was also politically significant. Best known for his command of the Mexican militia which defeated the U.S. Calvary under General Kearny at San Pasqual in 1847, Andrés usually aligned with his brother, with José Antonio Carrillo, and with Juan Bandini in advancing the interests of Southern California.

There were other political figures in the Mexican period who, although not as famous as the Pico brothers, were significant in their time. Manuel Domínguez, co-owner with his brothers of Rancho San Pedro, held many offices, including *regidor, alcalde, juez de paz,* and *prefect.* Tiburcio Tapia, son of José Bartolomé of Rancho Topanga Malibu, served as a member of the *diputación* and as mayor. José Sepulveda, a prominent ranchero, served several times as a councilman and as mayor, as did Manuel Requena, a prominent merchant who was born in Yucatán.[26]

Ygnacio Coronel and his son, Antonio, had migrated from Mexico City. Before long, they gained local respect for their skills and education. Ygnacio became school master in 1838 and held the post until 1840, when he advanced to secretary of the town council. He was later the receptor of customs at San Pedro in 1846. Antonio was involved in many of the major political machinations of Los Angeles throughout the Mexican national period. After the U.S.-Mexican War, for instance, he served as mayor as well as California state treasurer.

Abel Stearns, one of the non-Mexicans to exercise direct political influence in Los Angeles during the period, came from New England. A merchant and successful ranchero, Stearns eventually became a Mexican citizen and married the daughter of prominent San Diegan Juan Bandini. Publicly neutral in the War of 1846–48, Stearns is suspected to have worked secretly to further U.S. interests.

A series of events set in motion by the appointment of Colonel Manuel Victoria to the governorship in 1831 sheds light on the interplay of political forces in Alta California. Victoria was appointed by the Mexican government to replace José María de Echeandía. Once in office, Victoria angered political leaders throughout the territory by refusing to convene the *diputación* and by asserting his right to rule without consultation. In November 1831, a junta supported by former Governor Echeandía and led by Pio Pico, José Antonio Carrillo, and Juan Bandini initiated a revolt against Victoria at San Diego.[27]

Utah Street housing court. 1906.

(Courtesy of Los Angeles Housing Commission)

After issuing the "Pronunciamiento de San Diego" against the arbitrary rule of Victoria, the junta and its forces marched north. By December 4, 1831, they had occupied Los Angeles. Governor Victoria, who had marched south to meet them, reached the Cahuenga Pass on December 5, 1831. A brief battle was fought between a force of about 120 volunteers plus 30 soldiers led by José Antonio Carrillo, and 30 soldiers and an unrecorded number of Victoria supporters. Two men were killed and Governor Victoria was seriously injured. On December 9, at San Gabriel, the wounded Victoria resigned as governor. As senior vocal or speaker of the *diputación*, Pio Pico should have succeeded Victoria, but ex-Governor Echeandía indicated that Pico's claims were illegal and declared himself governor. Not to be left out of the competition, Agustín V. Zamarano of Monterey proclaimed himself governor. Rather than risk more chaos, Pico withdrew and without much further debate, Echeandía assumed the governorship.[28]

In 1833, a new governor, General José Figueroa, was appointed by the Mexican government. Unlike Victoria, he was a skilful politician and able to work with the *diputación* and local leaders in putting together a viable plan for secularization. The administration of the ex-missions was divided among various political leaders and their major supporters. As a result, serious political conflict was kept to a minimum.

Figueroa died in 1835 and in the year of political jockeying that followed, four interim governors held office. Finally, in December 1836, northern California leader, Juan Bautista Alvarado successfully established himself as governor. And in July 1837, he was formally recognized by the Mexican government as *jefe político* of the Department of Alta California. A skillful politician, Alvarado even managed to prevent Carlos Carrillo from taking office as governor despite the fact that Carrillo had been officially appointed by the Mexican government. In addition, through a policy of increased land grants, Governor Alvarado was able to reconcile his opponents and reward his southern California supporters.[29]

This, then, was the political ambiance of the Mexican national period. For 26 years, land, the creation of political networks, and an agile understanding of *realpolitik*, especially as it unfolded in Mexico City, defined the Mexican experience in Alta California. But in the end, all these concerns were overshadowed by the creeping inevitability of U.S. encroachment and invasion. Faced with no other acceptable option, loyal Mexican Californios chose to resist.

THE TWILIGHT OF MEXICAN DOMINANCE

The 1840s marked a decade of population growth, economic independence, and political influence for Los Angeles. Still, the town's prosperity and power were marred by the knowledge that foreign powers, including the United States, sought control of the region. The Mexican government, engrossed in its own economic, political, and social contradictions, failed to protect its most distant territory. And the relatively small pueblo populations and their officials lacked the military resources necessary to deter a strong invasion force.

In 1836, two incidents conspired to feed California's fears of invasion. First, Texas revolted against Mexico. Second, the United States tried to purchase land from the government in Mexico City. It was not long before rumors of war had spread throughout the entire northern territory. Many foreign settlers (especially U.S. citizens) made their home in upper California, near Monterey, but the southern pueblos remained constantly on guard against

what they saw to be a gradual infiltration of their land and culture.

Then, in the summer of 1842, the south's defensive postures took on a new meaning. In August, Commodore Thomas Ap Catesby Jones, commander of the U.S. naval squadron, received false word that war had broken out between Mexico and the United States. Believing these rumors to be true, he decided not to wait for official verification. Hurriedly sailing from the waters off Peru to Alta California, he and his squadron arrived at Monterey in late October. Despite the protests of Mexican officials, Jones ordered his men to occupy the town and raise the U.S. flag. When informed by the U.S. consul that no state of war existed, Jones apologized to Governor Manuel Micheltorena and withdrew. But the entire affair made it inescapably clear that the United States intended to annex Alta California at the first possible chance.[30]

The impending threat of invasion did not deter the growth of Los Angeles. In fact, the city's Mexican population increased considerably during the 1840s. Nineteenth century historian Bancroft once estimated that the population of *gente de razón* rose from 1,800 in 1841 to about 2,000 in 1845. Approximately 1,250 of these people lived in the ciudad and about 750 lived on ranchos or at ex-missions San Gabriel and San Fernando. Bancroft also estimated the total number of ex-neophyte Indians in the area to be near 1,110.

According to the last census of the Mexican period, taken in 1844, the total population of the Los Angeles District (from San Fernando to San Juan Capistrano) was approximately 3,041 persons — 1,200 Indians and 1,841 Mexicans.[31]

"A typical cholo court." Poorer housing in a Mexican immigrant community of Los Angeles. 1906.

(Courtesy of Los Angeles Housing Commission)

The basin population received a boost in 1842, when a cowboy named Francisco López routinely stopped to pick himself a wild onion in Placeritas Canyon, near the San Fernando Valley, and found much more than he expected. The small nugget of "sun's sweat" that he discovered led to a California gold rush that attracted prospectors from as far away as Sonora and New Mexico. Indeed, the number of visiting miners was grossly out of proportion to the amount of precious ore actually present in the region. But the flurry of activity hiked southern California's population by several hundred in just a matter of months.

The final years of the Mexican national period brought serious efforts to stimulate civic improvement. One municipal ordinance, passed in June 1843, required all owners of shops and cantinas to light the front of their establishments from dusk until 9 p.m. Old buildings were improved and new ones were constructed, including a capital building and a military barracks. The town council purchased land for a public cemetery and planned to present it to the town's church on the condition that no burial fees be charged. But the project ran into difficulty when the bishop declared that, once consecrated, the new burial ground would be church property and that a burial fee would be assessed.[32]

In 1844, a group of local residents organized their own social club, "Amigos Del País." The group built their clubhouse themselves on a large lot that had been purchased by donation money. Their ballroom and reading room were open to the public and frequently used for local activity. It was also in 1844 that Los Angeles first made a consistent effort on behalf of education. Before the year was up, a school teacher and headmaster had been hired.[33]

In February 1845, the departmental junta removed General Manuel Micheltoreña from the governorship of California and selected Pio Pico to serve in his place. As the first major step in his administration, Pico acted to transfer the capital from Monterey to Los Angeles. But just as they had always resisted moves toward transfer, northern Californios refused to accept the proposal. In a stand of defiance, they supported General José Castro, a northern military commander, in his unsuccessful bid for governor.

California had become a territory divided. But at a time when outside political threat so seriously jeopardized the entire region, both north and south saw the advantage of compromise. Not happily, but with conviction, both sides agreed on a split in territorial authority: the governor and the legislature would be headquartered in Los Angeles while the customs house and military authority would remain at Monterey.[34]

In April, Governor Pico turned his attention to the popular theme of pueblo renovation and issued a decree requiring the repair and whitewashing of all house fronts in the city.[35] But his plans were soon stalled and the broader issue of territorial consolidation was rendered a moot point. War between Mexico and the United States had finally begun.

Armed conflict was initiated in 1845, when, in the face of strong protest from the Mexican government, the United States annexed the Republic of Texas. This territorial acquisition was an overt act of war because Mexico had warned that any such action would bring about the end of diplomatic relations between the two nations.

At about this time, U.S. president John Tyler ordered that an army of 5,000 men, commanded by General Zachary Taylor, advance beyond the Nueces River (the historical boundary of Mexican Texas) and march toward the *Rio Bravo del Norte* (Rio Grande), which the present day state of Texas claimed as its southern border. From the Mexican perspective, this was outright invasion and Mexican patrols violently resisted the U.S. advance. Casualties resulted and Tyler's presidential successor, James Polk, falsely claimed that "American blood had been shed on American soil." In 1846, the U.S. Congress declared war against Mexico.

Not all members of Congress were in a war-mongering mood. Some, such as former president John Quincy Adams and Congressman Abraham Lincoln, demanded to see the spot on the map where American blood had been shed.[36] Nevertheless, their pleas for political reason came too late. Both the United States and Mexico had come to view the other as an enemy. And enemies, once made, are difficult to forgive.

News of the war prompted Governor Pico, General Castro, and the members of the departmental junta to meet at Santa Barbara in May 1846. There, they considered and debated California's various defense options. Among other plans, they discussed the possibility of asking British or French consuls for a protectorate over the territory. In this regard, Governor Pico has been viewed as an advocate of the English and has often been condemned for his position. It should be realized, however, that such a measure was considered—by him and others of his time—only as a last resort. With so little else to hope for, Pico may have thought it best to gamble that England would return Alta California to Mexico after the end of a war it had the strength to win.

Events moved rapidly over the next several months. In June 1846, a group of settlers from the Sacramento Valley rebelled against the Mexican government. In collaboration with a group of U.S. soldiers (supposedly in the area on a peaceful scientific expedition), they occupied the small settlement of Sonoma, north of San Francisco Bay, and proclaimed a mock California Republic under the Bear Flag. Under the military command of U.S. Captain Charles Fremont, the rebels publicly symbolized the imperialism that stood behind U.S. diplomacy. However, these political antics hardly inspired defeatism among the Californios. Combined with the wanton murder of innocent civilians, the incident served only to further solidify Mexican resistance.[37]

The Bear Flag revolt was followed almost immediately by the arrival of a U.S. Pacific naval squadron at Monterey. Under the command of Commodore John Sloat, the vessel's crew seized the capital on July 7, 1846. To the south, naval and marine units were occupying Santa Barbara and San Diego. And in August, Commodore Robert Stockton anchored off San Pedro, where he landed several hundred soldiers and proceeded to march on Los Angeles. Without time to prepare for the commodore's 400-man army, with a total adult male population of only 675 men—few of whom were soldiers—with only a small local militia at its disposal, Los Angeles was unable to oppose the landing.[38]

Just one day before Stockton's landing, Governor Pico had left Los Angeles and, with *jefe militar* Castro, headed for Sonora. His plan was to appeal to the Mexican government for regular troops and weapons. But Pico failed to accomplish his aim. In fact, he was ordered to remain in Sonora for the rest of the war. As it turned out, Mexico did prepare troops for the California fight, but they could not be spared after U.S. warships began periodically bombarding the southern coast cities of Guaymas and Mazatlán.[39]

Once he had successfully intimidated hostile Angelinos, Stockton moved on. But as a departing gesture, he gave Captain Archibald Gillespie and a garrison of 50 heavily armed marines orders to occupy the city. In charge of an entire pueblo, Gillespie arbitrarily humiliated the people of Los Angeles and placed many under arrest. Bancroft described the situation:

> "Gillespie had no special qualifications for his new position and his subordinates were still less fitted for their duties. They were disposed to look upon Californios and Mexicans as an inferior race, as a cowardly foe that had submitted without resistance, as Indians or children to be kept in subjugation by arbitrary rules."[40]

Needless to say, such open racism and wanton brutality angered the Angelinos. After a month's humiliation, a poorly armed contingent of pueblo residents rose up against the enemy. Under the leadership of Servulio Varela and Leonardo Cota, more than 300 Mexicans surrounded Gillespie's men. And on September 24th, a proclamation was issued to express the sentiments of the people of Los Angeles. Called "Pronunciamiento Contra Los Norte Americanos," it declared the Angelinos' loyalty to Mexico and their resolve to drive the invaders from Mexican soil. Signed by nearly half of the adult males in the District, it read:

> Citizens: For a month and a half, by a lamentable fatality resulting from the cowardice and incompetence of the department's chief authorities, we see ourselves subjugated and oppressed by an insignificant force of adventurers from the U.S. of N. America, who, putting us in a condition worse than that of slaves, are dictating to us despotic and arbitrary laws, by which, loading us with contributions and onerous taxes, they wish to destroy our industries and agriculture, and to compel us to abandon our property, to be taken and divided among themselves. And shall we be subjugated, and to accept in silence the heavy chain of slavery? Shall we lose the soil inherited from our fathers, which cost them so much blood? Shall we leave our families victims of the most barbarous servitude? Shall we wait to see our wives violated, our innocent children beaten by the American whip, our property sacked, our temples profaned, to drag out a life full of shame and disgrace? No! A thousand times no! Compatriots, death rather than that! Who of you does not feel his heart beat and his blood boil on contemplating our situation? Who will be the Mexican that will not be indignant, and rise in arms to destroy our oppressors? We believe there will not be one so vile and cowardly. Therefore, the majority of the inhabitants of this district, justly indignant at our tyrants, we raise the cry of war and with arms in our hands, we swear with one accord to support the following articles:
>
> 1. We, all, the inhabitants of the department of Cal., as members of the great Mexican Nation, declare that it is and has been our wish to belong to her alone, free, and independent.
> 2. Therefore the intrusive authorities appointed by the invading forces of the U.S. are held as null and void.
> 3. All North Americans being foes of Mexico, we swear not to lay down our arms until we see them ejected from Mexican soil.
> 4. Every Mexican citizen from 15 to 60 years of age who does not take up arms to carry out this plan is declared a traitor, under penalty of death.
> 5. Every Mexican or foreigner who may directly or indirectly aid the foes of Mexico will be punished in the same manner.
> 6. All property of resident North Americans who may have directly or indirectly taken part with or aided the enemies of Mexico will be confiscated and used for the expenses of war, and their persons sent to the interior of the republic.
> 7. All who may oppose the present plan will be punished with arms [put to death].
> 8. All inhabitants of Sta. Bárbara and the northern district will be immediately invited to accede to this plan.
>
> Camp near Los Angeles, Sept. 24, 1846.
> Serbulo Varela, Leonardo Cota, and over 300 others.[41]

Given the intensity of subsequent resistance, this document would seem to clearly express the sentiment of most Angelinos. After issuing the proclamation, officers were elected from among the retired veterans of the Mexican army and local military men were named to lead a campaign against the U.S. invaders. The pueblo chose Captain José María Flores to serve as *comandante general*, José Antonio Carrillo as *major general* (second in command) and Militia Captain Andres Pico as *comandante de escuadrón*. Varela was put in command of 50 volunteers and immediately sent to Rancho Chino. His orders were to arrest a garrison of 20 Anglo-Americans led by Isaac Williams. On September 26 and 27, Varela's detachment attacked and defeated the garrison in the Battle of Rancho Chino.[42]

Rebel attacks had pushed Gillespie and his troops to the foot of a hill where the Los Angeles Board of Education is now located. In late September 1846, the American troops surrendered. On October 4, they were marched to San Pedro, boarded onto a merchant ship (the Vandalia) and banished from the area. As a final slap of defiance, a group of Los Angeles women presented the departing and defeated Gillespie with a basket of peaches rolled in cactus needles.[43]

After the successful recapture of Los Angeles, hundreds of eager volunteers flocked to join *Comandante* Flores in his fight to retain a Mexican California. There were similar uprisings and victories at Santa Barbara and San Diego. For at least a moment in time, the people of southern California knew the sweet taste of proud victory.[44]

Resistance was not limited to California men. The women of Los Angeles also opposed U.S. invasion and contributed their energies to the pueblo's defense. One story that has been passed down through several generations clearly reflects the heroism that these women brought to the period. An old colonial cannon capable of firing 4-pound balls had long stood in the placita

Mexican women at graduation from an Americanization class. In the 1900s Los Angeles, as many other cities, established programs to Americanize new immigrants by teaching them English and skills. 1915.

(Courtesy of Huntington Library, San Marino, California)

near the church and had been used only to fire salutes during fiestas and other social celebrations. But when Francisca Reyes learned that Commodore Sloat's forces were occupying her city, she had the cannon buried on her property for safekeeping. After Los Angeles was liberated, the cannon was exhumed and nicknamed *el pederero de la vieja* ("the old woman's gun") in honor of Señora Reyes' courage.

By October, all of southern Alta California—from San Luis Obispo to San Diego—had been recaptured and again placed in Mexican hands. But the Californios lacked the men and weapons that might have permitted a large scale confrontation. They were facing an enemy with thousands of well-trained and well-armed soldiers. With more than 3,000 men at his land command, Commodore Sloat also had charge of just over five fully-armed naval vessels, each one capable of turning the coastal towns to rubble. For their part, the Californios had a volunteer force of perhaps 700 men, armed mainly with lances and reatas. They had only a handful of guns, most of which were old, outdated flintlocks. They did have the one small cannon but lacked gunpowder to fire it.[45]

On October 6, 1846, additional troops arrived at San Pedro aboard the warship Savannah. Commanded by U.S. Marine Captain William Mervine, 400 men marched on Los Angeles the very next day and, by nightfall, had occupied the Domínguez Ranch house. On October 8, Mervine and his men met Mexican resistance from a Los Angeles militia composed mostly of vaqueros with lances.[46]

The fighting did not last long and, against all odds, the Battle of Domínguez Ranch was a victory for the Angelinos. Pitifully armed and grossly outnumbered, the vaqueros killed six men and wounded another six with "the old woman's gun." There were no Mexican casualties and Mervine was forced to withdraw. He retreated to the safety of his ships and waited for reinforcements.

Support troops were slow in coming, but on October 23, Commodore Stockton arrived in San Pedro on the warship Congress. With his men added to the force, the total number of U.S. soldiers in the area was brought to over 800, excluding ship crews. Stockton and his men fought several short skirmishes with Angelinos in the San Pedro vicinity.

To intimidate the enemy, José Antonio Carrillo adopted special military tactics. By "displaying his men on the march among the hills in such a way that each man was counted several times over," Carrillo created the impression of a large Mexican force. In addition, "he also caused large droves of riderless horses to raise clouds in the distance." The approach proved a success. By early November, Stockton was convinced that he would need a larger force to take Los Angeles. He left the area and sailed south for San Diego.[47]

While Stockton was at San Diego, considering his options, another rebellion broke out and in this one, Mexican forces from Los Angeles played the leading role. The fight, which took place near Escondido in San Diego County, has been named the Battle of San Pasqual. Captain Andrés Pico and a command of nearly 80 men armed only with lances were dispatched to keep watch over the area. At the same time, U.S. Army General Stephen Watts Kearny was approaching Los Angeles from the New Mexico Territory—a land base that he had conquered several months earlier. Under the guidance of Kit Carson, and with orders from President Polk to assume control of land operations in Alta California, Kearny was traveling with a contingent of 140 soldiers. Rumor had it that Stockton had already occupied the region without

Children playing in the sandbox at a Mexican housing court. 1913.

(Courtesy of Los Angeles Housing Commission)

resistance and, on Carson's advice, Kearny chose to take only a small force of calvary with him. In fact, even the 140 men seemed to him unnecessary. When asked how many troops might be needed to take Los Angeles, Carson had reportedly told Kearny not to worry because "the greasers will not fight."

Just after first light on the morning of December 6th, Andrés Pico's men sighted the U.S. dragoons. Outnumbered nearly two to one, Pico chose to attack. First, he sent out a small group of vaqueros to draw the soldiers out into clear view and open space. As Pico expected, Kearny ordered his calvary to attack and the small Mexican contingent led their enemy into the small valley on San Pasqual. When Kearny's forces had strung themselves out over a mile in pursuit, Pico's lancers began attacking from all sides. Wielding their weapons, the Californios struck the dragoons too fast for them to retaliate with their carbines or their two mountain howitzers.

The fighting was brief but bloody. After just 20 minutes of fighting, Kearny's troopers were pushed to the side of a hill and surrounded by Pico's men. Somehow, Carson managed to escape and he rushed toward San Diego for Stockton's aid. This small battle, the bloodiest of the war in Alta California, resulted in approximately 20 wounded and at least 24 deaths for the U.S. forces. Only one Californio was wounded and none were killed. General Kearny lost his right arm, which had been pierced by a lance and amputated.

Kearny's men were rescued several days later by a force of over 200 men. Following his defeat, the general later claimed victory on the basis that he had remained in possession of the field of battle. This technicality was largely unconvincing since it was known that his men were completely surrounded and could not move until reinforcements arrived.[48]

The victory of San Pasqual was the high point of the Mexican Californio defense. But it was short lived. Within days, Stockton concentrated all his forces against Los Angeles and had additional sailors brought in to fight. Fremont's troops were called in from the north and two newly arrived regiments were also added to the U.S. force. Stockton marched north from San Diego with more than 600 men; Captain Fremont marched south from Monterey with another 600 troops. In addition to their numerical advantage, the U.S. force could boast more than enough modern artillery to silence "the old woman's gun."[49]

At this point, the Los Angeles lancers now numbered no more than 600 men. All of them were ready to oppose Stockton's march from the south. As many as another 100 waited and watched for Fremont's invasion from the north. Unimpressive as these numbers may seem, they suggest that, for the Angelinos, this was total war. The entire district had a population of only 575 adult males in 1844. Thus, the Angelino force included not only young, able-bodied soldiers but also old veterans of the presidios and pueblo youngsters.[50]

While the beleaguered Angelinos had been successful when U.S. forces lacked artillery and when quick hand-to-hand combat at San Pasqual gave their utter commitment the advantage, they could not hope to charge concentrated lines of riflemen or modern artillery. Nevertheless, two more engagements were fought. One was on January 8, 1847, at the San Gabriel River near the present city of Montebello. The other was on the following day at La Mesa, in what is now the City of Industry. In each battle, about 600 Californios faced about 600 troops under Stockton. The Californios charged but both times stopped short of rifle range. On January 10, Stockton's forces took Los Angeles as Fremont's troops entered the San Fernando Valley.[51]

At a meeting of the Mexican Californio officers under José María Flores, it was decided that there was no choice but to lay down their arms. To do otherwise would have resulted in the needless slaughter of hundreds of men. On January 13, Andrés Pico and José Antonio Carrillo, acting on behalf of the civil and military authority of the Mexican Department of Alta California, signed the Treaty of Cahuenga at a ranch house near the Cahuenga Pass. The capitulation of Cahuenga did not relinquish Mexican sovereignty over California or the allegiance of the Californios to Mexico. Instead, it was an armistice agreement by which the Mexican inhabitants of Alta California agreed to end armed resistance, to submit to occupation, and to await the final end of war between the two countries.[52] A new, uncertain period in the history of Mexican Los Angeles was about to begin.

A PAINFUL TRANSITION

In February 1848, the Treaty of Guadalupe Hidalgo officially ended the war. Alta California was ceded to the United States and the Mexican national period was over. Like the end of so many other historical eras, the end of Mexican dominance in Alta California came quietly. It was not accompanied by blasting trumpets of great proclamations. In the end, the loss of power and influence was grudgingly accepted, not as fair perhaps but certainly inevitable. It was a slow process and a painful one.

Still, for decades to come, the Mexican community would defy one rule. Despite constant efforts to incorporate them into an Anglo mainstream, the descendents of these early pobladores and rancheros would resist relinquishing their ethnic or cultural identity. Their land was gone and their political influence had been crushed. But their pride remained.

NOTES

1. Bancroft, *History of California*, 2:451.

2. Ibid., pp. 453-455.

3. Ibid., pp. 457-469.

4. Ibid., p. 557.

5. Bancroft, *History of California*, 3:652.

6. Ibid., pp. 643-645.

7. Bancroft, *History of California*, 2:568.

8. Ibid., pp. 561-562.

9. Ibid., p. 559.

10. Loc. cit.

11. Ibid., p. 558.

12. Ibid., p. 559.

13. Ibid., p. 560.

14. Ibid., p. 563.

15. Ibid., pp. 558, 560.

16. Ibid., pp. 560-561.

17. Bancroft, *History of California*, 3:641.

18. Ibid., pp. 420-521.

19. For a detailed discussion of political events in Alta California during the 1830s see Bancroft, *History of California*, volume 3, chapters VII, VIII, IX, XV, XVI, XVII, XVIII, XIX, and XX.

20. Bancroft, *History of California*, 4:518-20.

21. Bancroft, *History of California*, 3:301-38, 339-362. Also, Alan C. Hutchinson, *Frontier Settlement in Mexican California* (New Haven: 1969).

22. Bancroft, *History of California*, 4:553.

23. Ibid., pp. 633-634.

24. Bancroft, *History of California*, 2:745-746.

25. Arthur P. Botello, translator, *Don Pio Pico's Historical Narrative* (Glendale: 1973).

26. See "California Pioneer Register," in Bancroft, *History of California*, vols 2-5.

27. Bancroft, *History of California*, 3:633-637.

28. Ibid., pp. 181-215, 634.

29. Ibid., pp. 545-578.

30. Bancroft, *History of California*, 4:339-349.

31. Ibid., pp. 628, 637-638.

32. Ibid., pp. 631, 629-630.

33. Bancroft, *California Pastoral*, p. 496.

34. Bancroft, *History of California*, 4:513-45.

35. Ibid., pp. 631, 629-630.

36. David M. Pletcher, *The Diplomacy of Annexation: Texas, Oregon, and the Mexican War* (Columbia: 1975). K. Jack Bauer, *The Mexican War, 1846-1848* (New York: 1974).

37. Bancroft, *History of California*, 5:66-76.

38. Ibid., pp. 267-268, 281-282.

39. Ibid., pp. 275-279.

40. Ibid., pp. 305-306.

41. Ibid., pp. 310-311.

42. Ibid., pp. 311-312.

43. Ibid., p. 318.

44. Ibid., pp. 314-316.

45. Ibid., pp. 253-318.

46. Ibid., pp. 319-320.

47. Ibid., pp. 322-325.

48. Ibid., pp. 334-354.

49. Ibid., pp. 385-386.

50. Ibid., pp. 285-392.

51. Ibid., pp. 392-399.

52. Ibid., pp. 404-407.

Ricardo Flores Magon (1884-1922). An intrepid and progressive essayist, speaker, organizer, politician and one of the intellectual pillars of the Mexican revolution of 1910. Forced into exile in the United States for his opposition to the dictatorship of Porfirio Diaz, he began publishing a radical newspaper, *Regeneracion*, which by 1914 was headquartered in Los Angeles. Convicted of U.S. neutrality law violations and imprisoned, Magon and his brother Enrique languished in Leavenworth Federal Penitentiary where Ricardo died, perhaps by assassination, in 1922.

(Los Angeles Times)

CHAPTER FIVE

Initial Accommodations Cultural Maintenance and Community Isolation

The second half of the nineteenth century was an especially difficult time for the Mexicans of Los Angeles. They saw their small town transformed into a large industrial center, and, simultaneously, witnessed the dilution of their influence throughout Southern California. On a cultural level, too, transformation characterized the period. Initially, the small pueblo's Mexican majority moved toward a Mexican-Anglo mixture. This, in turn, led to a broad cultural diversity and, finally, to an Anglo-American majority.

On a more symbolic level, the years between 1848 and 1900 forced the Mexican community to relinquish important dreams. The town that they had founded and built was no longer their's to control. Their plans for the future and their visions of all that the city might have been, were rendered irrelevant by a political and cultural encroachment that they could not stop. If they had been formerly preoccupied with economic expansion and political in-fighting, they were now concerned with cultural solidarity and survival.

In the face of armed conflict with Anglo invaders and the threat of cultural extinction, Mexicans in Los Angeles persevered. Indeed, at the end of the nineteenth century, several experts were predicting that, as an organized force in community life, the Mexican population would soon disappear. Like American Indians, Mexicans were held to be a vanishing people. In this light, their ability to persist as a distinct culture and to maintain an identity separate from their new Anglo neighbors may be seen as their greatest victory of the post-war period. And just as the city's first fight for social continuity had been waged by poor farmers and artisans, this new effort to maintain cultural unity came from the community people themselves, from the laboring class majority of the Mexican population.

THE PASSING OF POWER

The most profound transition came between 1848 and 1860, as Mexicans made their initial accommodations to an imposed Anglo-American authority. For all practical purposes, the Mexican national period ended in January 1847, when Los Angeles was militarily occupied and the Treaty of Cahuenga was signed. Then, in February 1848, the Treaty of Guadalupe Hidalgo forced Mexico to cede Alta California to the United States.

Even before the formal transfer of power, Anglo interlopers imposed their political rule. From January 1847 until the end of 1848, Los Angeles was garrisoned by elements of the Mormon Battalion and Colonel J. D. Stevenson's regiment of New York volunteers.[1] Fort Moore was erected on the hill above the placita and its guns introduced Mexican residents to the political sovereignty of the United States.

Alta California was placed under the rule of a military governor. The Southern Military District, which included Los Angeles as the headquarters of the occupying troops, was handed to Colonel Stevenson for political safekeeping. Just as Major Gillespie had used the threat of violence to enforce strict regulation, Stevenson governed with weapons and intimidation rather than with political wisdom or cultural compromise. By the force of circumstance, Mexicans in Los Angeles suppressed their hostility and silently watched the enemy garrison take total control of their town.

In theory, Mexicans were at liberty to avoid the ordeal. The Treaty of Guadalupe Hidalgo offered all Alta California residents the choice of either returning to Mexico or staying in California. By treaty stipulation, all those who chose to remain were guaranteed automatic U.S. citizenship, the right to free worship as Roman Catholics, legally recognized and duly protected land grants and deeds to any property that they had owned when California was a Mexican territory.[2] In practice, equality of treatment for Mexican Californios took a back seat to the convenience and economic interests of Anglo settlers.

Almost immediately, military authorities stationed in Los Angeles made a mockery of treaty law and a sham of both the U.S. Constitution and the Bill of Rights. In January 1848, less than a year after occupation, Colonel Stevenson called an election for the office of mayor. The idea for the election actually came from Stevenson's commanding officer, the military governor of California. Turning to two of the most respected men in their community, the people of Los Angeles elected Ignacio Palomares and José Sepulveda to serve as first and second mayors of the city. Apparently, their choice did not please the military governor, who invalidated the election. The occupation forces wanted an Anglo mayor and, so, Stephen C. Foster was appointed to the post.

The Mexican response was simple and straightforward: the community ignored Foster and refused to acknowledge his authority. This social dynamic of Anglo military push versus Mexican community pull characterized Los Angeles — and most of California — for over a year. Official occupation ended in August 1848, but the military maintained a strong presence in the city and in several other Southern California pueblos. In December, Mayor Foster called an election for a new city council. But because his political appointment had so blatantly violated their civil rights, the people of Los Angeles boycotted the election and it did not take place. Later, a second election was called. Confident that they had made their point, the Angelinos chose to participate.

Then, in 1849, a constitutional convention was held. Anticipating California's formal admission into the Union, regional representatives were called upon to write a constitution for the "State" of California. Elected delegates from the Los Angeles area included José Antonio Carrillo, Manuel Domínguez, Abel Stearns, Hugo Reid, and Stephen Foster. The composition of this delegation reflects the working relationship that was emerging between members of the town's established Mexican elite and the area's developing Anglo upper-class. In the manner of true political consensus, the Southern California delegates proposed that Northern California be made a state and Southern California remain a separate territory called "Colorado." Both Anglo and Mexican *ricos* (wealthy people) favored this move because it ensured that they would not be outvoted by the north's 100,000 gold rush immigrants. Nevertheless, the proposal was defeated. California became a state in 1850 and Los Angeles became one of its newly created counties.[3]

Before county elections were held again, members of the still emerging Mexican-Anglo coalition met at the home of Agustín Olvera to prepare their own slate of candidates. When elections were held in 1850, several members of that slate were elected. Agustín Olvera was elected as county judge, Benjamin Hayes as county attorney, Ignacio Del Valle as county recorder, J. R. Connelly as surveyor, George Burrill as county sheriff, and Charles B. Cullen as county coroner. Over and above their elected office, Olvera and Hayes were the city's unquestioned political power brokers. Their off-the-record influence was not unique to Los Angeles politics. In fact, at the time, every county in California had its "boss" and "court house set."[4]

Despite this developing Mexican-Anglo elite — whose members collaborated for their own economic advantage — racial antagonism between the two cultures not only stayed alive but, in fact, escalated. Late in 1851, for example, a revolt among the Cahuilla, Kamayaay, and Cocopa Indians of neighboring San Diego County led to the disclosure of high-pitched political animosity.[5] The Indian rebels were led by Cocopa leader Antonio Garra. At his trial by military court-martial in January 1852, Garra revealed that several prominent Mexican Angelinos, including Antonio F. Coronel, had met with him before the uprising to discuss a joint Mexican-Indian revolt against United States rule.[6] Although Garra admitted that the Mexicans eventually backed out of any involvement, his testimony exacerbated prevailing racial tensions.

By 1854, the incidence of actual violence had increased alarmingly. A good deal of the crime can be traced to Anglo European outlaws, gamblers, and prostitutes who had been driven out of San Francisco by local vigilantes and had been drawn south, to Los Angeles, by the cattle boom. Many of these desperados worked for Jack Powers, a former New York street tough who had come to California as a soldier in Colonel Stevenson's regiment. But a number of men from the Australian "Sidney Ducks" gang also contributed to the city's dangerous atmosphere. They had first terrorized the entire San Francisco waterfront and when they were chased out of that town, turned to Los Angeles as the next best target.

There were, of course, Mexican criminals in California. And while they were as destructive and terrifying as their Anglo counterparts, the motive behind their lawlessness was different. By and large, Mexicans broke the law as a public reaction to the physical, economic, and political assaults levied against them by white intruders. First, they had seen the county's Anglo population gradually increase. In July 1851, they saw the establishment of El Monte, the first predominently Anglo town in the Los Angeles area. Founded by a group of settlers from Texas, including several former Texas Rangers, the new settlement soon earned a notorious reputation for anti-Mexican sentiments and a taste for racial violence.[7] In such a lawless atmosphere, Mexicans sometimes saw violence as their only option.

Still, the community made efforts at dialogue. One story has it that a group of Mexican ranchers, led by José del Carmen Lugo and Andrés Pico, once rode into El Monte and threatened to burn the town to ashes unless the "El Monte Boys" stopped terrorizing neighboring Mexicanos. For a while, at least, the brutality subsided.

As the 1850s moved toward their conclusion, the city of Los Angeles was repeatedly transformed. To begin with, the local population continued to grow. In 1850, there were 1,610 people living in town. By 1860, the figure had jumped to 4,385. Even more important, the ethnic composition of the city was shifting. Two years after the Treaty of Guadalupe Hidalgo, 75 percent of all Angelinos were Mexican. Only a decade later, Mexicans had become a slight numerical minority (47.1 percent of the population) of the city that their ancestors had founded.[8] Between 1850 and 1860, the city's Indian population ranged, according to season, from between 700 and 1,000 people, with the largest Indian immigrant population present during each year's harvest period.

Although a non-Mexican population remained the city's majority, Los Angeles was still very much a multi-cultural community. Indeed, well into the late 1860s, Spanish was the common local language.[9] Most important, even into the late 1860s, Los Angeles was a culturally Mexican city. Although the local population leaned slightly toward an Anglo European majority, the entire Los Angeles County maintained a marked Mexican majority.[10] Added to its economic importance, the community's numerical strength made Mexican culture the figurative blueprint for all of California.

Cattle ranching and agriculture remained the region's major economic activities. Then, after the Gold Rush of 1848, a massive influx of gold seekers resulted in a high demand for beef. Within just a few years, the cattle industry ascended to a position of unquestionable economic prominence in California and, for a short time, the price of beef went to $1,000 per head of cattle. Outstanding profits went to any rancher who could market cattle in Northern California. Throughout the 1850s, a small ranching elite—both Mexican and Anglo—reaped tremendous wealth.[11] Then, in 1857, beef prices plummeted and a period of economic depression began.

CULTURAL SOLIDARITY

Even during the early years of social adaptation, as Mexicans were forced to confront a rapidly developing Anglo mainstream, the community found creative ways with which to maintain its unique sense of cultural identity. One of the most fascinating mechanisms of ethnic survival was the Spanish-language press. Through their own local newspapers, Mexicans established a complex network of information dissemination and a forum for the exchange of ideas, opinions, news, and political concerns.

It is significant that Los Angeles had no newspaper throughout the Spanish and Mexican periods. In some sense, there had been no need for printed communication. The pueblo's population was small, few people could read, and the struggling settlers had very little need for knowing about affairs outside their immediate locality. But with the dawn of the American period, everything changed.

Suddenly, the town's population began growing faster than its long-standing residents could internalize. Only ten years after the conquest of California, Los Angeles had almost three times its pre-war population. Literacy became widespread. Faced with the imposing force of an intruding culture, the city's Spanish-speaking community had reason to be interested in news from Mexico. Politically divorced from what once had been their federal government and socially isolated from their families and friends to the south, the Mexicans of Los Angeles wanted and needed a connecting bridge between the cultural certainty of the past and the challenge of the present. That need resulted in a journalistic revolution. Fifteen Spanish-language newspapers appeared in the pueblo before the turn of the century.

By 1856, the city had two newspapers. *La Estrella de Los Angeles* (The Los Angeles Star) was a bilingual publication that, to a limited extent, bridged the two communities. *El Clamor Público* (The Public Clamor) was a Spanish-language newspaper established by the former typographer of the *Star*, 18-year old Francisco P. Ramírez.[12] Until it ceased publication in 1859, *El Clamor Público* functioned as the Mexican community's primary information source. It gave people an opportunity to voice their political viewpoints and, often, their outrage over the civic injustices directed toward them.

In his role as publisher, Ramírez never hesitated to criticize a destructive interplay that bound the city's Anglo-Mexican elite—even though that elite accounted for his subscription and advertising base. In particular, Ramírez printed strong criticism of local vigilante activities that had come to characterize the cross-cultural coalition. As just one example of his style of editorial expose, Ramírez once reported that Stephen Foster had resigned as mayor so that he could lead a local lynch mob. Once the "suspect" had been apprehended and lynched without a trial, Foster resumed his position, no questions asked.

The wave of violent crime did not subside until the late 1850s, when declining cattle prices slowed the local economy and edged gambling and sporting money out of town. As these developments took place, they were reported to the Spanish-speaking community via their local papers. In essence, the publications kept Mexicans a part of Los Angeles by informing them of the news and social trends that local Anglo media would have kept from them.

As more and more of these Spanish-language newspapers appeared on the scene, it became clear that the local Mexican press would have to reflect a broad diversity of public opinion. The city's Mexican population accounted for a broad spectrum of political and economic views. There was room for more than one Spanish-language publishing approach. Most of the papers gave editorial space to a variety of viewpoints but, in general, each reflected the political and cultural priorities of their publisher. Although too strict a classification would be misleading, there were two broad categories of Spanish-language newspapers, those which reflected native born Californians, and those which addressed themselves to newly-arrived Mexican immigrants.

The "Californio press," which included *El Clamor Público, La Estrella de Los Angeles, La Crónica* (The Chronicle) and *Las Dos Repúblicas* (The Two Republics), were usually financed and supported by the wealthiest members of the Spanish-speaking community. As a result, they were long-lived and influential. *Las Dos Repúblicas*, for example, had several branch offices throughout California, Arizona, and northern Mexico. And *La Crónica* was a fully incorporated publishing house with facilities for statewide distribution.[13]

The Mexican immigrant newspapers, however, were much less profitable and far more populistic in their editorial focus. In part a reflection of proud Mexican nationalism, papers like *La Voz de la Justicia* (The Voice of Justice), *El Eco de la Patria* (The Echo of the Homeland) and *El Eco Mexicano* (The Mexican Echo) began appearing in the early 1870s. Most all of them were started by poorly-financed Mexican immigrants and were unable to maintain publication for more than a few years. In general, they tended to express the more nationalistic sentiments of the Spanish-speaking population, sentiments sparked by the Mexican reform movement of Benito Juárez. Their existence, short-lived as it may have been, reflected an important shift in the political orientation of many Mexican Angelinos. With its overtly nationalistic slant, the immigrant press offered new symbols of cultural pride and new terms with which Mexicans could define themselves.

In both the Californio and immigrant press, *la raza* (the race) soon emerged as the community's single most important linquistic symbol. Although the phrase was used in different ways, *la raza* always connoted racial, spiritual, and blood ties to Latin American people—particularly to Mexican nationals. Most important, it implied membership in a complex cultural tradition that was separate and apart from that of Anglos. In everyday usage, *la raza* and its various Spanish derivatives served to nurture a strong sense of community solidarity.

A complete and complex set of Spanish terms came to describe a cultural cohesion that no longer went without saying. In *El Clamor Público*, Francisco Ramírez frequently used the words "nuestra raza" when referring to the Spanish-speaking community. *La Cronica* was dedicated "to the defense of La Raza Latina." In the 1870s, *El Joven* (The Young) published a serial novel and dedicated it to the defense of the "pueblo de la raza." And *Las Dos Repúblicas* frequently used the term "La Raza Mexicana" or "nuestra raza" in their editorials.[14]

In this way, the immigrant and Californio press worked in tandem to develop ethnic consciousness among Spanish-speaking Angelinos. They increased local awareness of a shared victimization, even as they encouraged a sense of tradition and cultural pride.

The press took the lead in condemning lynch mobs, job discrimination, illegal land seizure, and racial violence. Francisco Ramírez was one of the most outspoken opponents of land theft. In 1858, he wrote and published "Expresión Simultanea del Pueblo de California," a lengthy statement of grievances against local Anglo-American authority. He pointed to "the usurpation of lands," urged "nonconformity with the domination of the North Americans," and listed ten articles of resistance that he hoped would mobilize the community to resist the takeover of its lands. In his role of journalist activist, Ramírez was only one of many editors whose work exposed the meaning of local persecution.[15]

In 1877, *El Joven* editor José Rodríguez wrote a lengthy article in which he criticized the Los Angeles City Council for its racism. Specifically, Rodríguez reported that Anglo council members had proposed the destruction of Pio Pico's home. Located near the central plaza, Pico's home was in disrepair but it continued to hold fond and important memories for Mexican residents. Many people could still remember back to 1845, when the building was the official capital of the province and served as the meeting place for im-

A Los Angeles rally for José Vasconcelos during his unsuccessful campaign for president of Mexico in 1927. The Mexican political philosopher, historian, leading man of letters, and author of *la raza cosmica* had also served as Mexico's minister of education under President Obregon.

(Courtesy of Seaver Center for Western History Research, Natural History Museum of Los Angeles County)

portant local juntas. That Anglo authorities should regard the monument with such callous disrespect struck Rodríguez as a disgusting insult to all Mexican Angelinos.

Segregation and prejudice were also concerns for the editors of *La Crónica*: Pastor de Celis, Mariano J. Varela, and S. A. Cardona. In 1877, they observed that the "barrio latino" had inferior roads and inadequate public services. "Why," they asked, "don't they give us the same services that the others have?" The answer, they said, was the racist neglect of public officials. In strident language, they wrote: ". . . we still have a voice, tenacity and rights." They urged the community to remember that "we have not yet retired into the land of the dead."[16]

When discrimination took other forms, the *Crónica* editors were quick to react. In 1877, a smallpox epidemic broke out in Los Angeles, and a local Anglo physician argued before the common council that the unsanitary habits of Mexicans had caused the outbreak. The journalists ridiculed this idea in the first available issue, noting that only 21 smallpox cases had actually been reported. Their report acknowledged that most of the cases were among the

Mexican workers making adobe bricks. In the large brick factories which employed most of the Mexican brickmakers, more industrialized production methods were rapidly replacing these traditional methods of brick making.

(Courtesy of Seaver Center for Western History Research, Natural History Museum of Los Angeles County)

Spanish-speaking, but it also asserted that, by and large, the community was meticulously following all public health regulations.

In 1882, Juan de Toro wrote an ariticle for *El Democratico* (The Democracy) in which he revived memories of the Sumtuary laws passed by the common council in 1860. These restrictions on civil behavior stemmed from the moral code of California's Anglo, largely Puritan, population. In the author's view, they were statutes passed by "those who condemn our pueblo, submitting them to the principles and maxims of a small number of Puritans." De Toro hoped that by supporting the Democratic party in the next election, Mexicans might garner the political influence to repeal these ordinances. Indeed, the Democrats won the election. But the laws stayed on the books.

Although the press frequently rallied the community around a shared sense of victimization, it also nurtured a more positive sense of group solidarity. This was especially true in its coverage of Mexican national holidays. Well in advance of organized festivities, Spanish-language newspapers announced Mexican Independence Day, which lasted from September 15 through September 27 (later changed to the 15th and 16th), and *Cinco de Mayo* (Fifth of May), which celebrated the 1862 defeat of French forces in Mexico. As the holidays approached, *Las Dos Repúblicas* sometimes printed its front page in red, green and white—the colors of the Mexican flag. And local editors often devoted whole pages to the historical and nationalistic significance of each holiday celebration.

Just as the press increased ethnic awareness by awakening the community to its fate and by reflecting a proud sense of Mexican nationalism, a number of social, political, and cultural clubs drew the community together by sharply defining the boundaries of cultural identity. Between 1850 and 1900, at least 15 community groups were organized along ethnic lines. Most clubs were political in orientation and ranged from the conservative Spanish American Republican Club to the militaristic Compañía Militar and Los Lanceros. After 1863, the most influential of these organizations was La Sociedad Patriótica de Juárez, a Mexican nationalist group that sponsored the pueblo's Independence Day and Cinco de Mayo celebrations. As an organization, the group's most important function was its ability to mix a sense of Mexican nationalism with a strong sense of local culture.

Before almost every major holiday, La Junta organized a parade to preceed the day's speeches and fiesta. One of these parades stands as an important turning point in the public profile of Los Angeles Mexicans. For the 1878 Cinco de May celebration, the group's grand marshall, José J. Carrillo, headed a long procession that included a Mexican band and a flower-ladden carriage in which two respected orators, Reginaldo del Valle and Eulegio de Celis (president of La Junta) rode together through the city. After them came 200 members of La Junta Partiótica and Panteón Zabatela's Guardia Zaragosa. Finally, ten other units—each of them representing a Mexican social or political organization—marched through town.

Aside from the visual spectacle of the parade, this 1878 display symbolized a profound shift in the city's Mexican community. Before the Anglo-American period, community celebrations had religious overtones. But as the city became more and more an Anglo-controlled center, Mexicans found it less important to publicize their religion and more important to emphasize their political ideology and ethnic origin. Fundamental loyalties shifted away from the Church and landlords and toward idealistic sentiment of Mexican nationalism.

Nonpolitical associations were also important to the life of the Mexican community. The labor association, Los Caballeros de Trabajo, the music association, El Club Musical Hispano Americano, and the fraternal order of Corte Colón account for only three of the groups that attracted support from within the Mexican community. The most influential of these cultural organizations was La Sociedad Hispano-Americana de Beneficio Mutuo. This group was formed in 1875 as a *mutualista* (mutual aid society). Throughout the nineteenth century, privately financed mutualistas such as La Sociedad operated as self-help agencies. They gave business loans to local entrepreneurs, offered low cost medical and life insurance policies to people in the community, and provided a variety of necessary social services.

La Sociedad was not the first such mutualista in Los Angeles and it was not the last. Similiar self-help groups were organized well into the twentieth century. As early as the 1840s, several *rancheros* (wealthy land barons) had formed Los Amigos del País with the aim of providing social security pensions and stimulating local literacy. The group disbanded during the Mexican War and it was not until La Sociedad appeared on the scene that mutualistas again became commonplace in Los Angeles.

La Sociedad was incorporated under state laws to construct a hospital for the poor and to raise capital for charitable causes. To achieve these ends, the group sponsored concerts and dances. Still, its members had more specific interests than improving the quality of life for Los Angeles in general. La Sociedad was primarily concerned with its own community. In 1879, members submitted a petition to the common council proposing that a Spanish-language school be built. And in 1894, they ran ads in *Las Dos Repúblicas*, soliciting proposals for community development.[17]

In the most fundamental sense, these formal organizations developed ethnic consciousness among the Spanish-speaking by giving form to the life of the community. Even as California Mexicans confronted the tribulations of bigotry and discrimination, these organizations sponsored social and political activities that nurtured La Raza as a separate cultural entity. The very fact that the groups were so numerous indicates how eagerly the community sought constructive new avenues of communication and support.

THE REALITIES OF SEGREGATION

If the last half of the nineteenth century spawned a new cultural identity for the Mexicans of Los Angeles, it also inflicted upon them the hardships of isolation. Especially after the Mexican War, the city saw its mestizo population grow more and more segregated from the Anglo mainstream. As the county itself expanded, Mexican residents were literally and figuratively forced out of what was fast becoming an industrial boom town.

Concentrated in specific areas of the city, Mexicans were relegated to a second-class status that belied their ancestral claim to the City of Angels. Economically and politically, Los Angeles became a two-tiered city. Anglos lived, worked, prospered, and grew self-satisfied on the top rung of a mythical social ladder, while Mexicans operated from a position of imposed subservience. These are the disturbing realities of the history of Los Angeles, but they undeniably constitute a cornerstone to the experience of the city's Mexican population—then and now.

Whether they had been born in Mexico or in the United States, most Los Angeles Mexicans settled near the city's central business district, where

A major commercial street in "the Flats," a barrio around Lincoln Park. In the 1920s Mexicans were moving into the area where they intermingled with members of the Italian and Russian communities.

(Courtesy of Huntington Library, San Marino, California)

they could most easily find work. In the nineteenth century, the term *barrio* (neighborhood) was used by the community itself when referring to their residential area. To Anglo-Americans, this part of the city was known as "Sonora Town." Located north of the plaza and west of Main Street, the barrio was surrounded by Short, Main, Yale, and College Streets. The process of "barrioization" that had begun in the 1850s had, by the end of the 1880s, split the city into two mutually exclusive cultural entities.

In his study of Mexicans in nineteenth-century Los Angeles, Richard Griswold del Castillo states that "by the 1880s, the barrio was a well-defined enclave within the heart of the city surrounded by Anglo suburbs."[18] For downtown residents, life in Los Angeles meant long work days, low wages, and the unpredictable nature of unskilled employment. Still, the area offered proximity to the few job opportunities that existed. What's more, because Mexican workers were employed in occupations that demanded long hours for low pay, they needed to live near their worksite. For the sake of a job, a great many families accepted rundown, overcrowded, and unsanitary housing.

Because unskilled workers were hired on a daily basis, their employment tenure was, to say the least, uncertain. Most men were out of work a good deal of the time. In order to make ends meet, Mexicans were forced to take work wherever they could get it, which meant traveling from one end of the city to the other. On this level, too, living downtown proved to be their best option. It offered a fairly central base of operation from which they could contact the greatest number of prospective employers.

Nevertheless, something more than a constant job search drew Mexicans to the barrio. In the core area of the city, they found community institutions that were supportive to their unique social, economic, and cultural needs. In a very real way, the barrio provided psychological comfort to those who were new to town. Living downtown allowed for identification with their own ethnic community and for a sense of cultural solidarity amidst the stress of an otherwise foreign urban environment.

Some writers have argued that life in immigrant ghettos can result in social disorganization. For the Mexican community of Los Angeles, just the opposite holds true. There was a group consciousness and pride within the barrio, a complete social and cultural life that ensured positive reinforcement as an individual and as a member of La Raza. Indeed, the barrio helped ease the stress of the economic displacement and racism that had become part and parcel of life in an increasingly alien environment.

By 1880, Los Angeles was anything but what it had been when Alta Californians signed the Treaty of Cahuenga. It had become an industrialized center, managed almost exclusively by Anglo-Americans. As Glenn Dumke noted in *The Boom of the Eighties in Southern California*, by 1880, Los Angeles had "wiped out forever the last traces of the Spanish-Mexican pastoral economy."[19] Agriculture had become more important than livestock, and with the introduction of public transportation facilities, local expansion accelerated. These developments altered life for the Mexican community of Los Angeles.

In 1890, Mose H. Sherman and his brother-in-law, Eli P. Clarke, bought a number of local streetcar lines. Among them was the first electric railway line ever built in Los Angeles. Under the company name of Los Angeles Consolidated Electric Railway, Sherman and Clarke converted all their lines to electric power and slowly expanded their service toward Pasadena. After only five years, the high cost of construction and initially low profits crippled the small company. Sherman and Clarke were ousted by their bondholders in 1895. Not to be driven out of a good thing, the two men almost immediately formed the Los Angeles Pacific Railway Company. They built a line to the beach area of Santa Monica and soon expanded into western Los Angeles.[20] In 1898, their stockholders sold out to a group of San Francisco businessmen. One of those buyers was Henry Huntington.

Fascinated by the possibilities of growth and expansion, Huntington incorporated under the name Pacific Electric Railway Company, and in 1901 the geographical expansion and economic transformation of Los Angeles began in earnest.[21] Robert Fogelson has stated that "the Los Angeles and the Pacific Electric were crucial as a means of stimulating the subdivision of the countryside, and the expansion of the metropolis through 1910.[22]

As significant to the economic and geographical growth of Los Angeles as transportation was an enormous increase in local population. Between 1890 and 1900, the total population of Los Angeles more than doubled, from 50,395 to 100,479.[23] In 1890, the incorporated city of Los Angeles accounted for half the county's total population. By 1920, it was home to three-quarters of all county residents. But as the county's population had increased, the suburbs, population had declined from about 40 percent to only 15 percent of the regional total. Put simply, most people wanted to live in the central city, where a number of immigrant groups (including Mexicans) had settled.[24]

Los Angeles was not, as yet, an industrial or commercial center. But many local residents saw its economic potential. Thus, from 1890 to 1910 were two decades of rapid industrial development and an almost obsessive emphasis on commercial activity. According to Carey McWilliams, "expansion became the major business of the region, its reason for existence. Had the flow of population ceased or materially diminished, the consequences would have been as disastrous as a drought."[25] This rapid population growth, coupled with the physical expansion of the city itself, resulted in job openings in unskilled construction trades and service industries. Mexicans, along with other non-whites, held a large percentage of these positions.

Reflecting on California, Charles A. Stoddard remarked in 1894 that "Southern California is made up of groups who often live in isolated communities, continuing their own customs, language, and religious habits and associations."[26] This was certainly true of Mexicans and their patterns of local residence after 1890. Until about 1910, the Mexican population congregated in the city's central area, adjacent to the historic plaza. But new barrios were slowly established — always close to employment sites. In this way, the barrio provided local business with a reserve army of labor always available for immediate employment.

Some of the new barrios were initially established at the outskirts of the city, as agricultural labor communities. But as Los Angeles expanded, these neighborhoods were gradually absorbed into the city and their residents came to live a semi-urban existence.[27] These barrios retained their agricultural functions for a brief period of time and, depending on seasonal fluctuations, Mexican residents worked in both rural and urban occupations. Once the city's metamorphosis was fully underway, these rural enclaves were a luxury that Los Angeles business could not abide. The land was too valuable and the labor pool too precious. As a result, the metropolis expanded and Mexican workers were forced to find jobs in occupations other than agriculture.[28]

The number of farms in Los Angeles county increased between 1890 and 1920, but the total amount of farmland decreased. The large ranchos of the Mexican period had long ago vanished. Small farms, of under ten acres, had taken their place. For Mexican farm laborers, the change meant that job opportunities in agriculture were no longer plentiful and that men had to look for work elsewhere. This is not to say that Mexicans no longer worked in the fields. Large agribusiness did characterize the region. But the nature of California farming had changed. Along with so many other aspects of the economy, it had been industrialized. And with an industrialized agricultural system, it profited rich farmers to mechanize many of the farming functions that had once been done by human laborers. There were still jobs to be found in California's sweeping farmlands, but there were fewer of them. And the ones that did exist were not as they once had been.[29]

Yet another type of Mexican barrio was the former labor camp, or railroad worker's settlement. These areas formed the nuclei of emerging barrios, with only a small population remaining after the demand for their labor had ended. The direct relationship between residential patterns and employment opportunity determined the very existence of these neighborhoods. Again, Mexicans were segregated to areas that lacked the services provided to other city districts.[30]

Between 1900 and 1910, the population of Los Angeles tripled, from 102,479 to 319,198. The original Mexican barrio, adjacent to the plaza, continued to grow. But with the economic transformation of the city, the barrio underwent significant change. New railways and street cars allowed wealthier families to move away from the central city, away from urban poverty yet still within reach of political power and economic influence.[31] For the working classes of Los Angeles, the rural slums of the nineteenth century were becoming the urban slums of the 1900s. The residential areas of the central business district now housed only unskilled, low-income workers, who could afford nothing better. Although the city did not have tenements as they existed in the eastern United States, downtown Los Angeles offered mostly rundown rooming houses, hotels, adobe dwellings, and house courts.

Naturally, these changes affected the residential patterns of the Mexican community. First, because additional economic opportunity was attached to life in the central city, the population of the original barrio grew denser. Second, with an increase in the local Mexican population, other sources of housing were sought by the community's unskilled workers. The major movement was into east Los Angeles and, between 1900 and 1915, several new barrios were established. Significantly, the historic pueblo-plaza barrio remained the social, cultural, and economic center of the local Mexican community, but the appearance of more barrio areas had an impact on the eventual dispersal of the population.

As more and more Mexicans moved into town and settled alongside the descendents of the city's nineteenth century settlers, Los Angeles was well on its way to having the highest concentration of Mexicans anywhere in the country. In fact, by 1910, only San Antonio and El Paso, Texas had larger Mexican communities.[32] But unlike cities in Texas, Los Angeles was home to a number of other immigrant groups. Japanese, Chinese, and black communities were settling in the city. So were many European ethnic groups, including Italians, Russians, and Armenians. In essence, Los Angeles was becoming a city of vast ethnic diversity, a metropolis to which different races and cultural groups came looking for work and housing.

For Mexican Los Angeles, the area north of the plaza and west of Main Street was especially important. It was in this first barrio that Mexicans developed their earliest and largest residential concentration. Mexican families lived in small houses or house courts on Castelar Street (now part of north

Mexican gas company workers. 1920s.

(Courtesy of William D. Estrada)

Hill), Buena Vista, New High, Main, Olivera (now called Olvera), and Alameda Streets. Single men lived in the same area but usually in boarding houses or hotels. East of Main, on the fringe of the city's commercial district and developing industrial area, were metal shops, carriage and wagon businesses, blacksmith and horseshoeing shops, pottery factories, food preparation plants, foundries, wholesale vegetable markets, and a dozen other small industries. There, too, Mexican workers settled to look for work.

In "the Flats"—just east of the Los Angeles River, between the First Street bridge and Seventh Street—Japanese and European immigrant families moved onto Myers, Anderson, Rio Utah, and Clarence Streets. Los Angeles grew in population and expanded in size. The region east and south of the plaza—from Alameda Street to the Los Angeles River and between Aliso Street and First Street—became a Mexican area. Residents sometimes bought lots on installment plans and built homes out of hammered-out cans, old boxes, and burlap. Bad as these shacks may have been, they represented the pride of land ownership. As a result, the Mexican population was more permanent and stable here than in other parts of the city.

Less dense communities developed on Fickett Street, between Seventh Street and Whittier Boulevard in Boyle Heights, and on city-owned land on Olympic Boulevard and Boyle Street. After 1908, Boyle Heights in particular became a community inhabited by different immigrant groups. Small clusters of Mexican families also dotted north Main Street and Mission Road (near present-day Lincoln Park), Seventh Street and Sante Fe Avenue (west of the Los Angeles River), the corner of Santa Monica and Vermont Avenues (near the University of Southern California), the corner of Slauson and Hooper (in the city of Florence) Streets, and Pacoima in the San Fernando Valley.[33] In all these barrios, life was hard. But the city's Mexican underclass found the conditions affordable and acceptably close to their only employment options.

It is not too surprising that most of the city's luxuries eluded life in central Los Angeles and its neighboring barrios. In fact, the Los Angeles Housing Commission saw fit to condemn the area on east Seventh and Utah Streets in 1912 because of its slum conditions and inadequate sanitation facilities. With this move, of course, the Commission condemned more than architectural structure. It condemned 83 families to homelessness and utter poverty.[34]

According to Jacob Riis, who authored a classic study on living conditions among New York City's poor (*How the Other Half Lives*, 1890), housing conditions in Los Angeles were comparable to the worst tenements of Manhattan.[35] The house courts to which Riis referred were occupied primarily by Mexicans. When compared to local Japanese and black communities, Mexican neighborhoods suffered the worst housing in the city.[36] Historian Lawrence De Graff has written a good deal on the Los Angeles black community, yet he has stated that "Mexicans had the worst housing of any group. The poorest of all minorities, they composed most of the inhabitants of tent and shack colonies and occupied many of the poorest house courts, often dubbed 'cholo courts'."[37]

It was, in fact, an awareness of these conditions that led the city council to create a Los Angeles City Housing Commission in 1906. In order to make Los Angeles "a city without a slum," the commission was given authority to regulate living conditions in all local house courts, which were defined as:

> A parcel of area of land on which are grouped three or more habitations used or designed to be used for occupancy by families and upon which parcel or area the vacant or un-occupied portion thereof surrounding or abutting on said habitations is used or intended to be used in common by the inhabitants thereof. By habitation is meant a room or combination of rooms used or designed to be used for the occupancy of human beings.[38]

The commission was comprised of seven members, each of them appointed by the city council. As a local enforcement agency, they could order court owners to improve their property or see their building condemned. Although health officials and three inspectors could, at their own discretion, enter any unit and survey the facility, the commission had no power to actually regulate the crowded and unsanitary conditions of small cottages, shacks, or tenements.

Because most house courts were located adjacent to the city's expanding central business district, they were taking up extremely valuable real estate property.[39] Usually built in barrack-like rows, with only thin board walls separating one family from the next, individual dwellings frequently had only two rooms. One was used as a kitchen and the other as a sleeping and living room. Kitchens were typically six by ten feet and had a small wood-burning stove. The only other standard furniture in this room was a small table. Living room furniture included a bed and a chair. The buildings were built of pine board that was whitewashed on the inside and painted either red or brown on the outside. Floors were also made of pine. Because each room had only one window, they suffered from bad lighting and poor ventilation. Each apartment had one door, which was usually screened. Plumbing was virtually nonexistent; tenants shared a few outside toilets. There were no bathing facilities available and all water came from outdoor faucets.

Overcrowding was a serious problem in the house courts. According to William Matthews, most families of four or more lived in one or two-room

court apartments. He stated having seen ". . . congested living conditions in many cities, yet never anything worse than . . . (that) found in some of these courts."[40] A survey conducted by the housing commission in 1912 found that the average number of people living in a one-room unit was 3.3. In a two-room unit, the average was 3.7, and in a three-room unit, it was 3.9. Out of the 700 house courts surveyed, a total of 18 percent of all inhabitants were living in one-room houses, 60 percent in two-room houses, 16 percent in three-room houses, 3 percent in four-room houses, 2 percent in five-room houses, and 1 percent in six-room houses.

This same study found that 60 percent of all house courts were of a frame construction, 35 percent were classified as shacks, and 5 percent were built of brick. The commission listed 10 percent of the house courts as being in very bad condition, 45 percent in poor condition, 40 percent as fair, and 5 percent as good.[41] Lighting was usually by candlelight, although some tenants used kerosene lamps. Neither gas nor electricity were available, so most residents used wood stoves for cooking and heating.[42] Out of the 700 units surveyed, gas was available in 35 of them and none had electricity. Wood stoves were used in 85 percent of the units, gasoline in 10 percent, and gas in 5 percent. Most of the furniture—the kitchen table, cabinet, living room dresser, chair, and bed—had been made by the occupants themselves, usually out of boxes. Vacant lots next to house courts were often piled high with garbage, which created unsanitary conditions.[43] Only nine of the 700 units had an indoor toilet.[44]

Mexican children at the Lorena Street Elementary School, 1927. By the 1920s public education had begun to make a significant impact on the Mexican community. Educators regarded schools as a vehicle for Americanization. Teachers often had little sensitivity to Mexican children and Spanish was often banned from the classroom.

(Courtesy of William D. Estrado)

Rent for these house courts ranged between $3 and $16 per month, depending on location and condition. The average rental was $9.30 per month. The average income for the Mexican workers was $36.85 per month. After paying rent, the remaining money—$27.55—had to cover food, clothing, and all other monthly expenses.[45] Of the 803 adult men who lived in the house courts when the survey was conducted, 795 listed their occupation as common laborer and their average wage as $1.85 per day.[46]

Coupled with a high rate unemployment, this overcrowded, unsanitary, yet expensive housing created a difficult socio-economic situation for Mexican workers and their families.[47] In one way, men who worked for the railroads or the electric railway companies had an easier time of it because these employers provided their workers with free house court dwellings. Although these industries paid slightly lower salaries than other sectors, working for them meant freedom from all rental obligation.[48] For their part, railroad companies did not charge rent because they wanted their workers near the yards in case of an emergency. And it was far cheaper to build shacks than to pay high wages.[49]

Avila family on Bridge Street. 1920s.

(Courtesy of Rudecinda Lo Boglio)

By 1912, a little more than 2,000 of the city's 15,000 Mexicans lived in these house court apartments.[50] The exact population was 2,409 people: 887 men, 641 women, and 881 children under the age of 14. There were more men than women because of a sizeable bachelor group and also because some married men came to Los Angeles alone, hoping to eventually make enough money to send for their families or return to Mexico with some savings.[51] Of the 610 house courts under the supervision of the Los Angeles City Housing Commission in 1913, 18 percent were inhabited exclusively by Mexicans. The others were populated by a number of different racial and ethnic groups but almost always housed large concentrations of Mexicans.[52]

In 1915, Emory Bogardus undertook an exhaustive study of 1,202 house courts. He found that foreign-born Mexicans accounted for the largest number of renters, followed by Italians, and Russians.[53] Of the house courts surveyed, Bogardus found 40 percent were occupied by Mexicans. He also found that "the economic status of the Mexican is lowest on the whole of any race in the city."[54]

THE HARSHEST TRUTH

In retrospect, it is clear that as the city's commercial and business district continued to expand, Mexicans were forced to leave the historic central plaza barrio. This displacement was, in large part, due to a Mexican removal project that began in 1906 and lasted well into 1913. The program gave the housing commission the power to condemn house courts, tear down buildings, and sell cleared land to private developers. The commission took its job very seriously: between 1906 and 1912, it had 400 units demolished and ordered people to vacate another 50 units.[55] In theory, slum dwellers were to relocate to more sanitary and less congested housing. But better housing was not provided. So, Mexicans watched their barrios destroyed as they confronted the pain of total displacement. Without any other option, they began moving to other areas of the city.

It should not go without saying that considerations other than unskilled employment pushed the Mexican community to settle in substandard barrio areas. By the early 1900s, Los Angeles had become a city plagued by racism. Although there appears to have been no organized effort to confine Mexicans to certain areas of the city, members of the community could not rent apartments or buy property in certain neighborhoods. Even the Los Angeles Housing Commission admitted that "Mexicans cannot find homes except in a crowded district. They want to move away from the industrial district and the center of the city if restrictions and race feelings were not placed upon every new tract of land where lots were sold."[56]

Racially restrictive covenants were used to maintain segregation. The city's Mexicans found themselves alongside Japanese, Chinese, and black residents in the effort to overcome a minority status.[57] Despite their proud heritage, Mexicans in Los Angeles had become the economic castaways of an Anglo society fanatically engrossed in industrial expansion.

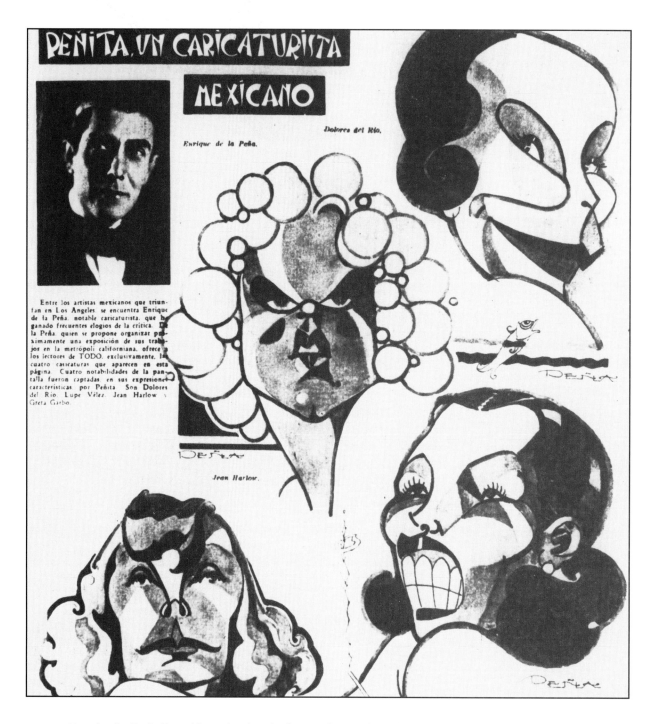

Drawing by De la Peña (shown here) and other Mexican caricaturists appeared regularly in local newspapers such as *El Heraldo de México* and *La Opinión*.

(Courtesy of Seaver Center for Western History Research, Natural History Museum of Los Angeles County)

NOTES

1. Bancroft, *History of California*, 5:626–627.

2. See Treaty of Guadalupe Hidalgo in David Hunter Miller (ed.), *Treaties and Other International Acts of the United States of America*, 8 vols, (Washington, D.C.: 1831–1848). Also, Tate Gallery, *Guadalupe Hidalgo: Treaty of Peace, 1848, and The Gadsden Treaty with Mexico, 1853* (Espanola, New Mexico: 1967).

3. Bancroft, *History of California*. 6:284–302.

4. Robinson, *Lawyers of Los Angeles*, pp. 31.

5. George Harwood Phillips, *Chiefs and Challengers: Indian Resistance and Cooperation in Southern California* (Berkeley: 1975).

6. Leonard Pitt, *The Decline of the Californios* (Berkeley: 1967), pp. 148–166.

7. Ibid., pp. 106-107, 172, 155-158, 163-164, 170, and 257.

8. Richard Griswold del Castillo, *The Los Angeles Barrio 1850-1890: A Social History* (Berkeley: 1979), pp. 35.

9. Harris Newmark, *Sixty Years in Southern California* (New York: 1916), pp. 56. Also, Pitt, pp. 123-124.

10. Pitt, pp. 262-263.

11. Robert Glass Cleland, *The Cattle on a Thousand Hills*, chapter VI, "The Rise and Collapse of the Cattle Boom," pp. 102-116. Also Pitt, pp. 120-129.

12. Pitt, pp. 181-194.

13. Richard Griswold del Castillo, "La Raza Hispano Americana: The Emergence of an Urban Culture Among the Spanish Speaking of Los Angeles, 1850-1880," (Ph.D. dissertation, University of California, Los Angeles, 1974), p. 213.

14. Ibid., pp. 219-223.

15. *El Clamor Público*, July 24, 1858.

16. Griswold del Castillo, pp. 218.

17. Ibid., pp. 226-228.

18. Ibid., pp. 276.

19. Glenn S. Dumke, *The Book of the Eighties in Southern California* (San Marino: Huntington Library, 1944), pp. 276. Also, Oscar Osburn Winter, "The Rise of Metropolitan Los Angeles, 1870-1900," *Huntington Library Quarterly*, 10 (1947):391-405.

20. Spencer Crump, *Ride the Big Red Cars* (Los Angeles: Cress Publications, 1962), pp. 39-40.

21. Ibid., pp. 60.

22. Robert M. Fogelson, *The Fragmented Metropolis; Los Angeles, 1850-1930* (Cambridge: Harvard University Press, 1967), pp. 92.

23. U.S. Bureau of the Census, *Thirteenth Census of the United States, Part 5* (Washington, D.C., 1913-1914), pp. 854.

24. Fogelson, pp. 146-147.

25. Carey McWilliams, *Southern California Country* (New York: Duell, Sloan and Pearce, 1946), pp. 134.

26. Ibid., pp. 314.

27. Alberto Camarillo, "Chicano Urban History: A Study of Compton's Barrio, 1936-1970," *Aztlan*, 2 (Fall, 1971): 79-106.

28. Joan Moore and Frank G. Mittelback, *Residential Segregation in the Urban Southwest*, Mexican-American Study Project, Advance Report 4, (Los Angeles: University of California Press, 1965), pp. 10-13.

29. Paul S. Taylor and Tom Vasey, "Contemporary Background of California Farm Labor," *Rural Sociology*, 1 (December, 1936) 401-419.

30. Gilbert Gonzalez, "Factors Relating to Property Ownership of Chicanos in Lincoln Heights, Los Angeles," *Aztlan*, 2 (Fall, 1971):107-143.

31. Sam B. Warner, *Streetcar Suburbs: The Process of Growth in Boston, 1870-1900* (Cambridge: Harvard University Press, 1962).

32. U.S. Bureau of the Census. *Fifteenth Census of the United States: 1930, Population* (Washington, D.C., 1932), Vol. 1, Table 23.

33. *U.S. Bureau of the Census, Twelfth Census of the United States* (Washington, D.C., 1901). Also, *Los Angeles City Directory*, 1910; McWilliams, pp. 314-324; Bessie D. Stockard, "Courts of Sonoratown," *Charities and the Commons*, 15 (December 2, 1905):295-299.

34. John Emmanuel Kienle, "Housing Conditions Among the Mexican Population of Los Angeles," (M.A. thesis, University of Southern California, 1912), pp. 6-7.

35. G. Bromley Oxnam, *The Mexican in Los Angeles*. (Los Angeles: Interchurch World Movement of North America, 1920), p. 6. Also William H. Matthew, "The House Courts of Los Angeles," *The Survey*, 30 (July 5, 1913):461.

36. John Modell, *The Economics and Politics of Racial Accommodation: The Japanese of Los Angeles, 1900-1942* (Urbana: University of Illinois Press, 1977), pp. 58-59.

37. De Graff, "The City of Black Angels," p. 339.

38. Matthews, p. 461.

39. Kienle, pp. 25-26. Also, Dana W. Bartlett, *The Better City: A Sociological Study of a Modern City* (Los Angeles: The Neurner Press, 1907), pp. 71-75.

40. Matthews, pp. 465. Also, Kienle, tables 5 and 7, pp. 41-42.

41. Oxnam, pp. 6, 8. Also, John Ihlder, "Housing at the Los Angeles Conference," *National Municipal Review*, 2 (January, 1913):68-75.

42. Kienle, pp. 12-13, 18.

43. Ibid., pp. 18-19, 22.

44. William W. McEuen, "A Survey of Mexicans in Los Angeles," (M.A. thesis, University of Southern California, 1914), pp. 40-41. Also Kienle, table 3, p. 40.

45. California Commission of Immigration and Housing, *First Annual Report*, January 2, 1915, pp. 237-238.

46. Kienle, table 9, p. 42.

47. California Commission of Immigration and Housing, op. cit. pp. 237-238.

48. *Report of the Los Angeles Housing Commission, February 20, 1906 to June 30, 1908*, pp. 8, 16.

49. Kienle, p. 11.

50. *Report of the Los Angeles Housing Commission, June 30, 1909 to June 30, 1910*, pp. 4-6. Also, *Report of the Los Angeles Housing Commission, July 1, 1910 to March 31, 1913*, p. 23; Kienle, table 8, p. 42.

51. Samuel Bryan, "Mexican Immigrants in the United States," *The Survey*, 28 (September 7, 1912):726-730. Also, Matthews, pp. 461-467; *Report of the Los Angeles Housing Commission, July 1, 1910 to March 31, 1913*, pp. 23-24.

52. *Report of the Los Angeles Housing Commission, July 1, 1910 to March 31, 1913*, pp. 31-32.

53. Emory Borgardus, "The House-Court Problem," pp. 391-399.

54. Ibid., p. 398.

55. Kienle, p. 26.

56. *Report of the Los Angeles Housing Commission, July 1, 1910 to March 31, 1913*, p. 22.

57. Modell, pp. 58-66. Also, De Graff, pp. 337-338.

Mexican men outside relief office.

CHAPTER SIX

A Delicate Balance: the Politics

of Survival

By 1900, relations between Mexicans and Anglos in Los Angeles had hardened into rigid patterns of behavior. In local business, politics, and social circles, Anglos were invariably on top, Mexicans below. As the city's Spanish-speaking community entered the new century, it saw that its economic position had worsened, its children had grown more accustomed to lack of opportunity, its young men were less able to find work, and its old people were condemned to almost inevitable poverty. Separation from the local mainstream was essentially complete.

But almost 50 years of Anglo dominance had changed something even more basic than socio-economic status. By the 1900s, the city's Mexican community had undergone significant internal change. Being a Spanish-speaking person had taken on a political meaning in California. By the very nature of their social and economic status, Mexicans in the City of Angels had become something altogether different from an ethnic constituency. They had become an enormous underclass. Up against racism and cultural bigotry, Mexicans grew increasingly preoccupied with their political future. In a burgeoning industrial center operated by an unsympathetic Anglo establishment, they saw reason to be suspect.

In terms of local residential patterns, the period marked a continued northeasterly movement. More and more Mexicans moved away from the central city to settle in new areas that allowed for land ownership and some measure of economic stability. The community's birthrate increased but the majority of Mexicans in Los Angeles had been born into a second class social status. What's more, the constantly growing immigrant population was also an underclass group, comprised mostly of unskilled Mexican nationals who hoped that the United States could offer a better life than their own country. For both these groups, the expectations of life in Southern California were very different from those of earlier generations. To be at the bottom of the social ladder was a hard reality but, for the majority of Mexicans in Los Angeles, it was an unavoidable truth.

Yet even in an atmosphere of economic exploitation and racial prejudice, Mexicans built supportive community resources. The importance of local Spanish-language media grew in proportion to worsening social conditions. No longer satisfied with the news itself, Mexicans looked to their own journalists and commentators for creative interpretation of events. Mutual aid societies and voluntary associations continued to help floundering members of the community bridge their private culture and life to the city's impersonal, industrial environment. In this way, twentieth-century mutualistas ensured that "pride" and "dignity" could remain operative terms for the Spanish-speaking population, even during times of crisis.

THE TWENTIETH-CENTURY SPANISH-LANGUAGE PRESS

The social and political life of the city's Mexican community can, perhaps, be best understood by examining its press. The number of Spanish-language newspapers published in Los Angeles grew steadily between 1910 and 1920. That fact alone suggests that the local Mexican population was rapidly becoming more literate and interested in the exchange of ideas. Equally important, the specific nature of the Spanish-language press tends to reflect a dynamic, self-directed community that viewed dialogue and debate as integral aspects of collective decision-making.

In downtown's Main Street area, from First Street to the Plaza, people gathered informally to read local newspapers and argue perspectives. There were several bookstores in the area, and most of them offered a selection of Mexican as well as U.S. Spanish-language publications. Magazines and newspapers were usually distributed by people pushing carts along Main Street and throughout the Plaza area. Articles and editorials in these papers were often the focus of political discussion among Mexican residents. Often, workers would meet in pool halls and billiard parlors spread along the northern sections of Main Street.[1] It was there that they would read newspapers aloud and discuss points of interest — political and otherwise.

Between 1910 and 1920, the most pivotal Mexican newspapers were the ones published weekly. *La Prensa, Regeneración, El Heraldo de México, La Gaceta de los Estados Unidos, El Correo Mexicano, El Eco de México,* and *Don Cacahuate* were the popular local weeklies. Each of them was thought to be a reliable source of local information. Monthlies such as *La Fuerza Consciente,* and even semi-monthlies like *La Pluma Roja,* were also influential. For the most part, they focused less on news events and more on the social trends or political issues of the day. As such, they served a unique role in the Mexican community.

In its own time, *La Prensa* (the Press) was considered a politically progressive paper. Published weekly between 1912 and 1924 by Adolfo Carrillo, *La Prensa* was dedicated to the laboring classes and to social reform. As both publisher and editor, Carrillo staunchly supported union organizing as a realistic way of improving life for local workers and their families. With its offices located at 108 Commercial Street in Los Angeles, *La Prensa* was published in the heart of the city's industrial center, where a large concentration of Mexicans lived and worked.[2] It was printed each Saturday and, at five cents a copy, offered weekend reading to many of the city's unskilled but literate Mexican workers.[3]

La Prensa was somewhat unique in that it was widely circulated throughout all of California and referred to itself as the state's most accurate reflection of "Latin American and Hispanic" people. As an editorial policy, Carrillo chose to focus on events in Mexico as well as on news related to the Mexican community in Los Angeles. In fact, many of his stories covered events pertaining to the Mexican Revolution (1910–1917) and analyzed the changes that war had ushered into the country.[4] The success of his publication suggests that the Spanish-speaking community in Los Angeles was, indeed, interested in the political machinations of its ancestral homeland.

Edited by Juan de Heras, *El Heraldo de México* (the Herald of Mexico) began publishing in 1915. Like *La Prensa,* the *Heraldo*'s offices were located in the city's central business district and its readership was made up primarily of unskilled downtown workers. Exceptionally well-received by the Mexican community, *El Heraldo* garnered a readership of 4,000 after only a year of publishing. It continued to appear on a weekly basis until the late 1920s.[5]

La Gaceta de los Estados Unidos (the United States Gazette) emphasized literature over news reporting. Its offices, at 314½ West Second Street, housed a bookstore also known as *La Gaceta.*[6] The newspaper was first published by Eduardo Ruíz in 1918 and, until the late 1920s, served as a weekly paper for Los Angeles and several other population centers throughout the Southwest. Like many editors of the period, Ruíz maintained that his publication was the true voice of Spanish-speaking people in the United States. Then, in May 1919, Clement G. Vincent assumed ownership of the paper and he moved its offices to 117 North Broadway. Insisting that the new *Gaceta* would be a "fraternity of the two communities" (Anglo and Mexican), Vincent initi-

Mexicans from Los Angeles at a Civilian Conservation Corps Camp in Idaho.

(Courtesy of Antonio Ríos-Ochoa)

ated an English-language page.[7] He was able to publish only through the mid-1920s.

Several of these Spanish-language newspapers gained reputations for their points of view. In fact, many of the publications appeared because of the socialist activity and worldwide revolution that characterized the 1910s and 1920s. Editors often took strong stands on emotionally-charged political issues. Mexico was itself in the throes of revolutionary upheaval and the Spanish-speaking community of Los Angeles wanted to read strident commentary on the subject. *La Pluma Roja* (the Red Pen), published by Blanca de Moncaleano, was only one of the publications to tread on political ice. But unlike most Spanish-language papers, *La Pluma Roja* covered socialist activism among both the Anglo and Mexican communities.[8] Moncaleano established the paper's offices at 1538 San Fernando and, for several years, she figured strongly in the city's newspaper publishing world.

La Fuerza Consciente (the Conscious Force), was even more radical in its orientation. A self-proclaimed anarchist newspaper, it was first published in Los Angeles and later moved to San Francisco. On the front page of each issue, editor Jaime Vidal wrote that the monthly was ". . . dedicada a la propaganda anarquica y revolucionaria" (dedicated to anarchical and revolutionary propaganda). Something of a regional legend in his own time, Vidal shocked California with his politics and personal prerogatives—among them, an unshakeable respect for liberated sexual activity.[9]

But in terms of radical journalism within the Mexican community, one newspaper stands above all others of the early century: *Regeneración* (Regeneration). Headed by Mexican anarchist, Ricardo Flores Magón, this journal was the literary voice of the Mexican Liberal party. A significant journalistic effort in the history of Los Angeles, especially in its coverage of Mexicans' political status in the region, *Regeneración* earned perhaps the most legendary reputation of all Spanish-language newspapers.

Flores Magón envisioned his newspaper to be a connecting communication link between the Mexican communities of the United States and Mexico. By exploring the issues of concern to both groups, Flores Magón believed that a radical shift in social status could begin. His paper was widely circulated in both countries, and after six years of publishing, it boasted a circulation of over 30,000. As publisher, Flores Magón called for a violent revolution that

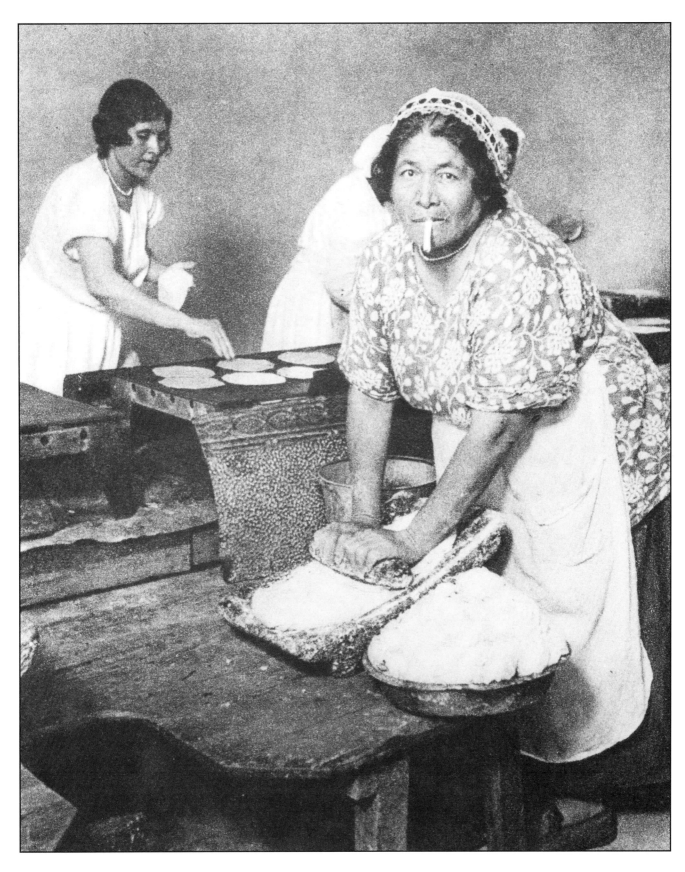

The number of Mexican women working outside the home, such as this tortilla maker, steadily increased during the twentienth century. 1930s.

(Courtesy of The Library of Congress)

would cross arbitrary borders, for an end to capitalism and foreign investment, and for political liberty for all Mexicans, regardless of their citizenship. He insisted that both societies were dominated by capitalists and believed that each was characterized by class conflict. As a spokesman for the working class, he felt that those who produced the wealth should own it. Under his direction, *Regeneración* became an influential symbol of political and social struggle among Mexicans in both countries.[10]

Originally, the newspaper was published in Mexico City. In 1904, Flores Magón's activities led to his expulsion from the country. He moved the journal to San Antonio, then to Chicago, next to St. Louis, and, finally, to Los Angeles in 1907. At first, he called the Los Angeles version *Revolución* (Revolution) but, in 1910, returned to the original *Regeneración*. Magón's local offices were located at 519½ East Fourth Street and his editor was Anselmo L. Figueroa. Members of the Mexican Liberal party were his contributors, and their essays and news reports advocated abrupt, uncompromising urban revolution. Before it became journalistically fashionable, he initiated an English-language page. It was written first by Alfred Sanfleben, later by Ethel Duffy Turner.

From 1912 to 1918, several Mexican Liberal party leaders—and a number of other writers and editors who had become involved in the newspaper—were repeatedly arrested and jailed. In 1912, Flores Magón and Figueroa were both imprisoned. Until their release in 1914, *Regeneración* was published on an irregular basis. Two years later, Flores Magón and a number of other party leaders were again arrested and jailed. In early 1918 *Regeneración* ceased publication.[11] It is often said that the paper's unprecedented popularity, coupled with its radical perspectives, led both the United States and Mexican governments to harass it into silence. The police, private detectives, and secret agents kept a close watch on Flores Magón and his staff. His offices were broken into as a way of intimidating the editors and members of the Mexican Liberal party. Still, for a number of years, his work stepped forward as a resilient voice of cultural determination and political resistance.

In short, the early twentieth century brought a strong cultural and social cohesion to the city's Mexican community. Spanish-language newspapers contributed a great deal to that solidarity. By 1920, several thousand copies of various publications were bought on a regular basis and either passed along to other readers or read aloud at public meeting places. By sharing and arguing political opinions, Mexicans were finding their way to a new cultural identity. The fact that so many publications appeared on the city's downtown and eastside newsstands implies that diversity had come to characterize the community. The rapid proliferation of these newspapers points to a literate and concerned populace. And the official disapproval that fell on *Regeneración* bears further witness to the power of the Mexican media throughout the period.

CULTURAL SELF-DEFENSE

For all its impact, the press was not the only means by which Mexicans in Los Angeles insulated their culture from a hostile mainstream society. In the tradition of their parents, twentieth century Angelinos continued to form new voluntary associations and mutualistas that could address new community concerns. Indeed, the combination of rapid growth and increased importance of these organizations stands as one of the most striking features of Mexican

social life throughout the period. On the level of cultural self-defense, mutualistas functioned as guiding institutions and regional anchors for a community
undeniably adrift in an Anglo city. Even more important, they offered small
scale networks of support in which Mexican leaders could emerge and serve
their own community.

There were very definite, pragmatic reasons for the development of
these institutions. First, local government was notoriously unresponsive to the
city's Mexican residents. Even when the power establishment attempted to
reach out, it was typically unable to meet crucial community needs. Housing
segregation, working-class alienation, and isolation from mainstream life were
among the many forces that led Mexicans to turn inward and seek a private
mechanism of protection. Often, these voluntary associations had more in
common with Mexican tradition than with North American practice. Most of
them emphasized *Mexicanismo* (pride in the Mexican heritage and culture)
and, in the process, reminded their members of an ancient and noble birth-
right. In the face of political oppression here in the United States, mutualistas
offered a constructive outlet for the nationalistic sentiments that were still
deeply ingrained in Mexican Americans. By reinforcing loyalty to the *madre
patria* (homeland or motherland), these organizations helped people make the
difficult adjustment to life in California.

In fact, many associations were established expressly for the "preserva-
tion of racial and patriotic principles."[12] In essence, they were the reflection of
Mexican nationalism as it functioned among Mexicans in the United States.
Despite the fact that most mutualista members had not been born or raised in
Mexico, recognition of ancestral roots remained a vital element in their self-
identity.

For this reason, the celebration of Mexican holidays took on great importance. Every year, the various clubs and lodge branches would plan patriotic parades and fiestas for the sixteenth of September and the fifth of May.[13]
In most cases, the entire community participated in the gala festivities. Beyond
the obvious purpose of providing culturally-tailored recreation, these annual
events reinforced pride in the Spanish language, the Mexican heritage, and to
some extent, the Californio way of life. Most important, they created a buffer
between the life of Mexican Los Angeles and the Anglo establishment.

Many of the early organizations were mutual benefit and protective
associations that functioned much like the social clubs of European immigrants.[14] By pooling their meager resources, Mexican immigrants learned that
they could provide each other with low-cost funeral and insurance benefits,
low-cost interest loans, and other forms of critical economic assistance. As
Paul Taylor notes, these mutualistas also provided ". . . a forum for discussion and a means of organizing the social life of the community."[15]

One of the most important charitable and social organizations in the
Mexican community was the Alianza Hispano-Americana. Established in
Tucson, Arizona in 1894, the Alianza offered its members life insurance, social
activities, and other financial services. In 1895, the group expanded and
established a second chapter in another Arizona community. Almost immediately, the local mutual aid society began to branch out of Arizona and into
other areas. Alianza chapters were established in New Mexico, Texas, and
California — usually in urban centers, where Mexicans were the most in need
of an insular support system. In each city, the association functioned as a fraternal insurance society serving middle-class and working class Mexicans. By
1913, there were 46 chapters established in four southwestern states.[16]

Some Alianza chapters were quite large. Most were small. Because economic uncertainty made membership more a luxury than a necessity, many people joined one year, dropped out the next and, when their income again allowed it, rejoined. In order to buy insurance through the association, members had to prove that they earned a steady income. As a result, Mexican migrants and unskilled residents found it very difficult to join. By and large, members were stable and employed Mexicans, usually from an upper middle-class background. According to Taylor, "the Alianza is generally regarded as somewhat more select than other societies."[17]

In 1918, the Alianza held its ninth annual convention in Los Angeles. Close to 250 delegates attended and elected Samuel Brown of Los Angeles as supreme president of the organization. Brown, whose mother was born in Mexico, identified himself as a Mexican. He worked as a blacksmith in Tempe, Arizona, where he involved himself in local politics—including a stint in the Arizona territorial legislature. As supreme president, he was instrumental in the growth and expansion of the association.[18]

By 1913, there were three association lodges in Los Angeles. According to reports in the Spanish-language press of the time, the Alianza was the only Latin American society in the United States to authorize health insurance policies up to $1,200, and to admit both male and female members. Even as they provided a solid insurance program, these Alianza branches served as a social and fraternal organization in which members could exchange ideas and reinforce community achievement. Still, for all their success, they were composed of a small, local elite. Mexican lawyers, doctors, merchants, owners of small businesses, and others with steady, relatively high-paying positions could meet the requirements of membership and afford to pay annual dues. Thousands of unskilled, working class Mexicans as well as victims of chronic unemployment and low wages could not.[19]

There were other social organizations in Los Angeles, and many of them allowed for a more diverse membership. El Club Anahuac, a young men's social club, sponsored a number of charitable and cultural activities. It also formed a baseball team to play against other teams backed by similar clubs. Like the larger mutualistas of the period, this club's members participated in Mexican national holidays and avidly supported a number of philanthropic causes.[20] For young Mexican women in Los Angeles, La Sociedad Moctezuma served as a popular and active association. Primarily a social club, La Sociedad sponsored dances, raised funds for various community activities, and participated in the celebration of Mexican holidays.[21] There were a few social clubs that functioned as mutual aid and recreational organizations for both men and women. El Club Alegria is an example. Similar to other Mexican associations, it sponsored dances, participated in various athletic teams, and helped in the celebration of various Mexican holidays.[22]

Although sometimes remembered as competitive social clubs, many of the voluntary associations worked together to nurture community consciousness. La Sociedad Mutualista Mexicana was specifically established to bring all groups together and to work toward a united Mexican community in Los Angeles.[23] At a dance to honor the first anniversary of El Club Juvenil Recreativo, one guest speaker urged the audience to work toward a better understanding and sense of brotherhood within their own local community. The evening's program also included drama and poetry readings that carried a nationalistic content.[24] In short, the evening reflected the overall orientation of the period's Mexican associations. Even as they balanced local concerns against nationalistic sentiment, they gave their members a social circle, community-oriented goals, and a connection to the heritage they might otherwise have lost.

They also provided a social network for what was fast becoming a substantial segment of the community—Mexicans who strongly identified with the United States and its ideals of patriotism and military duty. Indeed, the cultural penchant for organizing clubs led several Mexicans to organize Club

Beauty queen of a Mexican independence day celebration. 1933.

(Courtesy of Seaver Center for Western History Research, Natural History Museum of Los Angeles County)

Pro-Patria, a group dedicated to the preservation of the United States and to its defense throughout World War I. Both Mexicans and Anglos were encouraged to join this particular organization and it attracted a significant membership.[25] Still, it appears that the majority of Los Angeles Mexicans perceived themselves, first and foremost, as "Mexicans." Unlike most European immigrants, who wanted total involvement in the Anglo-American society, men and women of Mexican ancestry sought a middle ground between political and cultural loyalties.

As the 1910s moved into the 20s, many groups tried to involve their members in the political issues of the day. Some sponsored public meetings in order to provide a forum for community discussion and a safe environment in which people could voice their grievances on issues of importance to local Mexican residents. Working class Mexicans in particular were encouraged to attend because they generally faced the greatest employment difficulties and widest cultural gap.

In this way, the influence of these organizations reached far beyond the confines of any roll-call membership. Associations frequently extended financial aid to non-members and offered help to anyone in the community who was having problems with the police, employers, or discriminatory landlords. Even more important, the clubs became a hub of social activity and solidarity for local Mexican residents. With their commonly adopted motto ". . . the betterment of the Mexican community, socially and morally," they stood as public reflections of a community more concerned with its internal integrity than with its imposed subservience.[26] As early examples of social solidarity, the mutualistas and other voluntary associations sent a clear message to the community: pride and self-defense were community-defined concepts and, as such, were immune to the vagaries and bigotries of the outside society.

Throughout what sociologist Herbert Gans calls the creation of "urban villages," the continuity of Mexican tradition and culture—albeit with slight modification—became a constant process of self-assertion, self-affirmation, and self-protection for the city's Spanish-speaking community.[27] Cultural maintenance can be seen in the period's musical and theatre tastes. Throughout the 1920s, music was a popular recreation and many groups offered mostly Mexican audiences yet another connection to their roots. They often played at social dances and sometimes performed for large audiences at the plaza on Sundays.[28]

In their own theatres and clubs, members of the community could enjoy evenings of music, poetry, and live dramatic performance. The Teatro Zendéjas was located on south Spring, between Third and Fourth Streets. It regularly presented plays and other art events to a predominantly Mexican audience. The Teatro Hidalgo, located at 373 north Main Street, in the center of the Mexican commercial-social district of Los Angeles, also offered inexpensive forms of cultural entertainment.

Throughout the first 20 years of the century, Main Street—between Sixth and Macy Streets—constituted the businesses and social nexus of community life. Mexican restaurants, barber shops, theatres, pool halls, drug stores, tailors, jewelry stores, and other businesses spread throughout the area and offered a wide range of community services. On weekend evenings, the streets were filled with people on their way to the theatre, the plaza, or to restaurants.

On Sundays, the community would gather to hear bands play or speakers address issues of community concern. Newspaper carts filled with Spanish-language periodicals and journals were pushed about, old friends and relatives visited with each other, and new acquaintances were made. Indeed, the plaza was described as the "forum for the proletariat."[30]

In all of this, Mexicans found creative ways in which to live in Los Angeles even while they remained an insulated subculture within the city. Through their own press, social clubs, and business district, Mexicans drew together and erected a symbolic wall to protect themselves from the larger urban metropolis.

Nurturing a tradition that valued family, nationality, and cultural continuity, Mexicans in Los Angeles operated as a social entity unto themselves — even as they struggled to deal with an aggressive Anglo mainstream.

Thus, attempts to incorporate Mexicans into the industrial-urban order of Los Angeles met with failure. This is not to say that Mexican workers were not integrated into the city's economic structure. As cheap and exploited labor, they were certainly a part of local industrial expansion. Neither is it to suggest that all Mexicans remained unaffected by their exposure to the dominant society. There were significant adjustments made to life in an Anglo-run city. But the process of assimilation that affected most European immigrants did not occur within the Mexican population. Mexicans remained Mexican because they wanted it that way. If their defiance cost them economic advancement and political influence, they apparently considered it cheap at the price.

THE NEW BARRIOS

Although Mexican Angelinos diligently nurtured their social traditions and culture, unpleasant realities were affecting their lives. The segregated working class districts of the late nineteenth century gave rise to a serious housing crisis by 1900. An expanding economy called for more and more workers. The Mexican population continued to grow, both through immigration and high birthrates. Together with the rapid urbanization of the city in general, the local Mexican community was forced out of a single residential area and into outlying suburbs and new industrial sectors. Before long, new barrios had been created and segregation had become a firmly established fact of life in Los Angeles.

Residential dispersal did not bring improved housing. Restrictive racial convenants typically excluded the Spanish-speaking from desirable suburbs. The new barrios were established in sections of town that other, more affluent groups refused to inhabit. Just as proximity to jobs had determined settlement patterns during the late nineteenth century, the illusive goal of steady employment governed relocation trends of the 1900s. Be it near new business districts, the railroads or heavy industry, Mexicans moved close to economic activity, where they could look for work without the expense of daily transportation.

Several new barrios were settled east of the Los Angeles River. Low-income Mexican families moved into Boyle Heights, near Lincoln Park, and into Belvedere. Other barrios were created in central Los Angeles, in manufacturing areas near the old Chinatown, and in the southern part of the city. Like the old barrio near the Plaza, these new neighborhoods were physically isolated and almost inevitably lacked the basic services and facilities available to local Anglo communities.

Mexican neighborhoods in Los Angeles varied in size — from clusters of small homes and shacks to large tracts that housed thousands of people. No longer nestled in just one downtown district, Mexican families were scattered throughout the entire city and their barrios were transformed from a single urban center to a series of small-scale communities held together as much by their mutual poverty as by their ancestral traditions. The physical separation that kept Mexicans a long streetcar ride away from Anglo Los Angeles was not accidental; it was the result of consciously constructed economic and racial barriers. Carey McWilliams pinpointed the basic reasons for the historical development of Mexican barrios: "Site location has been determined by a combination of factors: low wages, cheap rents, low land values, prejudice, closeness to employment, undesirability of site, etc."[31]

The dominant economic and political powers of the time essentially forced Mexicans into segregated housing. Rarely did the Anglo establishment attempt to integrate Mexicans into the dominant social structure. Even when the industrial complex did embrace the Spanish-speaking community, it offered employment opportunities that effectively ruled out all possibility of financial security, professional advancement, and, consequently, improved housing. What's more, the urban migration of the Mexican working class doomed even community-based efforts at economic improvement.

After the outbreak of World War I, the development of barrios accelerated. An increase in war-related industries boosted Southern California's economy. In turn, the rise in production and sale of goods ranging from ships to fruits created a new demand for workers. Again, the rush of Mexican newcomers made it impossible for many families to find housing in the crowded Plaza neighborhood. Without other options, men and women moved into the northeast part of town, where affordable housing was still available. Within a few years, the area north of the Plaza—from Elysian Park on the east to Broadway on the west and from Avenue 10 on the north to Alhambra on the south—had become known as a working class community.[32] Indeed, one research survey found that, by 1916, Mexicans and Italians constituted 80 percent of the ethnic groups in the Elysian Park neighborhood.

In a survey conducted by the Los Angeles Society for the Study and Prevention of Tuberculosis, researchers questioned some 1,650 individuals in 331 homes about their health. Of the respondent group, 51 percent was Mexican and 30 percent Italian. The study found that, for Mexicans, youth was a common denominator. Only 2 percent of the Mexican residents were over 30 years of age, compared to 13 percent for the other groups. A hefty 56 percent of the Mexicans living in the area were between the ages of five and nine. Although the average Mexican family consisted of five members, more than half of the Mexicans interviewed lived in small apartments or house courts.

By the end of the war, the Mexican community had already moved in a northeasterly direction and was about to begin its major thrust to the eastside.[33] As early as 1920, numerous local developments pointed to the eventual movement of Mexicans to the eastside of the city. Almost prophetically, one observer of the period suggested in 1920 that "it is quite likely that the Mexicans now situated around the Plaza and in the Macy School District, will be forced to go to other parts of the city within the next five years."[34]

Still, factors other than overcrowding figured decisively in the relocation patterns of the local Mexican community. For one thing, it was almost certain that the state railway commission would place the Union Pacific passenger depot in an area adjacent to the Plaza community. This area, with its boarding houses, small hotels, and one- and two-room shacks, was extremely popular among new Mexican immigrants. To one observer of the time, it seemed almost inevitable that the Plaza would be chosen for construction, and he explained the consequences that such a decision would have for Mexican residents:

> This means that between five and ten thousand Mexicans will have to move to other sections of the city. It is thought that a large number will go to the Palos Verde region . . . that a larger group will cross the river and locate around Stephenson Avenue, in what may be called the South Boyle Heights section. Still another group will seek the new Industrial District just south of city limits.[35]

Ironically, resettlement served to unite rather than divide the Mexican community. Had it not been for the regular service and inexpensive fares provided by the city's interurban railway system, the community might have splintered into disconnected residential areas. But the electric trolley made it possible for Mexicans to relocate to residential areas several miles away from the central business district yet remain physically and culturally in touch with relatives, friends, and employers. Because movement into the "new" eastside occurred just as the Los Angeles Pacific Electric Railway opened new lines to Brooklyn Heights, Boyle Heights, and Ramona, rail service to outlying communities such as Maravilla and Belvedere actually made it possible for many working class families to leapfrog the older Mexican communities immediately east of the Los Angeles River. The scattered communities of the eastside soon became one enormous subcultural barrio. In contrast to the Anglo population, Mexicans had become a tightly clustered group by 1930. It was, ironically, appropriate for Mexicans to be the chief beneficiaries of the interurban railway system. After all, Mexican labor had been largely responsible for its construction.

While Mexicans continued to rely on the Red Cars, more and more Anglos turned to the automobile for their daily transportation. The rising popularity of this new vehicle had a remarkable impact on the urban structure of the city's Mexican residents. After the first World War, auto registration in Los Angeles soared. Nationally, one out of every seven Americans owned an automobile by the mid-1920s. In California, one out of every four residents owned one. In Los Angeles—the city soon hailed the auto capital of the world—the rate was one car for every 2.25 people. The ultimate impact of this car "craze" was simple: drivers enjoyed greater mobility than their streetcar-dependent neighbors. As auto registration increased, the general population gravitated toward outlying areas.[36] Like other cities around the country, Los Angeles gradually annexed many of the new commuter communities. A city of just 100 square miles in 1910, Los Angeles claimed 441 square miles by 1930. As the population of the city spread, vast tracts of single-family homes emerged. As families dispersed, so did industry.

Even as the new eastside community continued to grow, older Mexican enclaves found ways of surviving the impact of suburban development. One such community—itself split into three sections—was located in Pasadena. According to a 1922 survey, the three barrios of Pasadena accounted for 1,736 Mexicans and 396 families. According to Christine Lofstedt, the area was hardly an urban hideaway "located in that narrow strip of land south of Colorado Avenue, traversed by two railroad tracks, having gas tanks, electric power plants, several factories, laundries, and a heterogeneous huddle of abodes."[37] Living in Pasadena made it possible for Mexicans to find seasonal agricultural work in nearby citrus farms and ranches. "Most of their work," one observer wrote, "is in orchards, picking fruit, gardening, stone work, cement work, digging, hod carrying, and laundering."[38]

La Opinión February 27, 1931. "11 Mexicans Arrested in a Raid at the Placita." During the depression thousands of Mexicans were repatriated to Mexico. Many raids took place at the Placita which remained a popular meeting place for Mexicans.

(Courtesy of La Opinión)

In another southwestern barrio of Los Angeles, researcher Elizabeth Hummer found housing conditions little better than those in the Mexican colonia of Watts. In 1924, she wrote that the community is "a heterogeneous racial group, with Jewish, negro, and upper class Mexican predominating." One survey revealed that nearly two-thirds of them wanted American neighbors—an indication that they had "a definite desire to become a part of the fabric of the American social order."[39]

Greater industrial diversification in Los Angeles brought greater economic opportunity. Tire industries and meat packing companies, for example, viewed the inexpensive real estate, low taxes, and ample work force to be had in outlying areas of town extremely enticing. Other companies, such as those that relied on ocean shipping, were drawn to the harbor area surrounding San Pedro and Wilmington. For companies doing major business via the rail system, the eastside offered many attractive advantages.

Tire manufacturers, in particular, chose the eastside for the construction of their plants and factories. Most of these companies had received their first industrial impetus after World War I, when the automobile gained widespread popularity. By the mid-1920s, the tire industry employed 8,000 workers and produced an annual payroll of $14 million. A sizeable share of its workforce was Mexican and, while the pay was poor, work was available. The Samson Tire Company was a particularly large eastside employer. When it bought 40 acres of land on Atlantic Boulevard from the Union Pacific Industrial Park complex, it positioned itself to tap an enormous Mexican labor pool. Thanks to Samson and other manufacturers who settled in the area, the eastside grew more and more popular among Mexican immigrants looking for jobs.[40]

By the mid-1920s, a phenomenal migration of Mexican national families to Los Angeles contributed to the city's new reputation as the "Mexican capital" of the United States. Indeed, between 1920 and 1930, the Mexican population in the city tripled—from 33,644 to 97,116. The city soon surpassed San Antonio in its number of Mexican residents. The county as a whole counted 167,000 Mexicans, a number significantly greater than the population of all but a few cities in Mexico.[41]

The greatest growth occurred in areas east and south of downtown Los Angeles. The Central Plaza District and the Boyle Heights community (referred to as Assembly Districts 60 and 61 in 1930) recorded the largest increases. In District 60, which in 1930 included the Central Plaza, Lincoln Park, and sections of Boyle Heights, the Mexican population numbered nearly 35,000—or about twice the size of the second largest barrio located in Assembly District 61.[42]

Many of the social and religious centers serving the Mexican population followed the eastward shift. In 1928, the Brownson House Settlement, the

oldest center for Mexican immigrants in Los Angeles, relocated its facilities to the Eastside's Pleasant Avenue. Only by such a move could it hope to continue servicing the city's Spanish-speaking community. Originally built in 1901, near the Plaza just west of the Los Angeles River, the Brownson House was compelled to change with changing times. Mary J. Desmond, the head resident of that settlement house, recalled its very first days: "It was in a valley surrounded by pleasant homes and attractive gardens, but in recent years the encroachment of commercial enterprises was so rapid that the settlement house found itself entirely surrounded by factories and carried on its work beneath three huge towering gas tanks."[43]

By the late 1920s, Belvedere—with its 30,000 Mexican residents—had become home to the largest Spanish-speaking population of any Los Angeles district. It was larger than even the Mexican population of the city's central barrio. Mexicans had begun moving into the area during the late 1910s, when its lots and houses were significantly cheaper than in other welcoming suburbs. Like Santa Ana, this eastside community was served by a rail system that made movement in and out of the central city inexpensive and relatively swift.[44] This transportation system helped give Mexicans increased opportunities for property ownership by allowing them to live far from their place of employment, in areas that offered property values which were within their economic reach.

Belvedere, which was even closer to the central city than Watts or Santa Ana, flourished during the ten years following World War I. Significantly, the 1930 census shows that only 13 black residents lived in the area. In other low-income parts of town, Mexicans and blacks rivaled for a numerical majority and for the jobs offered by nearby employers. The competition that often characterized black/brown relations in these areas led to a long-lived tradition of urban conflict between the two groups. On the eastside, Mexicans were the unquestioned majority. Their sheer strength in numbers ensured first rights to all available job opportunities—especially in adjacent brick, lumber, clay, and heavy manufacturing plants.[45]

As additional industries established new plants in areas east and south of Belvedere, Mexicans enjoyed greater employment options. By city ordinance, meat packing, steel, and auto assembly firms were required to operate in areas outside the residential sections of town. By establishing their headquarters in the cities of Vernon, Maywood, Commerce, Bell, and Cudahy, these plants offered a growing Mexican community a wealth of industry-related jobs.

None of this addressed the fundamental employment status of working class Mexican laborers. Despite the abundance of available jobs, social worker Mary Lanigan once noted that second generation Mexicans in Belvedere had become a disillusioned group. "Accustomed to segregation and [referring to] Americans as 'white people'," she wrote, they had come to understand "that there are certain types of jobs for Mexicans and certain kinds for Americans." As to anything akin to true economic integration, Lanigan concluded that "America has repulsed the Mexican immigrant in every step he has taken toward that goal."[46]

The city's new subdivisions blatantly catered to white Americans and to immigrants of northern European ancestry. In an article entitled "Land of Sunny Homes," one writer warned that "for the man whose capital consists principally of his bare hands, the opportunities in southern California are limited. Though the district has made a remarkable industrial growth, thanks to cheap oil and cheap electric power, though the number of factories is doubling every five years, still the influx of labor usually exceeds the demands."[47]

The Spanish-speaking branch of the International Ladies Garment Workers Union (ILGWU) in a Labor Day parade. In the 1930s Mexicans in Los Angeles were involved in labor organizations. Mexican women, by now a major sector of garment workers in Los Angeles, played a critical role in the ILGWU and the garment workers' strike of 1933.

(Courtesy of Jaime Monroy)

Thus, most of the region's so-called "golden opportunities" benefited skilled and semi-skilled Anglo workers.

The findings of a study by the Interchurch World Movement (IWM) of Los Angeles suggested that life for Mexicans in Los Angeles had improved considerably by the end of World War I. The IWM research indicated that 50 percent of all Spanish-speaking residents lived in four or five-room dwellings, as opposed to only 5 percent in 1912. Even when this optimistic data was first released, the advancement it explored seemed all too remarkable. Indeed, the figures have been subsequently refuted by a number of other studies. More telling than its percentage totals was its final recommendation "that a reasonable rental commission be appointed to investigate the exorbitant rent now charged Mexicans."[48]

In terms of Mexican-owned businesses, the post-war period did usher in rapid growth and expansion. By 1922, 239 Mexican-owned establishments had opened their doors in the Eastside. Their emergence reflected a sense of permanency with regard to the Spanish-speaking community and helped to dispel the myth that Mexicans in Los Angeles contributed to the local economy only through seasonal work. Prior to the War, most Mexican businesses operated in the Plaza community. As time passed, entrepreneurs faced the same problem as individual families: higher rents and lack of space made the central city area inaccessible. As the community itself spilled over into new eastside districts, small business followed.

By 1920, close to one-sixth of all Mexican-owned grocery stores were located on Brooklyn Avenue in the Eastside. Evidently, the grocery business was a popular market for Mexican businessmen because grocery stores accounted for 25 percent of the community's commercial activity. The next two most popular businesses were restaurants and cleaning establishments—probably because so many single men lived in the area.[49]

In many ways, these businesses signaled a new phase in the on-going history of Mexican Los Angeles. Although they often operated without adequate financial backing and proved less profitable than their Anglo-owned counterparts, they managed to survive. Their survival stood as yet another reflection of a community that insisted on shaping its own way of life, even as a whirl of industrial change shaped the rest of the city.

A SOCIAL PORTRAIT, CIRCA 1930

By sifting through the available literature and plumbing a variety of obscure sources, a general portrait of the Mexican community, circa 1930, can be outlined. The process reveals a picture of a growing population and a community repeatedly pushed into the less desirable areas of town. Above all else, it reveals the way in which one group confronted racial prejudice and economic malfeasance with a tenacious drive to survive.

Demographic data show that, by the end of the 1920s, the Mexican population of Los Angeles was increasing at a phenomenal rate. In 1929 and 1927, the excess of births-over-death among the white population of the unincorporated area of Los Angeles was 241. For Mexicans, it was 4,070. Between 1918 and 1927, Mexicans accounted for 20 percent of the local birth-over-death excess. A study of 769 Mexican households, conducted during this same period revealed that among the people interviewed, the average number of children per married couple was 4.3. Over 45 percent of the families surveyed had five or more children, and only 40 percent had fewer than three.[50]

The study also confirmed the low wages earned by most Mexican laborers in Los Angeles. Of the 701 Mexican families for which average monthly incomes were available, 69.2 percent averaged less than $100 per month, 10.5 percent averaged between $100 and $150, 5.9 percent earned between $150 and $200, and only 4.4 percent grossed $200 or more. Because of the low salaries, every able person in the household was encouraged to contribute to the family income. A second study, which analyzed 435 Mexican families residing in Los Angeles, reported that 35.2 percent of all respondents admitted to having their children working full-time or, more commonly, part-time.[51]

As the Mexican population increased and dispersed throughout much of the city, neighborhoods began to divide along racial lines. For example, in Watts, one investigator observed that "Main Street divided the community into two sections; north of Main Street became settled by white people, mostly those who segregated themselves, while the greater part of south of Main Street was occupied mostly by the Mexicans and later by both Mexicans and Negroes."[52]

Although Mexicans resided in every district of Los Angeles, a general and deeply embedded housing discrimination prevailed in most communities. Prior to World War I, and by using restrictive mortgage contracts, Anglo residents of the Central Avenue District had successfully resisted the "invasion" of Mexican neighbors. Like blacks and Asians, Mexicans experienced segregation in housing in nearly every section of the city and its outlying areas. In Santa Ana, one woman explained how the Mexican population came to live near the railroad tracks, in an area known as the Santa Fe District:

> The Mexicans went down there to live because the rents were cheap. Then, too, there was a terrible feeling among the white people in Santa Ana at that time. They did not like to live near the Mexican people. A white man would let his house stand vacant all of the time before he would rent it to a Mexican, even if the Mexican and his family were clean and could pay the rent. So whether or not the Mexican people wanted to live in a district by themselves, they had to. There was no other place they could get a house to live in.[53]

But after the World War I, increasing numbers of Mexicans settled in areas where Anglos already owned homes. Such relocation was often the catalyst to utter isolation. As sociologist Clara Smith concluded: "When the Mexican buys property in the white district, he becomes an outcast of his former group and is rejected by his American neighbors."[54]

According to social worker Helen Walker, Mexicans in the Santa Ana community wanted "to put their children in schools with Americans." She reported that "many of the Mexicans feel that the Mexican schools, with their old and ugly buildings, are not as good as the schools to which the Americans go."[55] But the urge to give their children a better education meant additional shifts in the residential patterns of the new immigrant population.

In 1927, the Los Angeles Chamber of Commerce asked surrounding, incorporated cities to report on their rate of population growth and industrial development. The results of its survey shed light on the problem of local segregation and, more importantly, on the attitudes of community leaders toward new Mexican residents. The coastal city of El Segundo stated proudly that its city "had no negroes or Mexicans." In 1930, Lynwood—one of the new industrial areas southeast of the central area—reported that: "Lynwood, being restricted to the white race, can furnish ample labor of the better class." These comments were not aberrations of their time. Apparently, every city that wished to attract new Anglo homeowners and renters felt compelled to

The Lugo family. 1930s.

(Courtesy of Antonio Ríos-Ochoa)

deny a large number of foreign born or racially-mixed residents. Long Beach, a city that, indeed, had a large Mexican population, once advertised that "Long Beach has a population of 140,000—98 percent of whom are of the Anglo-Saxon race."[56]

Most housing discrimination was directed toward poor, working class Mexican immigrants. Real estate agents and homeowners were willing to bend the unwritten rules of segregation if it appeared that the prospective minority buyer had attained an acceptable level of social status. Ramon Navarro and Dolores del Rio—two of early Hollywood's most successful stars—bought homes in the nearly all-white area of the Westside, but only after they had been well-established for sometime.

A few other affluent Mexican immigrants settled on the Westside, in fashionable homes on Adams and Wilshire Boulevard. In general, they were ex-Mexican nationals who had been members of the ruling elite during the dictatorship of Porfirio Díaz. These residents included the ex-land baron of Chihuahua, Luis Terrazas, who had once ruled over a cattle and mining empire valued at $200 million. The ex-governors of Baja California and Oaxaca were also L.A. residents.[57] In private Westside dwellings, they could shelter themselves amidst spacious gardens reminiscent of pre-Revolutionary Mexico. And for their part, Anglo sophisticates were happy to socialize with these members of the "Spanish" community. The *Los Angeles Times* once reported that on West Adams Boulevard, near the popular *Centro Hispano Americano*, Mexican *señoritas* mixed with the city's upper crust.[58]

More than undesirable housing characterized the life of Mexicans in Los Angeles during the late 1920s and early 1930s. The community suffered the plague of a distorted public image. Perhaps the most difficult myth to overcome was the one of vagabond transience. The California Development Association would have liked for the public to believe that all Mexican Angelinos were engaged in agriculture and returned to Mexico at the end of each harvest season. In an effort to persuade the U.S. Congress that Mexico should not be placed on the quota list—as it had done for eastern European countries—the association fostered a wide array of misleading perceptions. Its main argument was that "the Mexican coming to California has evidenced little mass tendency to remain in permanent colonies."[59]

Young man and car. 1930s.

(Courtesy of Antonio Ríos-Ochoa)

It was almost politically fashionable to portray Mexicans as a casual labor force. The Los Angeles Chamber of Commerce, for instance, contributed to the myth of the transient Mexican laborer. In 1929, prominent chamber spokeman, Dr. George Clements, authored an extensive report, which he filled with typical misconceptions of the day. Out of three arbitrary categories of workers—permanent, casual, and climactic—Clements placed Mexicans in the latter two. He noted that Mexican laborers in the casual sector met both agricultural and public utility demands and argued that "climactic labor calls for a class of workers who are by habit and ability capable of standing up under desert conditions."

Clements further asserted that the casual labor needs of the region, which "are totally un-American since they are nomadic, are supplied by Mexican people, both immigrant and American citizens of the Mexican stem." The latter part of his statement revealed a common myth of the period: that even the American-born Mexican held no claim to American society. Responding to a question concerning the extent to which unskilled immigrant laborers (especially Mexican) had replaced American laborers, Clements wrote that "in general industry, alien labor—especially Mexicans—are drawn upon to supply a short labor market in industry. An American laborer willing to work has the first preference." The Mexican, Clements concluded, "comes to America primarily to sell his labor for American money so that he may return to Mexico and be a landed citizen."[60] The utter absurdity of his claims, and the fact that many Mexicans in the United States raised families, bought homes, and sent their children to school did not stand in the way of widespread acceptance for the Clement paper.

Robert McLean, a religious leader and writer of the early 1930s, challenged the image of Mexicans as nomadic wanderers who returned to Mexico for each year's winter. In a dozen settlement houses from San Antonio to Los Angeles, McLean found that of "1,021 individuals studied, 833 had been in this country for five years or more. Of that group, 982 remarked that they intended to live permanently in the United States; 15 were not sure; and 24 said they desired to return eventually to Mexico." Of the latter group, "not a single one stated that it was his habit to spend the winter in Mexico." In an earlier study, researcher Gladys Patric found that 31 percent of the 495 Mexicans surveyed in one northeast Los Angeles community had lived in the city for five to nine years. An even larger portion, 34 percent, had been in the city between ten and 19 years.

Still a third survey, this one conducted in the mid-1920s, provides some insight into the settlement and migration patterns of Mexican immigrants. Just over half of all respondents said that they expected to eventually return to Mexico. Another 35 percent chose not to answer the question. When the same question was re-phrased, 29 percent expressed a desire to remain permanently in the United States while 49.2 percent chose not to answer this particular question.

A TURNING INWARD

Even as the early twentieth century ushered in industrial expansion and increasing employment opportunity, it failed to include the Mexican community of Los Angeles in the harvest of technology's bounty or in the abundance of wartime affluence. If the years between 1900 and 1930 taught the Spanish-speaking residents of California's growing metropolis nothing else, it taught them that the outside society would not look after their needs or ensure their rights.

By then an assumed underclass, Mexicans spent the period mastering the politics of survival. While the Anglo mainstream gave up close-knit cultural bonds in favor of economic expansion, Mexicans turned inward. Within the confines of their run-down barrios, they sowed the seeds of a cultural renaissance that would flower in the years to come.

The Logia 'Juventud Latina' #222 of the Alianza Hispano Americana. Seventh Anniversary. Los Angeles. 1936. Social and fraternal organizations played a significant role in the cultural life of Mexicans in Los Angeles. The Alianza Hispano Americana, the largest fraternal organization in the United States, had over 30 lodges in Los Angeles county in the 1930s.

(Courtesy of Seaver Center for Western History Research, Natural History Museum of Los Angeles County)

"America Tropical." In 1932 the Mexican muralist David Alfaro Siqueiros visited Los Angeles and was commissioned to paint a mural on the wall of the Plaza Art Center on Olvera Street. When Siqueiros recreated the jungle of capitalist America rather than a lush tropical pastorale envisioned by the owners, Siqueiros was fired and the controversial mural whitewashed.

(Courtesy of Los Angeles Times)

NOTES

1. William W. McEuen, "A Survey of Mexicans in Los Angeles" (M.A. thesis, University of Southern California, Los Angeles, 1914), pp. 67-68.

2. Julia Norton McCorkle, "A History of Los Angeles Journalism," *Historical Society of Southern California* 10 (1915-1916):24-43; Herminio Rios and Guadalupe Castillo, "Toward a True Chicano Bibliography, Mexican-American Newspapers, 1848-1942," *El Grito* 3 (Summer, 1970):17-24.

3. *La Prensa*, December 8, 1917, p. 5.

4. Ibid., February 2, 1918, p. 5.

5. *El Heraldo de México*, April 22, 1916, p. 6.

6. *La Gaceta de los Estados Unidos*, April 30, 1919, p. 1.

7. *La Gaceta de los Estados Unidos*, April 30, 1919, p. 1.

8. McCorkle, "A History of Los Angeles Journalism," p. 39.

9. McEuen, "A Survey of Mexicans in Los Angeles," pp. 87-94; *La Fuerza Consciente*, January 15, 1914, p.1.

10. Juan Gómez-Quiñones, *Sembradores, Ricardo Flores Magón y El Partido Liberal Mexicano* (Los Angeles: Aztlan Publications, 1973), pp. 45-65; *Regeneración*, September 2, 1910.

11. Armando Bartra (ed.), *Regeneración, 1910-1918* (Mexico City: Ediciones Era, 1977), pp. 13-58; *Regeneración*, September 3, 1910, p. 1; Gómez-Quiñones, *Sembradores*, pp. 31-42; Robert E. Ireland, "The Radical Community, Mexican and American Radicalism; 1900-1910." *Journal of Mexican American History* 2 (Fall, 1971):22-32.

12. *La Opinión*, June 4, 1927, p. 5.

13. On September 16, 1810, a priest, Miguel Hidalgo y Costilla, declared Mexico's independence from Spain. On May 5, 1862, the French army with a loss of more than a thousand men was defeated at the Battle of Puebla by the Mexican army and was driven back to the coast. Both of these historical events are celebrated annually in Mexico and by Mexicans in the United States as national holidays.

14. See: Nelli, *The Italians in Chicago*, pp. 170-181; Rischin, *The Promised City*, pp. 104-105, 182-183; and Virginia Yans-McLaughlin, *Family and Community; Italian Immigrants in Buffalo, 1880-1930* (Ithaca: Cornell University Press, 1977), pp. 110-111, 130-131.

15. Paul S. Taylor, *Mexican Labor in the United States* (Berkeley: University of California Press, 1928), p. 45.

16. Kaye Lynn Briegel, "Alianza Hispano-Americana, 1894-1965: A Mexican American Fraternal Insurance Society," (Ph.D. dissertation, University of Southern California, 1974), pp. 19-22, 47, 48, 68-70.

17. Paul Taylor, *Mexican Labor in the United States: The Imperial Valley* (Berkeley, University of California Press, 1928), p. 64.

18. *La Prensa*, February 2, 1918, p. 5 and Kaye Briegel, "Alianza Hispano-Americana," pp. 50-53.

19. *La Prensa*, December 22, 1917, p. 5.

20. *El Heraldo de México*, April 22, 1916, p. 8.

21. *La Prensa*, December 15, 1917, p. 5.

22. *El Heraldo de México*, November 11, 1919, p. 4.

23. *La Prensa*, September 21, 1918, p. 5.

24. *La Prensa*, February 23, 1918, p. 5

25. *La Prensa*, May 18, 1918, p. 5.

26. *La Opinión*, June 4, 1927, p. 5.

27. Herbert Gans, *The Urban Villagers* (New York: The Macmillan Company, 1962).

28. *La Prensa*, January 26, 1918, p. 5.

29. *El Heraldo de México*, October 17, 1919, p. 3; *La Prensa*, May 25, 1918, p. 5.

30. Paul Herbold, "Sociological Survey of Main Street; Los Angeles, California," (M.A. thesis, University of Southern California, 1936), p. 128.

31. Carey McWilliams, *North From Mexico, The Spanish Speaking Peoples of the United States* (New York: Greenwood Press, 1968), p. 217.

32. Walter V. Woehlke, "Los Angeles—Homeland," *Sunset Magazine* 36 (January 1911):11.

33. Baist's Real Estate Atlas, "Survey of Los Angeles," (Philadelphia, 1910) Los Angeles County Museum of Natural History, plates 4, 5, 12. John S. McGroarty (ed.), *History of Los Angeles County*, Vol. I (New York, 1923), pp. 13 and 281.

34. Oxnam, "The Mexican in Los Angeles," p. 23.

35. Ibid., p. 23.

36. Ashleigh E. Brillant, "Some Aspects of Mass Motorization in Southern California, 1919-1929," *Southern California Quarterly* 47 (1965):191-206.

37. Lofstedt, "The Mexican Population of Pasadena, California," p. 260.

38. Ibid., p. 262.

39. Elizabeth E. Humer, "A Study of the Social Attitudes of Adult Mexican Immigrants in Los Angeles and Vicinity," (Master's thesis, University of Southern California, 1924), pp. 2, 3, and 25.

40. John C. Austin, "Pioneering the World's Second Tire Center," *Southern California Business* 8 (February 1929): 9, 10, 47.

41. U.S. Bureau of the Census. *Fifteenth Census of the United States, 1930—Vol. II: Population* (Washington, 1933), p. 266. Richard Romo, "The Urbanization of Southwestern Chicanos in the Early Twentieth Century," *New Scholar* 6 (1977):185.

42. U.S. Bureau of the Census. *Fifteenth Census of the United States, 1930—Vol. III: Population* (Washington, 1933), p. 287.

43. Mary J. Desmond, "New Brownson House." *Playground* 22 (November 1928):456.

44. Crump, *Ride the Big Red Car*, p. 236.

45. *Fifteenth Census of the United States, 1930—Vol. II: Population* (Washington, 1933), pp. 259-263.

46. Mary Lanigan, "Second Generation Mexicans in Belverdere" (Master's thesis, University of Southern California 1932), p. 45.

47. Walter V. Woehlke, "The Land of the Sunny Home," *Sunset Magazine* 34 (1915):472.

48. Oxnam, "The Mexican in Los Angeles," p. 8.

49. Figures computed from data published by Los Angeles Directory Company. *Los Angeles City Directory* (Los Angeles: Southern California Publishing Co., 1920-30).

50. U.S. Department of Labor, Bureau of Labor Statistics, "Labor and Social Conditions of Mexicans in California" *Monthly Labor Review* 32 (January 1931): 86-87.

51. Ibid., p. 89.

52. Smith, "The Development of the Mexican People in the Community of Watts, California," p. 10.

53. Helen Walker, "The Conflict of Cultures in First Generation Mexicans in Santa Ana, California" (Master's thesis, University of Southern California, 1928), p. XIV.

54. Smith, "The Development of the Mexican People in the Community of Watts, California," p. 10.

55. Walker, "The Conflict of Cultures in First Generation Mexicans in Santa Ana, California," p. XIV. Also by the same author, "Mexican Immigrants and American Citizenship" *Sociology and Social Research* 13 (May 1929):465-471.

56. Los Angeles Chamber of Commerce Files. Letters located at the City Hall Library under the title "Industrial Surveys of Los Angeles Chamber of Commerce." The letters were written by local Chamber of Commerce secretaries and presidents to the main headquarters in Los Angeles. Box 4330-779.

57. *Los Angeles Times*, January 2, 1916.

58. *Los Angeles Times*, November 22, 1922.

59. Ofra J. Shontz, "The Land of 'Poco Tiempo'," *Family* 8 (May 1927):78-79.

60. George P. Clements Papers. Los Angeles Department of Special Collections, University of California, Los Angeles.

During World War II over 200,000 Mexicans served in the armed forces. Most fought as combat troops, receiving more Purple Hearts than any other ethnic group. While only 10% of the Los Angeles population, Mexicans composed over 20% of the city's war casualties.

(Courtesy of William D. Estrada)

CHAPTER SEVEN

Depression, War, and Resistance

When the Great Depression of the 1930s began, most Mexicans in Southern California were employed at least part of the year. But by 1933, many had been forced to ask for government subsidy. As the city's business community desperately struggled to survive, employers all across the country laid off thousands of workers. Almost inevitably, Mexicans were the first to be eliminated. Still, hard as their forced departure was, it constituted just one more link in what had become a long chain of employment problems. In short, while the 1930s ushered in dramatic economic change for most Americans, it simply brought the Mexican community of Los Angeles another round of job instability and insufferably low wages.

In 1929, Los Angeles claimed a higher level of employment than any other city in California; not even San Francisco could offer its residents as many employment prospects. By the spring of 1930, the situation changed, and, for several years, Los Angeles stood in the shadow of the Bay City's economic activity. In fact, it was not until much later in the Depression, when large corporate branch plants and new aircraft firms set up offices in Los Angeles, that the Southern California metropolis regained an employment opportunity edge. Even then, the upswing had little impact on Mexican workers. By 1940, Los Angeles had jobs to offer but, by and large, they went to Anglos, whose educational background better prepared them for the available work.

With the outbreak of World War II, tens of thousands of Mexicans found reason to enlist. In part, their military involvement was the reflection of a community that still believed it could enjoy the privileges of the dominant culture—if only it were willing to pay the price. The collective assumption proved tragically ill-founded. By the end of the war, the community had lost many of its young men and remained as disadvantaged as ever.

AN EMPLOYMENT PROFILE

It is difficult to establish a precise occupational distribution of the Los Angeles Mexican population during the 1930s. It is certain, however, that the community was relatively static rather than growing. Between 1911 and 1920, roughly 219,000 Mexican citizens crossed into the United States. Another 460,000 arrived during the 1920s. It is a telling fact that by 1930, only 97,116 Mexicans still lived in Los Angeles. With a total county population of 167,024, the community did constitute over 13 percent of all regional residents but only 22,000 additional Mexican nationals entered the United States during the Depression decade.[1]

The majority of Mexican Angelinos lived in the central and eastern areas of town. A great many worked in urban occupations, primarily in the downtown garment and furniture industries. However, close proximity to the fields of eastern Los Angeles also allowed them to work in agriculture for at least part of the year. In fact, agriculture was the chief income industry for Mexicans living in the San Gabriel Valley. Those in north San Gabriel probably worked the citrus groves of Pasadena while those in the eastern parts of the valley worked in truck farms around El Monte. Many Mexicans lived in the San Fernando Valley and they, too, worked in agriculture. So did the Spanish-speaking residents of Culver City and Venice. Some Mexican families lived in the Watts area and, along with Spanish-speaking laborers from the local Harbor areas, the men often took jobs in either the city's small harbor industry or one of its lumber companies.

Wounded veteran of the North African and Italian campaigns with his fiancee. 1945.

(Courtesy of Antonio Rios-Ochoa)

Based on the marriage records of 1936, over 77 percent of all Mexican men in Los Angeles worked as unskilled or semi-skilled laborers. A hefty 31 percent of these men listed their occupation simply as "laborer." The rest listed a specific unskilled or semi-skilled job title. Nevertheless, these records also indicate the emergence of a fairly successful Mexican middle class. Almost 10 percent of all the men surveyed claimed to be holding a "skilled" job. What's more, a sizeable share, over 13 percent, listed their job as either "white collar" or "small business ownership."[2]

According to these 1936 records, one-third of all Mexican women worked outside the home. The vast majority, over 85 percent, worked in unskilled jobs. Less than one percent had a skilled trade although close to 14 percent held either a white collar job or owned a small business. (It is worth noting that all women who listed themselves as "sales" or "saleslady"—3.3 percent of all surveyed women—were counted as "white collar" workers. Because this work lacked prestige and offered low wages, the label may be somewhat misleading.) Just over 34 percent of all these working women listed their occupation as "housekeeper." Nearly as many worked in *la costura* (the garment industry), almost 19 percent as "dressmakers" and nearly 5 percent as "machine operators."

Other research surveys conducted during the 1930s corroborated these findings. One study was conducted by the city itself between 1934 and 1935. Its researchers found that out of 99 Mexican families living in the city, 56 percent had a semi-skilled wage worker as the chief income earner. Another 29 percent depended primarily on an unskilled worker, 8 percent on a skilled worker, and 7 percent of all Anglo families depended primarily on a clerical worker, 17 percent on a skilled worker, 28 percent on a semi-skilled worker, and only 10 percent on an unskilled worker.[3]

Although these statistics offer some insight into the employment realities that confronted Mexicans throughout the 1930s, they cannot paint the full picture. This is especially true because a high degree of job mobility characterized the Spanish-speaking workforce of the period. "The Mexicans are like swallows at the old mission," agricultural employers would say. "They come and go about the same time every year." They came and went all right—but always in search of other jobs in Los Angeles, not back to Mexico.

Attention was first drawn to this employment cycle during the depression of 1907–13, when public officials noticed that Mexicans would live in local barrios all winter. Then, each spring, they would vanish. Similar patterns of migration operated in other parts of the country, but Los Angeles was unique in that it was a year-round agricultural city. Thousands of farmworkers had settled permanently within the county limits. Each year, when the harvest season ended, they turned to urban industry for winter work. Unfortunately, they had to compete with an annual rush of winter-only residents—farmworkers who traveled from one agricultural center to another, looking for seasonal work wherever they could find it. Despite the fact that local industry was booming, it could not employ all the winter-time jobseekers. And because there was so large a labor surplus, those who did get jobs were forced to work for extremely low wages.[4] Then came the Depression, and with drastic workforce cutbacks, there were virtually no jobs available. By the mid-1930s, winter had become a harsh season for Mexicans in Los Angeles.

The entire problem was exacerbated by the fact that many Mexicans worked in fruit and vegetable canning, which was an agriculture-related urban occupation. In 1928, nearly one out of every four cannery workers in Los Angeles was Mexican. Yet even then, when industry was booming, the canneries could not employ their workers for long periods of time. When the Depression hit, things became that much worse. If 100 were considered the average number of workers to be employed in a cannery at any given time, then during the mid '30s, only 16 workers were on the job in December. Only 17 were working in January. In August, however, 354 could find cannery work. Throughout California, between 60,000 and 70,000 people found summer cannery jobs while only 10,000 to 13,000 found them during the winter. Average employment amounted to a mere ten to 11 weeks per year.

Nevertheless, thousands of cannery workers managed to live on their meager earnings. With average wages of $26.64 per week, half of all male employees earned less than $300 per year. For women, the average salary was only $16.55. That meant that less than 25 percent earned an annual wage of $300 or more. One might imagine that many of these workers took winter jobs in other city industries. But they did not. In fact, the California Unemployment Reserves Commission of 1937 found that only 1 percent of all male cannery workers found off-season employment outside the canning factories. Only

10 percent of all cannery workers held a job throughout the entire year. Given the nature of the California employment situation, it is doubtful that Mexicans comprised much of this group. In short, over 70 percent of all male cannery workers found either casual employment or no employment at all for the winter months. For women, the statistics are just as shocking, although somewhat more difficult to analyze. It seems that their cannery wages were considered only a supplemental family income. In fact, 61 percent of all women cannery workers surveyed were unemployed through the winter and had no desire to find a job. Still, over 31 percent of the Mexican women who worked in local canneries did want a winter job but could not find one.

Figures such as these expose the way in which seasonal industries left many Mexicans underemployed or out of work altogether for a good portion of the year. Although cannery workers in Los Angeles suffered less than those employed in the rest of the state—because they lived in the hub of all Southern California agriculture and could count on a wider variety of products to be canned—the effects of seasonal employment were devastating.

Of course, there were other industries in which Mexicans found work. But with few exceptions, they all offered unsteady, seasonal employment. Spanish-speaking workers in the textile, furniture, woodworking, and construction industries found themselves at the mercies of on-again, off-again employment. While every Angelino working in these sectors lived with the nagging threat of winter lay-off, Mexicans fared worse than most. Generally occupied at the bottom rung of every employment ladder, they were the first to be fired when the slow winter months rolled around. As a result, their seasonal unemployment rate was higher than any overall, industry-wide figure would suggest.[5]

In all this data, a trend is obvious: winter was the off-season for just about every industry that employed Mexicans. Thus, a cannery worker could not find a winter job with a local construction gang or in a downtown dress shop because it was the off-season there, too. Along with the thousands of agricultural workers who wintered in Los Angeles with friends or relatives, and in addition to people rendered chronically unemployed by the Depression, these urban laborers produced an enormous surplus labor pool each and every winter.

Mexican workers were not concentrated in these seasonal industries by accident. The economy of Los Angeles demanded a group of workers who would accept such seasonal work. Because better-paying, steadier occupations were generally unavailable, the Spanish-speaking community was forced to take undesirable jobs in any industry that could hire them for even a fraction of the year. Thus, a racially identifiable work force, against whom discrimination and racism could be rallied, was earmarked and exploited. In a manner that had become traditional, a few members of the community acquired professional expertise while the majority remained unskilled. In such an environment, the Spanish-speaking of Los Angeles were affected less by the skill level attained by a few and more by the instability of employment that plagued so many.

The entire issue of employment stability points to a community gap that began dividing Mexican Angelinos during the 1930s. Put simply, a new segment of the Spanish-speaking population was emerging: the white collar professional. Although most Mexicans in Los Angeles were poor, a small contingent of the community was decidedly geared toward career advancement and economic security. In El Monte, for example, most Mexicans lived in the deplorable Hicks Camps. But some lived in comfortable homes where the houses and yards were well kept. These homes were humble dwellings of four and five rooms, but infinitely better than the rest.

Mexican home ownership was not at all unusual in Los Angeles of the 1930s. According to a special 1933 census, less than 5 percent of all local Japanese families lived in homes that they owned themselves. Among Chinese residents, the figure reached to over 8 percent. For Mexican families, it stretched to over 18 percent. This same survey found that annual income varied a great deal among the Spanish-speaking. Out of 99 Mexican households, 21 had an annual income of between $500 and $900. Another 35 families relied on between $900 and $1,200 per year and 24 households relied on between $1,200 and $1,500. A total of 12 families lived on between $1,500 and $1,800, and seven of the 99 families claimed an annual income of over $1,800. For those living on between $500 and $1,500, the average number of gainful workers per family did not vary significantly. On the average, they depended on between 1.34 and 1.58 salaried workers. But families with incomes of over $1,800 relied on an average of 3.28 gainful workers.

The average Mexican family's net income amounted to $1,201 per year but, again, the community was not uniform in its earnings. In terms of annual income and home ownership, Mexicans in Los Angeles differed a great deal from one another. Their differences cannot be completely explained by their divergent skill levels. Only the fact that some Mexicans were able to find steady, dependable work can explain the community's annual earning spectrum—a spectrum that brought different families different levels of consumption luxury, home ownership prerogative and physical and psychological security.

One of the ways in which some Mexican workers ensured steady employment was unionization. For example, 10 percent of the Teamster's Local 1 were Mexican. Among organized Los Angeles cement workers, there were

Chavez Ravine, shown here in the 1940s, was one of the largest and poorest Mexican barrios in Los Angeles, and without sewers, water facilities or paved streets. As the value of the land soared, pressure began to build to take over the area for commercial development. In a fight lasting over 18 years, Chavez Ravine was eventually condemned, its citizens removed and the city council deeded the land to build Dodger Stadium.

(Courtesy of Los Angeles City Planning Commission)

many Mexicans who had been in the union since its inception. Although they worked in the industry's least appealing jobs, Mexicans also comprised 10 percent of the Hollywood Ornamental Plasterers Local. In packinghouses, Spanish-speaking workers held relatively undesirable but steady jobs, and they had a local reputation of being residents of long standing in the industry. A business agent of the local Lumber and Sawmill Workers union once recalled that his union's Mexican workers were an old local population which had been in the work force since the thirties.

Less formal factors also helped ensure job stability. Family contacts and on-going relationships with local employers and foremen are only a few of the contact networks that contributed to what little employment stability there was for local Mexican workers. Of course, men and women who had been north of the border for a while tended to have an easier time of it. Organized as they were by unions, community contacts, and familiarity with the dominant California culture, these workers sometimes achieved a significant measure of job security. In essence, they understood the city. They had lived within its economic and social structures long enough to feel somewhat at ease with its Anglo residents and its employment patterns. Although their wages were low, they did manage to work all year. That gave them a decided advantage over the less acclimated members of the community, people who withstood daily culture shock and only seasonal employment opportunity.

THE WORST OF TIMES

By the mid 1930s, job stability drew a decisive line between the Mexican and Anglo communities of Los Angeles. Indeed, it distinguished even between local Mexican families—some of whom could rely on steady income and others who had to survive all year on a few months' wages. Still, there was one employment problem that plagued all Mexicans, regardless of their professional background: racism. Widespread discrimination had come to determine more than social status in the City of Angels; it dictated income, professional mobility, and economic security.

For example, in 1928, Mexicans comprised nearly 54 percent of all California brick, tile, and pottery workers. By 1940, there were 2,000 Mexicans in the United Brick and Clay Workers Union, but numerical strength did not result in employment. To the contrary, Spanish-speaking workers were systematically segregated into "production" jobs and rarely were promoted to management positions. In fact, the Mexican field representative for the local union once noted that the importance of Mexicans and Mexican-Americans in this industry was mainly due to the subnormal wages at which "wetbacks" could be forced to work during the early days (1920–1935), as well as the strenuous and "dirty" nature of many jobs. Concentrated in specific areas of the factory, Mexican workers fulfilled an important function within local industry. They could be employed at substandard wages and, especially if they were undocumented, they could be forced to take on the dirtiest, least desirable jobs. Such was the pattern and function of segregated labor in Los Angeles during the 1930s.

Other employment patterns affected local Mexican laborers. Many of them worked in one of the city's innumerable and competitive service industries, where low pay, underemployment, seasonal jobs, and bad workplace conditions were long-standing employment realities. What's more, because these markets tended to be local, they were prone to instability, seasonality,

Los Angeles. 1940. The Second World War initiated major changes in the community as thousands of Mexicans enlisted in the armed forces and/or entered industries from which they had been excluded. This youth gazing across the roof tops of the Alpine barrio toward City Hall evokes the uneasy mood of the 1940s.

(Courtesy of Los Angeles City Planning Commission)

the absence of an incentive to stabilize production, and a lack of real career opportunity. Overcrowding typified the service sector because, equipped with a relatively small capital investment, almost anyone could try his hand at it.

For precisely this reason, the service industries were undesirable work environments. Too many small shops tried to win the edge on a local market—usually by cutting their operating expenses to almost nothing. From the Mexican worker's perspective, this meant undesirable working conditions within industries that concerned themselves exclusively with bottom line profits. Still, unable to find full-time, year-round, well paying work in the more appealing sectors of California's economy, the Spanish-speaking were compelled to accept barber shop, restaurant, service station, and laundry jobs on virtually any terms.

The garment industry provides a good example of just how the employment dynamics of the late 1930s and 1940s affected Mexican workers in Los Angeles. By 1939, there were 634 dress factories in the city. Together, these factories employed 15,890 workers, 75 percent of whom were Mexican women and girls. Garment factory owners, a union organizer once claimed, regarded their employees as casual workers, in the same class as migrants who harvested fruit and vegetable products. With few exceptions, these employers exploited the language barrier that separated their Spanish-speaking employees from full industry participation. They operated a vicious kick-back system whereby workers were forced to give back some of their substandard salary. As a way of guarding against internal workplace dissent, they consciously maintained a high employee turnover rate.

Even after the strikes of the 1930s and the establishment of a clothing workers' union, the $20-per-week wage of women's garment workers was the lowest salary earned in California—with the exception of hotel and restaurant workers, who made even less for their labor. In 1935, prior to unionization and despite the fact that the state-sanctioned minimum wage was $18.90 per week, wages in the garment industry averaged between $13 and $17 per week. During the Depression, when the minimum wage dropped to $16 per week, unregulated garment employers could chisel wages to less than $5 per week.

Furniture, too, was an important local business for Mexican workers. In 1929, local furniture companies employed 5,904 people. While the Depression hit this industry with a particular vengeance, by 1939 it had climbed back to a workforce of 5,888. Indeed, by 1940, Los Angeles was the fourth largest furniture manufacturing center in the United States. Several large firms—such as S. Karpen, Nachman Spring, Gillespie, L.A. Period, and Angelus—dominated the industry. But the average establishment was small and typically employed about 25 people.

Just as individual garment industries went in and out of business with an unnerving frequency, furniture shops were extremely susceptible to bankruptcy. In 1929, for example, there were 193 furniture factories in the city. By 1933, the number had dropped to 126. Statewide figures show that, after the crash of '29, the entire industry went through an economic slump 50 percent greater than that experienced by industry as a whole. In 1933, wages fell to $1.50 per day in unorganized shops. Many workers faced unemployment. By the mid-1930s, things had begun to pick up; in 1935, there were 166 furniture shops in the city and by 1937, up to 182. Then, in 1938, the United Furniture Workers' Union gained local strength. Wages shot up to between $.50 and $1.25 per hour and, by 1939, 268 furniture shops existed in Los Angeles.

Still, Mexican workers remained segregated into the lowest-paying, least desirable jobs. Southern whites usually dominated the skilled woodworking trades. Jews had cornered the upholstering trade and, so, Spanish-speaking job seekers were left to fill the industry's finishing and unskilled labor slots. Only after World War II—when black workers became a sizeable workforce population—did the situation change. When these black workers came along, they were pushed into the unskilled jobs and, by default, Mexicans were pushed a rung or two up the industry ladder.[6]

Obviously, employer priorities conflicted with the human needs of Mexican workers. While it took some time to fester, a level of dissent began to develop within the Spanish-speaking community. Frustrated and angry over so many aspects of their urban experience, Mexicans took initial steps toward a loud public outcry. Sometimes in all-Mexican unions (such as the Confederación de Uniones de Campesinos y Obreros Mexicanos) and sometimes in interracial unions (such as the American Federation of Labor or the Congress of Industrial Organizations), Mexicans began to stand up to the economic exploitation that was dictating the contours of their lives.

Political viewpoints were also made public. In organizations such as the Communist party, Mexican workers stepped forward to express their disdain for employers who would have liked to preserve the right to treat all their Spanish-speaking employees like ignorant children. These political struggles, like their labor counterparts, were only one aspect of an on-going battle between local labor and capital investment. More important, they gave rise to a new and crucial element in the Mexican community's evolving self-concept.

In the summer and fall of 1933, a strike against Japanese growers broke out in El Monte. The majority of strikers (75 percent) were Anglo; 20 percent were Mexican and 5 percent Japanese. Initially, all the strikers claimed that wages were too low. But by winter, the Mexicans were as disenchanted with the strike itself as they were with their employers. After almost half a year's hardship, they could be certain of only one thing: they had lost their summer earnings. What's more, the growers blamed them for having stirred up trouble in the first place and were furious over the loss of their season's produce. The local community tended to side with the growers, primarily because the Japanese farmers enjoyed a reputation for hard work, long hours, and low prices. For Mexican laborers who sought integration into the American labor movement, the entire El Monte episode was a decided setback. Nevertheless, the strike suggested to the local Spanish-speaking workforce that their long-term economic future would be decidedly affected by a collective acceptance or rejection of the labor movement.[7]

Field workers were not the only Mexicans to attract the attention of union organizers in the early 1930s. Rose Pesotta, a leading organizer for the International Ladies Garment Workers' Union (ILGWU), came to Los Angeles in September 1933 with hopes of organizing Mexican women in local dressmaking factories. She found that 75 percent of the women working in the city's garment industry were of Mexican descent and that they desperately needed a union. On October 12, 1934, the Mexican women went on strike, contending that local manufacturers were not obeying the industry codes set forth by the National Industrial Relations Act and Administration. In November, garment industry employers promised to pay closer attention to industry codes. The women went back to work and, in December, the ILGWU became an official union group in Los Angeles.

An important political group also emerged during the 1930s. "The largest secular organization that has ever existed for Mexicans," the Congress of Spanish-Speaking People of the United States (popularly known as the Mexican Congress) "was organized in 1938 and disbanded with the war." Historian John Burma once described the organization as a Southwestern federation of many groups, with a total membership estimated as high as 6,000. With its goals tied to the economic, social, and cultural advance of Mexico, and to the promotion of better relations between Anglo-Americans and Mexicans, the Congress fought discrimination by the use of local boycotts. It tried to promote organizations of working people by aiding trade unions and by fighting workplace bigotry. In all its activities, the Congress emphasized the economic, political, and civil rights of both citizen and non-citizen Mexicans. Ironically, its orientation cost it the support of many community members, particularly some older people who considered it politically radical.

The Federation of Spanish-Speaking Voters was, perhaps, the first exclusively political group ever organized by Mexicans in Los Angeles. It ran candidates for state and local offices in 1930, none of whom were elected. Prior to World War II, the Mexican-American Movement to Promote Athletes was a non-political group, although after the war, some members used the organization to promote their own political agenda. Indeed, it was not until after the war, when organizations such as this one began to publicize the political realities of Mexican life in Los Angeles, that the community achieved any significant social advances.[8]

Even as these political factions began to develop, the local Spanish-speaking community confronted one of its most trying tests. Ostensibly due to a tightening economy, but clearly the manifestation of deep-rooted racism and cultural hegemony, Mexicans in Los Angeles were subjected to a strenuous new immigration policy, constant social pressure, and outright deportation. By 1930, the country's Mexican population had reached 1,422,533, (619,998 foreign born and 805,535 born in the United States). But as the Depression settled in, the federal government decided to limit the number of people who could come from Mexico. The rate of legal entrants was reduced from a yearly average of 58,000 to only 16,000. During fiscal year 1927-1928, a total of 58,146 visas were issued to natives of Mexico. Between July 1933 and June 1934, the number dropped to 1,523 — an immigration reduction of 97 percent. Between 1928 and 1933, 160,000 Mexicans from California were repatriated. In 1931 alone, 7,500 Mexicans left the Los Angeles area and returned to Mexico.

Throughout the 1930s, more Mexicans returned to Mexico than immigrated to the United States. Many left because they could not survive economically in U.S. cities. Racism compelled many to return home, particularly those who had retained their Mexican citizenship. In a country devastated by rampant unemployment, bread lines, and shantytowns, a furor was made of the fact that Mexicans were out of their native land and taking American jobs away from *real* Americans. While poor Anglos walked the streets without work or money, it did not seem fair — at least from the mainstream vantage point — that Spanish-speaking immigrants should be allowed to hold any job in this country. Only a few years before, the work they performed had been considered too menial for Anglo workers. But hard times shifted priorities, and any job was a good job during the Depression — too good for men and women who had come from Mexico.

During more prosperous times, the deportation of Mexican nationals was left to faceless immigration authorities. After the economic collapse of 1929, public hysteria took control of America. The country needed a scapegoat. People needed to feel that some identifiable force was responsible for the chaos that had overtaken them. In some places — and Los Angeles was the most prominent among them — Mexicans became that scapegoat. By the end of 1933, tens of thousands of Mexicans had been returned to Mexico.[9]

By and large, the forced repatriation of Mexicans was engineered by local governments. In January 1931, the burden of financial relief became particularly heavy in Los Angeles. The Mexican consul went to the Associated Charities, pleading for repatriation funds. It would be better, the consul argued, to pay for indigent Mexicans to return home than to support them all winter in Los Angeles. The Southern Pacific Railroad Company graciously offered to cooperate by fixing very low "charity Mexican fares" out of town.

Mexican teenagers at the Nu-Pike Amusement park in Long Beach. In the middle is former United States Ambassador to Mexico, Julian Nava.

(Courtesy of Ernesto Collosi)

For their part, many Mexican immigrants feared that all welfare would be withdrawn if they did not leave the United States. With all employment options eliminated, and confused by a body of new immigration law, many Mexicans chose to return home. Initially, 9,000 Los Angeles residents were sent to Mexico—at a cost to the county of $155,000. Still, considering the fact that one year's welfare cost for this same group would have amounted to $850,000, the repatriation program seemed an irresistible bargain.[10] By 1940, between 80,000 and 100,000 Mexicans had left Los Angeles County and there were fewer Spanish-speaking residents in the area than there had been prior to the Depression.[11]

Ultimately, of course, repatriation was a sort of tragicomic affair. The tragedy revolved around the many hardships which resulted from the progress. The comedy concerned the fact that most of the Mexicans sent back to Mexico eventually returned to Los Angeles, having had a trip back home at the expense of the county government.

ON THE BRINK OF WAR

By 1940, and with the Great Depression just barely behind it, the Mexican community of Los Angeles slowly began to move forward. But just as it had been among the first groups to suffer from the country's financial misfortune, it was among the last to benefit from the economic recovery of the 1940s. The Depression had left an ugly mark on Mexican Los Angeles. It had slowed the community's growth and, as a result of revised immigration policy, had arrested the expansion of local barrios.

It had also affected many Mexican-owned businesses and community organizations. During the boom years of the 1920s, a large number and wide variety of Spanish-speaking ventures emerged to serve the local Mexican community. Operating on a small margin of profit, most of these businesses were constantly in debt and had minimal access to credit. Always on the edge of collapse, these small ventures were devastated by the first tremors of 1929.

The 1920s had also seen the flourishing of local mutualistas and social clubs. As a result of the Depression's massive unemployment rates, decline in wages, and slowed immigration, many of these organizations disappeared. Annual dues and membership incidentals were suddenly too expensive. People's limited funds became precious and, for the city's unemployed Mexicans, time was better spent looking for a job than organizing social dances. There was another factor that contributed to the decline of Mexican social clubs and local business. Many middle-class Spanish-speaking immigrants, some of whom had been pivotal leaders within the community—the presidents of clubs and the entrepreneurs of downtown and eastside barrios—had returned to Mexico. Lacking a solid base of social operation and stripped of all economic security, many of the community's most respected members had left Los Angeles.

The United States census of 1940 showed a total Los Angeles population of 1,504,277 persons. Of that number, 107,680 were listed as Mexican.[12] For all of Los Angeles County, the total population was 2,785,643 persons, but a separate figure on Mexicans was not listed. Nevertheless, the United States Bureau of the Census acknowledges that in the censuses of both 1930 and 1940 population figures on Mexican residents are inadequate. In short, far more Spanish-speaking people lived and worked in the area than were listed on either census count. In part, the problem stems from inconsistencies in the definition and methods of counting the population. For instance, in 1930,

Hollenbeck junior high school
students. 1940.

(Courtesy of Ernesto Collosi)

Mexicans were listed as a separate racial group. In 1940, they were listed as "white," but could identify themselves in a separate count by reporting Spanish as their mother tongue. General racial and cultural bias and the near absence of Spanish-speaking census takers also account for a probable undercount of the actual Los Angeles Mexican community.

At any rate, knowledgeable observers of the period estimate that, during the 1940s, the Mexican community of Los Angeles City and County was close to 10 percent of the total population. At that, the community had been significantly handicapped by the effects of the Depression. Had it not been for slowed immigration and forced repatriation, Mexicans would have constituted an even larger portion of the city. Later, with these constraints removed, the community burgeoned.

Geographically, the city's largest Spanish-speaking population remained concentrated in the downtown area and in East Los Angeles. Small Mexican enclaves were also scattered throughout other areas of the county. By 1940, there were 52 incorporated cities in the county.[13] With the exception of very few communities—areas incorporated specifically for the wealthy, such as Beverly Hills, San Marino, and Rolling Hills Estates—each of these new cities had their own Mexican barrio. In Santa Monica, Azusa, Burbank, Glendale, Torrance, Pacoima, Pasadena, Monterey Park, Pomona, San Gabriel, Culver City, Long Beach, Placencia, Fullerton, La Puente, San Fernando, Norwalk, El Monte, Gardena, Florence, North Hollywood, Inglewood, Vernon, Claremont, La Habra, and Venice, Mexicans established their own communities. They shopped on their own business streets, joined Spanish-language churches, organized their own social clubs, and planned separate celebrations of annual Mexican holidays.[14]

Barrios were also established in unincorporated areas of the county. Communities sprang up in a number of small, hillside colonias and labor camps which had been originally built for low-paid railroad and agricultural laborers. In several of these outlying areas, there were sizeable Mexican communities.

Surrounding downtown Los Angeles, in the Central District, there were still other barrios. Extending from Palo Verde or Chavez Ravine on the north (where Dodger Stadium now stands) past Figueroa Street on the west and nearly to Exhibition Boulevard on the south, large Mexican communities were buying homes and raising families. Mexicans also lived in multi-ethnic communities. On the east, for intance, the Central District merged across the Los Angeles River with the still culturally-mixed populations of Lincoln Park, Boyle Heights, and Belvedere Park. In tracts more recently annexed to the city, there were large Mexican communities in Sawtelle, San Pedro, Wilmington, Watts, West Los Angeles, Van Nuys, Hollywood, and Northridge. In most of these areas, small Mexican neighborhoods existed within larger Anglo communities. Even so, they developed their own sense of suburban identity. Even as the urbanization of the post-World War II era transformed them from small, independent enclaves to check points on a map of sprawling Los Angeles, some of these Mexican areas managed to retain their own distinct identities.

In what had become a kind of tradition, these new Mexican residence patterns were closely related to housing, income, and employment discrimination. Although Mexicans lived in most every city in the county, they were inevitably segregated into specific areas of those cities. For example, in the westside beach community of Santa Monica, the Mexican barrio La Viente stretched along Olympic Boulevard. And recognizably Mexican people were not allowed to purchase homes or rent apartments north of Wilshire Boulevard.

Similarly, Santa Monica was respected for its excellent public schools, but Mexican children living within the city limits did not reap the benefits of superior public education. Restricted by attendance zones to inferior elementary and junior high schools, only a few managed to attend the city's one high school. Even for them, discrimination was an almost insurmountable barrier to education. Systematically tracked into non-academic classes and kept apart from the rest of the student body, Mexican youngsters were denied the educational skills that their schools provided to other ethnic groups.

In Los Angeles, Glendale, Burbank, Pasadena, Culver City, Pomona, and El Monte, the story was the same. Discrimination differed only in its intensity and, all too often, was much worse than that experienced in Santa Monica.

In 1940, the overwhelming majority of Mexicans in Los Angeles were poorly-paid wage workers.[15] For the most part, employment was marginal, temporary, and irregular. Nevertheless, people who still held full-time, regular jobs considered themselves lucky. After all, over 10 percent of the national workforce remained unemployed. Even those Spanish-speaking laborers who had advanced into skilled or semi-skilled industry occupations during the boom years of the late 1920s faced unemployment by 1938.

Discrimination meant that any Mexican still working in 1940 was holding down the lowest-paying, dirtiest, and most dangerous job in the factory, field, or local service shop. Grossly under-represented in skilled, white collar, civil service, semi-professional, and professional occupations, Mexicans were usually relegated to the ranks of agricultural workers, day laborers, and domestic servants. Construction industries employed large numbers of Mexicans during the 1940s, as laborers, plasterers, hod carriers, and cement finishers. Canneries also hired the Spanish-speaking—as cutters and packers. In furniture factories, they worked as millmen and upholsterers. In garment manufacturing, they accounted for most of the machine operators, finishers, and pressers. The city's laundries continued to offer jobs as shake table workers and washmen. Warehouses used Mexican workers for loading, grading, and separating scrap iron. Meat packing companies paid them for manual labor and skinning, and fruit packing firms used them for packing. The railroads always needed section hands, and agriculture always needed seasonal field labor. Brick firms needed kiln workers; nurseries needed laborers; and domestic services needed maids. Mexicans constituted an exploited labor pool from which all these industries could pick and choose however many one-day, one-week, or one-month workers they needed.

For doing the hardest work, Mexicans and other minority laborers received the worst pay. In 1941, with industry buzzing along at a wartime pace, the median income for a Mexican family in the United States was still only $700—a full $520 less than what the federal government deemed necessary for a decent standard of living for a family of five.[16] Even after the attack on Pearl Harbor, when the nation shifted into full wartime production, Mexicans earned less for the worst jobs. Despite employment policies that forbade workplace discrimination, many war industries refused to employ Mexicans. As one major employer said in 1942, "Americans simply will not work with Mexicans."[17] Ironically, they found it easier to die alongside them.

BATTLEFIELDS: HOME AND ABROAD

United States involvement in World War II changed life for Mexicans in Los Angeles, just as it changed life for everyone in the country. The employment situation improved slightly and, as war production accelerated, jobs became easier to find. Responding to the government's demands for increased military production and to its promise of guaranteed "cost plus" profits, employers all across the country began hiring women, blacks, and Mexicans into jobs that had once been denied them. Thousands of Los Angeles area Mexicans, including a large number of women, were able to enter semi-skilled and even skilled occupations.

Nevertheless, life for the Spanish-speaking hardly became an exercise in equal opportunity. The advances made during the period, substantial and important as they may have been, were unquestionably less impressive than the progress made by the dominant society. It is certainly true that the United States became a land of expanding opportunity, but its opportunities typically expanded in the direction of white America. Indeed, the social, educational, and economic gains made by Anglo-Americans so far exceeded the gains made by Mexicans that the gap between the two communities only widened.

Not all segments of the Mexican community shared in the advances of the 1940s. Often curtailed by a lack of education—itself the result of discrimination— a large sector of the community remained excluded from better jobs and higher wages. Thus, many Mexicans lagged not only behind Anglo-Americans but also behind the more fortunate members of their own community. The most recently arrived immigrants suffered the most. Although frequently advancing by the sheer dint of their will and hard work to a better economic status, these Mexicans were forced by discrimination to start at the bottom of America's social and economic ladder. Typically, these immigrants settled in one of the city's older barrios. They took up residence in low-rent apartments that more fortunate Mexicans had left behind when, with a higher income and a skilled trade to rely on, they moved on to a blue collar suburb. In this way, then, the War exacerbated a community division that had begun years before. Mexicans were no longer isolated from only the outside, Anglo society. They were splintering from within, breaking apart into a multiplicity of social, economic, and even cultural classes.

The War itself changed the community because it took many of its finest young men. During the Second World War and Korean War, tens of thousands of Mexican youths from Los Angeles City and County served in all branches of the United States armed forces. It has been estimated that throughout World War II, Mexicans comprised only between 5 and 10 percent of the city's population, yet Spanish surnames accounted for nearly 25 percent of the names on local casualty lists.[18] Why Mexicans would have so eagerly sought to defend a nation that had denied them equal access to opportunity—indeed, a country that has deported them from its borders— remains one of the tragic ironies of the community's recent history. Part of an explanation surely rests with a U.S. publicity campaign that depicted World War II as a noble fight for democracy, a war against fascist aggression, a war in the defense of civil rights for people everywhere. For a community that had suffered the injustices of racism and bigotry, concepts of freedom and liberation engendered strong passions. The federal government spoke of post-war abundance and Mexicans throughout the country believed in the promise. They listened to assurances that military service today would bring veteran security tomorrow, and they acted on those assurances.

For all these reasons, most draft age youth in the Mexican community eagerly responded to the call for volunteers. Young men and women from the Los Angeles Spanish-speaking community served in all theatres of the war—from Berlin to Tokyo. Indeed, many sought the most dangerous assignments possible. Many died. Due to their extraordinary acts of heroism in combat, more Mexicans earned the Congressional Medal of Honor than did any other ethnic group—with the possible exception of Japanese Americans. Yet only a handful of Spanish-speaking soldiers ever received battlefield promotions. Bravery, like hard work, was evidently to be its own reward.

The end of the war brought Mexican veterans a staggering disappointment. In short, they learned that the Distinguished Service Medal, the Navy Cross, even the Congressional Medal of Honor could not persuade a racist real estate agent to accept their Cal Vet or GI loan as a down payment on the new home they wanted to buy in an all-white housing tract. Their battle scars could not get their children enrolled in the superior all-white schools built on the other side of an attendance zone boundary line.

Indeed, even before the war ended, it had become clear that Mexican sacrifices on behalf of the United States could not alter deeply ingrained social bias. Wartime tensions, initially manifested in the internment of Japanese Americans, fastened onto Mexicans in 1942, when a malicious newspaper campaign depicted all Mexican youths as "Pachucos"—Zootsuiters who were mislabeled "criminal elements" and accused of attacking servicemen.[19]

Despite the fact that informed police sources admitted that Mexican youth had a lower crime rate than Anglo youth and that out of more than 30,000 Mexican teenagers in Los Angeles, no more than 1,000 were Pachucos, local terror escalated. Before long, a manufactured panic took control of the city.[20] Pomona Police Captain Hugh D. Morgan once said that "when it comes to juvenile delinquency of the Zootsuit variety, there is involved a far lesser

Padua Hills Mexican Players. Claremont.

(Courtesy of Sara Cardenas)

percentage of Mexicans youths than of American born boys of American born parents." But newspapers were more interested in sensationalism than in facts. So, journalists concentrated on the more dramatic remarks of public officials and law enforcement officers who found scare tactics an easy route to larger police and sheriff's department budgets.

Zootsuit sensationalism culminated in the Sleepy Lagoon case of 1942, in which a group of Mexican youths were framed on a murder charge and convicted more because of the press than because of courtroom evidence. Admittedly among the small number of actual Pachucos in the city, these young men were acquitted only after a lengthy defense campaign by community activists and civil libertarians. Then, in 1943, the infamous Zootsuit Riots ignited new and even more lurid tales of alleged Pachuco violence. Most often, the tales were fabricated. At best, they were distorted by prejudice and fear. The actual street fights between sometimes intoxicated servicemen and Mexican civilians were not terribly unlike the bar fights that occur in any large city. But in the charged atmosphere of 1943 Los Angeles, the altercations were transformed into widespread "Pachuco terrorism."[21]

Like all fads, Zootsuits really had far more to do with teenage flamboyance than with ethnic dictate. What's more, Mexicans were not the only youths to wear Zootsuits, nor were they the majority of boys who popularized the look. Anglo, black, and some Asian youths also sported their Zootsuits and "drapes" around town. And even among the Mexican youths who did ritualize the look, there were very few real Pachucos. Nevertheless, the culturally specific elegance of the Los Angeles Pachuco—with his Zootsuit and exaggerated pompadour—was a means of cultural expression by which some young people demonstrated their community-oriented savvy and defiance.

Although these facts were well known to both local police and the city press, a *Los Angeles Times* scare campaign eventually led to violence. On June 3, 1943, large scale rioting erupted. Mobs of servicemen and armed bigots first invaded the downtown area and then moved toward the Mexican and black neighborhoods, where they attacked and beat Zootsuiters and any other minority youth they happened to see. Many police and sheriff officers, themselves primed by explosive newspaper stories, chose either to stand aside in tacit approval or to participate in the beatings. Sporadic rioting continued for several days. Then, on the evening of June 7, a mob pulled a black man off a local streetcar and gouged out one of his eyes. Almost immediately, and to prevent any further lawlessness, military authorities declared the entire downtown area off-limits to servicemen on passes.

Even at the time, and especially to the Mexican community of Los Angeles, the situation was quite clear. The riots were a result of local racism that had always existed but which had been pushed suddenly beyond its threshold by the tensions of a war-weary society. For a few years, local government and neighborhood church groups made an effort to support programs that provided increased recreational and leadership activities for Mexican teenagers. Still, the fundamental community disquiet that had given rise to the Pachucos remained unexplored. Left unattended, it did not vanish. It only festered.

NEW CULTURAL EXPRESSIONS

It was the rare social scientist of the 1940s who sought to define, much less understand, Mexican American culture. Those who did try, usually viewed it as a culture in transition, somewhere between a traditional rural culture and an urban industrial one. The assumption, of course, was that such a transition was tantamount to progress. Virtually all social dynamics within the Spanish-speaking community were thought to be extensions of deep-rooted tensions, manifestations of an internal cultural class that supposedly tore at the heart and minds of bewildered Mexican people. Implicitly, such social disorientation was thought to be the result of a failure on the part of the Mexican immigrant population—its failure to seek full assimilation into Anglo-American society, its failure to escape a self-imposed cultural dichotomy. To the myopic mainstream mindset, total acculturation seemed the only practical solution to this intense internal conflict and social displacement.

Social scientists were not alone in this view of Mexican culture. Most public officials endorsed the same conceptual framework. Even more frightening, many Mexican observers and some Mexican-Americans themselves stereotyped the culture. For instance, upper-class Mexican nationals often viewed U.S. Mexicans as unquestionably inferior. From this class-biased perspective, Mexicans in Los Angeles were considered lower class renegades who had abandoned Mexican society when they crossed over into California. "Pochos," as these immigrants were sometimes called, were considered nothing better than culturally assimilated non-Mexicans who would no longer speak refined Spanish, grasp the pride of their Mexican heritage, or guard against the most unbecoming qualities of American culture.

Only a few studies diverged from these stereotypes. Foremost among them was the work of Mexican sociologist Manual Gamio. Studying the Mexican immigrant population of the United States during the late 1920s and early 1930s, Gamio conducted hundreds of oral interviews with a diverse cross-section of the U.S. Mexican community. Many of these interviews and much of his research concerned the Spanish-speaking population of Los Angeles which, by the late 1920s, had become home to the largest Mexican population in the United States. Above all else, his work revealed that Mexicans in the United States were a far more complex group than researchers had previously supposed.

Gamio found that Mexican Los Angeles was made up of various class, income, regional, and age groups. What's more, the community did not exhibit a stressful division between two or more conflicting cultures. Indeed, it seemed to have creatively integrated a complex amalgam of both Mexican, United States, and even international culture. Composed, in part, of pre-1848 Mexican descendents and, in part, of more recently arriving immigrants from nearly every social strata in Mexican society, the Spanish-speaking community of Los Angeles was no more determined by the rural culture of Mexico than by the industrial culture of Southern California. And it was certainly not stagnant. In short, Gamio concluded that Mexican Los Angeles not only reflected the interaction of modern Mexican and North American popular cultures but also produced a new cultural expression that was separate and apart from either of its interactive influences.

Indeed, because of the size, diversity, and sophistication of its Mexican population, Los Angeles beckoned with seemingly boundless potential as a major Spanish-language media market. Mexico was intrigued by the area's possible profitability because, by its standards, California was a land of economic abundance. The average working American earned more for labor and spent more on leisure activity than Mexican nationals could ever imagine. Thus, as early as 1920, local Spanish-speaking audiences could attract, and pay for, the biggest, best-paid entertainers of Mexico. Then, with the invention and rapid diffusion of radio, almost every home received daily communiques from the society and popular culture that operated outside its front door. By 1930, Spanish-speaking media exercised a significant but seldom acknowledged influence on the city's evolving Mexican culture. In fact, local box office receipts suggest that Los Angeles was the world's biggest Spanish-speaking audience outside Mexico City and Guadalajara.

Nevertheless, the local Mexican community lacked adequate funding and the commercial organization that it would have taken to fulfill its media potential. More often than not, local talent was absorbed into powerful Anglo American companies. Film stars like Anthony Quinn, singers like Andy Russell, and theatre personalities were forced by the racism of their time to hide or downplay their ethnic background. In short, self-denial was the price for media recognition.

The cultural machinations that controlled the U.S. entertainment industry also controlled other large institutions. Virtually every social establishment that reached large numbers of people—from the Catholic and Protestant churches to local boxing arenas—were the reflection of Anglo bigotry and condescension. Always, Mexicans were prevented from controlling even the institutions that they supported. Oppression and cultural domination were maintained through unequal wages, denial of credit, and the crudest forms of social discrimination. During the 1940s, racism was overt. Movie theatres were segregated, youngsters were, by policy and practice, kept from speaking Spanish on local school grounds. In its subtler forms, prejudice was hidden. A condescending paternalism viewed Mexican culture and the Spanish language as quaint reminders of life in ol' Mexico, where easygoing peasants took their afternoon siesta today and thought about their economic exploitation tommorrow.

Thus, in both obvious and subtle ways, the cultural life of Southern California's Mexican community was limited by the active bias of dominant groups and institutions outside its realm of influence. This bias affected all Mexicans in Los Angeles, but it impacted most severely on the youth and long-time residents of the city. Since the barrios of Mexican Los Angeles were neither totally isolated nor completely self-sufficient, most Mexicans interacted with people outside their community. And when work, parish, or recreational activities brought the Spanish-speaking in contact with Anglos, the results were nothing more than awkward stabs at communication. Whenever Mexicans met Anglos, they met on unequal ground and invariably left the encounter resentfully aware of their imposed inferiority.

Had Mexican Los Angeles truly existed in a vacuum, such contacts would have been impossible. But as a distinct community within a larger social network, the barrio was unable to fully insulate itself from the brutalities of racism and cultural hegemony. When Mexican youngsters first went to kindergarten and found their Spanish names suddenly transformed to a more accessible English equivalent, they learned public education's most fundamental and long-lasting lesson.

In essence, Mexican Angelinos were at a disadvantage in every major institution with which they made contact. Prior to the mid-1940s and the discrimination revealed by the hearings on the Zootsuit riots, city and county

Sleepy Lagoon Defendants. In 1942 a group of Mexican teenagers were arrested during a frenzy of sensational newspaper coverage about Mexican 'pachucos.' Accused of murdering another Mexican teenager in a fight at the Sleepy Lagoon, the case quickly became a cause celebre in Los Angeles. After a celebrated trial they were convicted and served two years in jail before they were finally acquitted in 1944.

(Courtesy of Los Angeles Times)

officials took little account of the Mexican community. As much out of ignorance as malice, the city's cultural institutions were always located outside the
Mexican community's reach. The Hollywood Bowl, Greek Theatre, Los Angeles County Museum of Natural History, parks, and public libraries were
erected in parts of town that Mexicans rarely visited, much less inhabited. Virtually no Mexicans were on the boards, administrations, or staffs of these
institutions and almost no activities or programs were planned with the Spanish-speaking community in mind.

When public facilities did exist in Los Angeles barrios, it was usually
because the area had once been a predominantly Anglo neighborhood. But as
Mexicans had gradually moved in, white families had rushed out, taking little
notice of the public institutions that they left behind. Sometimes, local officials chose to move major public programs out and away from the barrio.
More often, however, libraries, schools, and parks were simply allowed to de-
teriorate. As funds for maintenance were reduced and diverted into facilities
in new Anglo communities, Mexicans were left with neighborhood eyesores
and architectural dead weight.

Ironically, the decision to cut funds from barrio programs was based on
the absurd argument that Mexicans never use their community facilities. In
part because of their lower income levels, and in part because of their cultural
preferences, Mexicans actually made greater use of public facilities than most
other local groups. In many cases, expensive facilities located in high income
suburbs went unused even while dilapidated, inadequately funded facilities
in the barrio were over-utilized by a community that lacked more expensive
leisure time options.

Social club of East Los
Angeles. 1950s.

(Courtesy of William D. Estrada)

Edward R. Roybal campaigning for city council, 1947. He was defeated in this election but won two years later as a result of a grass roots voter registration campaign.

(Courtesy of Congressman Edward R. Roybal)

In a similar fashion, religious institutions denied the Mexican community a role in church administration. Toward the end of the 1940s, the Catholic church in particular developed a deep concern for the Spanish-speaking community of Los Angeles. But in keeping with the period, that concern was most often expressed in patronizing gestures of Christian charity. As early as 1930, the Roman Catholic archdiocese recognized that numbers alone made the predominantly Catholic Mexican population a congregation worth nurturing. Although its primary concern was spiritual, in temporal policy, in parochial school policy, in religious organizations, and in parish administration, the church was obsessed with cultural assimilation.

Spanish-language services were usually offered in predominantly Mexican areas of town—but only as a transitional measure, a sort of spiritual bridge between the congregation's past and its future. There were very few Mexican or even Spanish-speaking priests or ministers to attend to the community. The few who did exist seldom rose to decision-making positions within the church hierarchy. Even more problematic was that a majority of these Spanish-speaking clergy were culturally and politically conservative exiles from Mexico or Spain. Although they could speak the language of the local Mexican community, they were grossly out of touch with its social and economic welfare. In essence, the attitudes and policies of the Los Angeles archdiocese reflected benign paternalism toward the community. The archbishop and other policy-makers within the church viewed Mexicans as a spiritual burden which, as good pastors, they were bound to carry on their shoulders. But their heart and soul remained bound to the Anglo-American population from which they had come and of which they would always remain a part.

THE NEW CHALLENGE

By the end of the 1940s, Mexican Los Angeles had passed through some of its roughest history. It had withstood the hardships of a major Depression, the tragedy of war, and the bitterness of disillusionment. In every way relegated to a second class status, the community was no longer an isolated cultural entity able to operate entirely on its own. The size of the city, the speed at which it functioned, the complexity of its economic network—these realities demanded that Mexicans be part of the larger, Anglo-controlled society. Yet in each encounter with that society, the Spanish-speaking were confronted with their own oppression.

Still, for all its negative impact, racism and discrimination did not divide the Mexican community in any clear-cut fashion. Histories of the period, often use the Spanish language as a symbolic and defacto line that cut through the barrio communities of Los Angeles. On one side of the line, we are told, Mexican traditionalists stood silent and unable to speak whenever the language of communication was not Spanish. On the other side of the boundary, we are to imagine English-speaking Mexicans as members of the community who aspired toward a better, more Anglicized lifestyle. Reality, as always, is far more complex.

The diverse elements of the city's Mexican community constituted a cultural continuum that was time and again intersected by variables such as income, regional origin, age, sex, religion, education, and personal preference. Indeed, the entire notion of primarily English-speaking Mexicans had no real meaning until 1940. Until then, all but the most assimilated Mexicans could speak colloquial Spanish. In practice, most Mexicans living in Los Angeles during the first half of the twentieth century were bilingual, equally comfortable in Spanish and English. Unfortunately, theirs was a limited bilingualism. Because most people had only an informal education in either or both of the languages, their verbal skills were limited to rudimentary colloquial speech.

Thus, if the Mexican community's greatest challenge had once been to somehow enter the city's mainstream, then the test it faced in 1950 was to retreat somewhat from that mainstream, to insulate itself from the cultural encroachment of Anglo Los Angeles. The years that followed reflect precisely that struggle. By electing their own politicians and by focusing on their own culturally-defined problems and abilities, the Mexicans of Los Angeles built a symbolic wall around their barrios. And within the perimeters of their own community, they pursued a public profile that could fit their new self-concept.

NOTES

1. Douglas Monroy, "Mexicanos in Los Angeles, 1930–1941: An Ethnic Group in Relation to Class Forces" (Ph.D. dissertation, University of California, Los Angeles: 1978), p. 74.

2. Ibid., p. 77.

3. Ibid., p. 78.

4. Ibid., p. 79.

5. Ibid., pp. 79–81.

6. Ibid., pp. 85–90.

7. Robin Scott, "The Mexican American in the Los Angeles Area, 1920–1950: From Acquiescence to Activity" (Ph.D. dissertation, University of Southern California: 1971), p. 108.

8. Ibid., pp. 109–110, 147–148.

9. Abraham Hoffman, *Unwanted Mexican Americans in the Great Depression; Repatriation Pressures, 1929–1939* (Tucson: 1979), pp. 39–51.

10. Ibid., pp. 85–107.

11. Ibid., pp. 100–101.

12. United States Bureau of the Census, *Sixteenth Census of the United States: 1940*. Also, "Population: Special Report: Nativity and Parentage of the White Population," *Mother Tongue*, p. 34.

13. Robert Michael Demuth (Ed.), *Los Angeles County Almanac: A Guide to Government*, nineteenth edition, (Los Angeles: 1980), pp. 214–215.

14. Kay Lyon Briegel, "Alianza Hispano Americana, 1894–1945: A Mexican Fraternal Insurance Society" (Ph.D. dissertation, University of Southern California: 1974).

15. Leo Grebler et al., "Patterns of Work and Settlement," *The Mexican American People* (New York: 1970), pp. 82–100. Also, Fred E. Ramero, *Chicano Workers: Their Utilization and Development* (Los Angeles: 1979); Frederico López, "A Historical Analysis of Occupational and Employment Patterns of Mexican Americans in California, 1950–1965" (honors paper, University of California, Los Angeles: 1976); Fred H. Schmidt, *Spanish American Employment in the Southwest* (Washington, D.C.: 1960).

16. Robin Scott Fitzgerald, "The Mexican American in the Los Angeles Area, 1920–1950" (Ph.D. dissertation, University of Southern California: 1971), p. 195.

17. Ibid., p. 205.

18. Fitzgerald, pp. 156, 195, 256, 261. Also, Raul Morin, *Among the Valiant* (Alabama: 1966).

19. Mauricio Mazón, "Social Upheaval in World War II: Zoot Suiters and Servicemen in Los Angeles, 1943" (Ph.D. dissertation, University of California, Los Angeles: 1976).

20. Fitzgerald, p. 220.

21. Ibid., pp. 222–232.

In the 1960s the United Farm Workers' union symbolized the beginning of a new civil rights movement among Mexicans and inspired the birth of the Chicano Movement.

(Courtesy of Devra Weber)

CHAPTER EIGHT

The Road to Power: Making
Numbers Count

The past 35 years constitute a period of astonishing growth and development for Mexican Los Angeles. In ways that would have been impossible only a generation ago, the city's Mexican community has asserted itself as a cultural and political force. Thanks to a constantly growing rate of immigration from Mexico and a spectacular rise in their U.S. birth rate, Mexican Angelinos now find themselves on the cutting edge of a new regional influence.

Simultaneously, they face unique challenges. In a high technology, capital-intensive society, Mexicans remain limited by the income and educational gaps that separate them from their Anglo-American counterparts. What's more, they find themselves in need of new ways to convert their sense of common identity into an organized movement toward social advancement. In order to transform their various social classes and backgrounds into a single constituency, the community must grapple with the hard decisions that stem from the choice between cultural assimilation and social isolation.

A BICULTURAL REALITY

The roots of this choice can be traced back to the late 1940s and early 1950s. Even then, some Mexicans knew that the community faced a difficult challenge: could it take from the dominant society the valuable techniques for economic survival without abandoning its own cultural heritage?

That question echoed throughout the 1950s, when Mexicans suddenly found themselves caught between opposing cultural messages. On the one hand, Spanish-language popular culture implied that they were part of a unique cultural tradition distinct from white America. On the other hand, the English-language educational system told Mexicans that they had best become something altogether different from their ancestors. Throughout that decade and into the 1960s, individuals diligently tried to balance Spanish-language newspapers, magazines, movies, live performances, radio programs, and television with a school experience that sought to envelop them in an English-speaking, Anglo-defined mainstream.

By the mid-1950s, the community had splintered and Mexican Los Angeles had become a spectrum of biculturalism. Some individuals could—or would—speak only Spanish. Others could not speak Spanish at all. Of course, there were many Mexicans who were completely bilingual and bicultural. They represent the most recent process of transculturation in that they transformed rather than abandoned their culture. Mexicans did not bow to an outside culture; instead, they blended cultures. In the process, they reached toward an altogether new collective entity.

Nevertheless, the mixed cultural messages that barraged Mexicans during the 1950s were not always blended well. In the abstract, it may seem that an exposure to Anglo-American culture would have had positive effects on Spanish-speaking youngsters, that it might have led to a healthy, multicultural perspective. Unfortunately, this did not occur often. Due to racism, cultural bias, distorted stereotypes, and assimilationist pressures, Anglo-American culture did not present itself as an attractive alternative system of social behavior. It presented itself as an *a priori* superior way of life. Most Anglo Americans of the period automatically assumed that their tradition was superior to anything Mexicans had to offer.

The Mexican response to such visceral racism was complex. Although most members of the community continued to value their ethnicity, they lacked the institutional mechanisms with which to counter cultural bias. They most surely lacked the means to pass on a literate Spanish-language education. An active Spanish-speaking cultural life was sustained in Los Angeles, but it was limited to the barrio. To appeal to the greatest number of people, it typically emphasized non-controversial, commercial entertainment including romantic and comic films, radio programs, a few weekly TV shows, and local newspapers.

Just as the community was struggling to maintain a sense of its unique ethnic identity, outside indicators would have suggested that it was a strong constituency within Los Angeles. Indeed, the 1940s and 50s were golden years for the Mexican cinema. Spanish-language theatres sprang up all across the city. The largest chain of these theatres was owned by just one businessman, Francisco Fouce. He owned the Teatro Maya, Teatro Mason, Teatro Liberty, and the Teatro Roosevelt, where he presented not only films but live entertainment as well. Singers, orchestras, actors, and comedians were welcomed in theatres that catered primarily to a Spanish-speaking audience.

The flagship of the Fouce chain was the Teatro Maya—which proudly advertised itself as "el maximo teatro de la Raza" (the greatest theatre of La Raza) and was explicitly "dedicated to the presentation of the greatest attrac-

National Chicano Moratorium. August 29, 1970.

(Courtesy of Devra Weber)

tions of Mexico, Argentina, Spain, and other Hispanic countries." To attract an audience, Fouce brought the greatest stars of Mexico, Latin America, and Spain to Los Angeles. Jorge Negrete, Pedro Infante, María Félix, Rosita Quintana, Luis Aguilar, and Cantiflas are just some of the stars that he booked into his theatres. Sometimes the events were so large that they could not be presented at even the biggest indoor theatre. Instead, they were held at open-air arenas like the Greek Theatre and the Hollywood Bowl.

Spanish-language radio also flourished during this period and Rodolfo Hoyos, Sr. served as its most popular local celebrity. In fact, his regular program, "La Hora de Rodolfo Hoyos," was broadcast on KWKW radio from 1932 until 1967. Initially, Hoyos and every other Spanish-language programmer purchased surplus air time from English-language stations. Eventually,

Unity Conference. 1974.

(Courtesy of Rosemary Quesada-Weiner)

the glimmer of potential profit led many stations, including KWKW, to convert to all or mainly Spanish-language programming. Along with music and interviews, these radio stations ran public service shows and aired news that was of special interest to the city's Spanish-speaking community. Although most over-the-air advertisements aimed to sell Anglo brand goods, some promoted Mexican-owned businesses in the area. Through its musical programming, public service announcements, advertisements, and sheer presence as a viable entertainment and news source, Spanish-language radio played an essential role within local Mexican culture.

Los Angeles was one of the first cities in the United States to offer regular Spanish-language television. Following the precedent set by radio, the first one-hour TV shows were broadcast on English-language television stations that had "empty" time slots to sell. The earliest regular TV program appears to have been Lupita Beltran's "Latin Time," which aired on KCOP every Sunday. The show first appeared in late 1955 or early 1956 and featured entertainer Rita Holguín, composer Lalo Guerrero and his orchestra, and Aura San Juan. Then, in April of 1956, "Fandango" premiered on the local CBS station, KNXT. It, too, was a variety show and enjoyed a popular run in the city.

Important as Spanish-language radio and television were in transmitting popular culture, Los Angeles Mexicans nurtured a less dramatic but equally important cultural information system: extended-family gatherings. As Anglo society moved further toward the nuclear family emphasis, Spanish-speaking people encouraged a multi-generational concept. At baptisms, confirmations, weddings, birthdays, and other special occasions, members of extended families gathered to talk, eat, and relax together. Such gatherings were not, of course, unique to Mexican culture. But they were, and have remained, an important mechanism of Mexican cultural maintenance. Grandparents recalled tales of earlier times and parents bowed to the traditions that had preceded their suburban lifestyle. In this way, young children learned more than family history—they learned a value system.

A NEW CONSTITUENCY

Throughout the late 1940s and then especially during the 1950s, a substantial segment of the Mexican community moved from downtown and eastside barrios into the city's emerging post-war suburbs. With that migration, more than mailing addresses changed. Optimistic young family men and women frequently found middle class enclaves to be the breeding ground of cold discrimination. In response, they began organizing various groups into a formidable voice for workplace reform and created their own political organizations. Yet like many other progressives of the period, they experienced the repressive effects of unbridled McCarthyism. In short, the period was characterized by a few hard-won victories and a multitude of valuable lessons salvaged from defeat. In all of this, Mexicans learned to bide their time and organize for a future success.

The 1950 census revealed an amazing population growth among Mexicans in Los Angeles. Indeed, out of a total city population of 1,970,368, the Mexican community accounted for 272,000 people.[1] Officially, the community had more than doubled in just ten years. Combined with a modicum of economic advancement in some workplace sectors, these numbers led to the geographic dispersal and expansion of existing Mexican communities.

Many Spanish-speaking families moved further east, into blue collar communities such as Montebello, Monterey Park, and Pico Rivera. But like past relocations, the exodus did not come easily. The right to purchase homes outside the barrio had to be upheld in courtrooms throughout the city. In many areas, restrictive covenants blatantly stated that "no person of African, Latin American, or Oriental descent shall reside on these premises except as a domestic servant."[2] In each of these suburbs, Mexicans moved in only after a high legal and emotional cost had been paid.

Many young Mexican veterans of World War II were profoundly disillusioned to find that rampant discrimination still prevailed on the home front. They were disappointed to discover that democracy and civil rights remained distant ideals. While some of the more superficial forms of racism (such as Mexican nights at swimming pools and movie theatres) had been outlawed within the city itself, they remained commonplace in surrounding communities. Educational discrimination, whether overt or subtle, was prevalent throughout the County of Los Angeles. Mexican war heroes were also forced to witness the spectacle of constant police brutality and immigration raids that targeted only persons who looked Latin American.

But perhaps the most debilitating effect of prejudice was the dominant Anglo attitude toward Mexicans. Confident that Mexicans should be grateful for just being allowed to live in the United States, many Anglo residents considered it a charitable favor to address their brown neighbors and co-workers as "Spanish" rather than "Mexican." In effect, the mid-twentieth century ushered in a renewed cycle of distorted social grace. In an environment that considered the word "Mexican" a derogatory term, Spanish-speaking people often stepped out of their private, insulated barrios, only to find themselves swept into a whirlwind of cultural ignorance and economic oppression.

These were the ugly realities that motivated many Mexican war veterans to organize groups for the express purpose of fighting discrimination. The Unity Leagues, Community Service Organization, the Asociación Nacional Mexicano Americano (ANMA), and the American G.I. Forum are only a few of the organizations born during the late 1940s and early 1950s. As a symbolic reflection of Mexican demands for first-class citizenship, most of these associations publicly referred to themselves as "Mexican American" — a cultural duality that they proudly embodied.[3]

The Unity League was organized in 1947 by Ignacio López, a veteran of World War II's Office of War Information. With its membership congregated primarily in the eastern part of Los Angeles County — in the Pomona Valley area and even San Bernardino, Riverside, and Orange Counties — the League campaigned vigorously against housing and educational discrimination. In part, because López was publisher of the Spanish-language Pomona Valley newspaper, *El Espectador*, his Unity League was able to publicize issues of concern to a growing suburban Mexican community. Throughout the late 40s and early 50s, the group scored several local successes. They were especially victorious in San Bernardino county, where members won lawsuits against segregated schools and swimming pools. By 1949, the league had helped elect the first Mexican member of the city council in Chino, California.[4]

Perhaps the best known and most successful group to emerge during the period was the Community Service Organization (CSO). Operating within the city itself, this organization actually emerged from Edward R. Roybal's unsuccessful campaign for city council in 1947. A graduate of UCLA and himself a veteran of World War II, Roybal was a social worker and former educational

director of the Los Angeles County Tuberculosis Association. Above all, he was deeply committed to solving the social problems that faced his community. After his defeat in 1947, he and a group of his supporters reconstituted the election committee into CSO. Their aims were straightforward: to effectively challenge the social problems that plagued the city's Spanish-speaking people, and to provide the community with a level of political representation that it had lacked for almost 100 years.

Roybal's defeat had served to alert the group to an important reality. Mexicans who were not registered to vote could not elect sensitive representatives to positions of local influence. Consequently, CSO's first major undertaking was to ensure that, next time around, the community's numerical strength would translate into election day influence. In a large scale voter registration campaign, the group was supported by many Mexican unionists and by some members of other ethnic groups throughout the city. By 1949, CSO had registered thousands of voters in the city's ninth council district. Roybal challenged the incumbent council member, defeated him by a two-thirds margin and became the first Mexican to serve on the city council since 1881. Roybal's victory lent that much more credibility to CSO. The organization continued their effort and by 1950, claimed to have added 32,000 new Mexicans to the registration rolls.

Next, CSO turned its attention to the defense of Mexican immigrant rights and to controlling racist police brutality. As a member of the city council, Roybal supported many of these activities, particularly those that fought against police harassment. In fact, he himself demanded the removal of a number of police officers with racist reputations. He also joined CSO in its battle against housing discrimination. Nevertheless, the effort was only partially successful. It is true that a series of CSO-supported lawsuits eventually

Demonstration against Carter immigration plan. August 29, 1977.

(*Courtesy of* Los Angles Times)

forced real estate agents to sell homes in Montebello and several other suburban communities to Mexicans. Nevertheless, it was not until the 1960s that restrictive covenants were categorically struck down by the courts. Even then, de facto discrimination based on income continued to flourish.

By 1954, McCarthyism was in full swing. Needless to say, the country's political shift to the right did not auger well for the Mexican community. Along with other minority groups, the city's Spanish-speaking population was suddenly suspect. Mexican efforts to enforce their own civil rights had always been unpopular but, in the climate of the times, progressive political associations were considered possible "fronts for Communist activity." Several organizations, especially those associated with labor unions, were subjected to open repression. Members were blacklisted and their careers destroyed. As a result, more cautious Mexican groups chose simply to mark the time during the mid-1950s. Worried that if they failed to "toe the line" they might be labeled "Communist sympathizers," they waited for national sentiment to change.[5]

Toward the end of the 1950s, a wave of political liberalism swept across the United States. By 1960, the McCarthy era had come to a bitter end and America's social conscience was aroused by the black civil rights movement. For their part, Mexican organizers and politicians began to glimpse the potential power of their constituency. After all, the community was the largest minority group in all of Southern California. They watched with great interest as the black community in Los Angeles gained widespread media coverage through its struggle against all forms of discrimination.

The new political atmosphere was initially exploited by the more farsighted Mexican politicians. In 1958, Hank López campaigned for California secretary of state and City Council Member Roybal ran for the county board of supervisors. Both men lost, but in Roybal's case, the race was extremely close. In fact, many observers believed that it was only because of voter intimidation that his opponent, Ernest Debs, managed to squeak through. It seems that some of Debs' supporters challenged the qualifications of Mexican voters at the polls.[6]

At any rate, these two 1958 defeats stimulated even more political activity within the Mexican community. For instance, in 1959, a group of Mexican Democratic party regulars formed the Mexican American Political Association (MAPA) to serve as a vehicle for better representation.[7] At that time, there were no Mexicans in the California state legislature or in the U.S. Congress, and Roybal was the only elected Mexican official in Los Angeles. Along with other groups of the period, MAPA intended to change that reality. Although its activities throughout the 1950s were not always successful, it did provide the concrete foundation for a series of future electoral victories. More importantly, it roused a new social consciousness among Mexican youth.

THE SLEEPING GIANT STIRS

As the 1950s wound down and while America looked toward the coming decade, the Mexican community in Los Angeles continued to grow. Again, the U.S. census provides a fairly reliable measure of the local Spanish surnamed population. In 1960, 2,479,015 people lived in Los Angeles; 260,000 had a Spanish surname.[8] For Los Angeles County, the results were more dramatic. Out of a total population of 6,038,771, there were 576,000 Spanish surnamed people. It also revealed that Mexicans were no longer residentially restricted to the Eastside. Although the figures suggest that the community's largest popu-

(Left) Mexican garment workers. Mexicans and other Latinos have been the backbone of the work force since the beginning of Los Angeles garment industry and the major drive behind labor organization of the International Ladies Garment Workers' Union.

(Courtesy of Ernesto Collosi)

Woman at welfare office. Due to occupational discrimination and low wages, a large percentage of the Mexican community has hovered near the poverty line. Many are women with little job security and low incomes. As a result, social services are a major issue in the community and a focus for community organization. Since the 1960s the East Los Angeles Welfare Rights Organization, headed by Alicia Escalante, has been a major advocate for welfare recipients in the East Los Angeles community.

(Courtesy of Rosemary Quesada-Weiner)

lation remained in East Los Angeles, a major relocation pattern was spreading Mexicans east and south of the main barrio. There were many Mexicans living in the Venice-Santa Monica-Culver City area. The community was significantly present in the San Fernando-Pacoima area, just as it had moved into the Torrance-Norwalk suburbs.

For the most part, Mexicans were unaware of how rapidly the community was growing and relatively unconcerned that the population increase was primarily due to the growing number of U.S.-born Mexicans. Nevertheless, the census figures unmistakably implied that, by the sheer strength of numbers, Mexican Angelinos would become a formidable political constituency within the City of the Angels. Indeed, a number of local newspapers ran stories in which the city's Mexican community was termed a "sleeping giant."

It is significant that this population explosion within the Mexican community was matched by a zero population growth within the Anglo sector. What's more, a great many Anglos left Los Angeles County during the early 1960s for the suburban comforts of Orange, San Bernardino, and Ventura counties. The city's black population was also beginning to shrink in proportion to the growth of Mexicans and Asians. In fact, local central city neighborhoods were rapidly shifting toward a Mexican and Latin American majority. In effect, and for a variety of reasons, other ethnic groups grew smaller and moved out of Los Angeles proper while Mexicans increased their numbers and moved in.

The results of the two most recent censuses bear out this pattern. For example, the 1970 census showed a total Los Angeles city population of 2,811,801 people. Of that number, 545,000 were Spanish surnamed.[9] In Los Angeles County, the population was 6,938,457 and an impressive 1,289,000 were Spanish surnamed. The preliminary 1980 figures suggest an even more amazing growth rate. They point to a total city population of 2,966,763 persons, 815,989 of whom were Spanish surnamed.[10] Looking at the entire region, there appear to have been 7,477,657 people in the County of Los Angeles in 1980. Of that number, 2,065,727 had a Spanish surname.

Given this shift in population, experts predict that, by the end of the 1980s, Mexicans and other Latins will constitute the largest ethnic group in the entire county. This is quite a change from the predictions of the late nineteenth century, when Anglo scholars and politicians thought that within a few decades the Mexican as a unique ethnic group would be extinct in California. Asian Americans are the only other ethnic group growing at a similar rate. Thus, by the year 2000, Los Angeles will be a largely Mexican and Asian metropolis.[11]

Despite these dramatic predictions, the average Mexican living in Los Angeles now earns less than the average Anglo resident, enjoys less educational opportunity, and suffers a relative lack of local political power. Perhaps more alarming, the community itself is somewhat divided by internal social stratification. Entrepreneurs, professionals, semi-professionals, technicians, entertainers—a new upper-middle class Mexican has certainly emerged. But the Mexican population as a whole is not benefiting from their affluence. Indeed, the community's status remains static at best and may well have worsened in recent years.[12]

Ironically, members of the would-be Hispanic bourgeoisie often wield little power within the institutions that employ them. They are usually subject to the social, cultural, economic, and political influence of their Anglo employers and creditors. This is particularly true in the ownership of productive real estate and the holding of policy-making positions in corporate, financial, civic, and educational institutions. Yet their stake in the Anglo mainstream is sometimes a large one, large enough to shift their allegiance and even their self-image.

Although the 1960s spurred this internal division, the decade also took the community to new economic and political plateaus. Through hard work and painful business and campaign lessons, some Mexicans gradually began to climb the career and government ladders. Mexicans have served as members of the U.S. House of Representatives and the California state legislature. They have been mayors and city council members within several smaller cities. They have served as members of the Los Angeles school board. Mexican judges have risen to the municipal and county court levels. And even greater numbers have held appointed office at the federal, state, and municipal levels.

Each of these gains can be traced to more effective political organization and keen political awareness. Both skills followed from the enthusiasm that overtook Mexican Los Angeles during the very early 1960s. It is often said that when John F. Kennedy sought the community's support in his bid for the presidency, something fundamental changed. It is certainly true that the 1960 campaign generated an electoral vitality among Mexicans, particularly among the community's college students, that had never existed before.

Kennedy openly identified himself as a friend to Mexicans and other minorities. That position alone did a great deal for his political standing within the community. But without question, Kennedy's Catholicism contributed significantly to the almost unanimous popularity that he enjoyed among Mexican Americans. In a very real way, they saw him as the symbol of a new political climate. Their hopes bordered on a belief that his "new frontier" would include equality for Mexican people in the United States.

After the 1960 election, Mexican politicians and Democratic party regulars secured their new gains. In 1962, Council Member Edward R. Roybal was elected to the House of Representatives and became the first Mexican from Los Angeles County to serve in Congress. It was also in 1962 that Phillip S. Soto and Manuel Moreno were elected to the California State Assembly. They were the first Mexicans elected to that body since the 1890s.[13]

The widely heralded War on Poverty got underway in the 1960s and had its own long-lasting effect on the nation's Mexican community.[14] Despite initial enthusiasm, especially among the people hired to run various social service agencies, Mexicans and other minority groups soon realized that the programs could not solve their social or economic problems. Indeed, many community organizers believed that these programs had been intentionally conceived to be operated in full accord with the institutions and practices that perpetuated urban poverty and discrimination. There were exceptions to the rule. Some health clinics in particular provided necessary medical services. Overall, however, people grew bitter over innumerable unkept promises and their disappointment gave rise to a rigid distrust of virtually all government programs.

The most vocal critics of such programs were Mexican college students and other young people from the community. Without apology, they charged that the actual purpose of the War on Poverty was the pacification of minority people through the cooptation of all potential leaders. These young people were motivated by an acute awareness of the plight of their community. Having watched the failures and achievements of the Black movement, the grape boycott, farm workers strikes and the land grant movement of López Tijerina in New Mexico, they saw the need for a fresh strategy with which to mobilize the community.

Their collective dissatisfaction climaxed in the late 1960s. On college campuses throughout Los Angeles, Mexican students organized groups and planned meetings at which they could discuss common political concerns and work toward social reform. Their efforts were accompanied by a drive within the community to create organizational unity and cultural coalition. As a result of this latter effort, the Mexican Unity Council was formed in 1967. The late 60s also brought about a renewed support for Mexican candidates like Richard Calderón, who ran unsuccessfully for state assembly in 1966, and Julián Nava, who won election to the Los Angeles school board in 1967.[15]

It was in 1967 that a fully-developed social movement swept through Mexican communities in Los Angeles and the entire Southwest. It has become known as the Chicano movement.[16] "Chicano" was taken as a contracted form of the word "Mexicano" and was adopted by many Mexicans to signify their common political and cultural identity. It was intended to stand as a verbal counterpoint to "Mexican American"—a term that many associated with a passive acceptance of the status quo.

One of the Chicano movement's most dramatic and impressive moments in Los Angeles occurred when its members focused community attention on the abysmal conditions within the city public school system. In March 1968, thousands of Mexican students literally walked out of their classrooms. The Blowouts, as the staged demonstrations were called, involved only five high schools in the East Los Angeles area, but their impact reverberated throughout the entire Los Angeles Unified School District. With the support from older Chicano activists and from one of their teachers, Sal Castro, the students dramatically drew attention to the racist attitudes held by many Anglo teachers and to the inferior educational conditions that plagued East Los Angeles schools.[17] These conditions were epitomized by a 50 percent dropout rate for Mexican high school students.

The Blowouts precipitated a wave of community outcry and a series of confrontations between local Mexican residents and the Los Angeles Board of Education. Students, parents, and community activists demanded bilingual and bicultural school programs. In all of this, the Chicano movement gained a level of respect even among the Mexican middle class. In some sense, Chicanos had made a public issue of the racism and inequality that less vocal members of the community had somehow grown afraid to mention.

Not long after the Blowouts, a group of local Chicanos began organizing the community around a number of other social issues. Perhaps their best-known effort was the 1970 National Chicano Moratorium. On August 29, Chicano anti-war activists staged a large march and rally to protest United States intervention in Vietnam and to publicize the staggeringly high rate of Mexican war casualties. Records indicate that approximately 30,000 people attended the demonstration.

Perhaps born of idealism, the Moratorium ended with the terror of police brutality and the horror of blood stained streets. Unaccustomed to large and militant demonstrations within the Mexican community, and unable or unwilling to comprehend the real reasons for the rally, local law enforcement agencies overreacted. By nightfall, several demonstrators had been violently attacked by Los Angeles police officers and three people were dead, among them a *Los Angeles Times* reporter named Ruben Salazar.[18] With a frenzy that sometimes accompanies fear, Chicano organizers spent the next few months staging a series of demonstrations throughout Los Angeles. Although that effort changed very little in the day-in day-out lives of local Spanish-speaking people, it did solidify ties between the Chicano movement and the Mexican community in Los Angeles.

First established in Texas and later organized in Colorado, La Raza Unida Party emerged in Los Angeles in 1971 as an independent political party made up primarily of Chicanos. On one level, it was successful in its appeal to the community's social conscience: it gained ballot status in California and ran a series of candidates for local and state office. But in terms of real political power the party made little headway, for as it began to garner local

Chicano newspapers.

(Courtesy of the Chicano Studies Research Library, UCLA)

attention, Mexican American Democrats like Art Torres and Richard Alatorre were elected to office.[19] Perhaps an independent political party appeared superfluous to many members of the community.

By 1975, the Chicano movement had shifted its emphasis to the defense of undocumented Mexican immigrants and began founding organizations like Centro de Acción Social Autónoma (CASA) to aid Mexican nationals in their efforts to remain in the United States. Because of Mexico's proximity to California and because of its historical significance to Spanish-speaking Los Angeles, the issue of immigration policy remains a top priority for many Mexican organizations and is likely to preoccupy the entire community for a long time.[20]

By the late 1970s, the Chicano movement had diffused. The intensity of the decade had worn many activities down into an awkward silence. As Los Angeles prepared to enter the 1980s, a new political and cultural phase began for the city's Mexican community. Mexicans were no longer a single, homogeneous community. Rather, they had become a complex amalgam of interests, backgrounds, and goals. A growing number of professional politicians surfaced from a variety of the city's Mexican communities, each of them espousing the concerns of a unique political constituency.

In hindsight, the Chicano movement can be seen to have served as a social catalyst within the city's larger Spanish-speaking community. By 1970, many young Mexicans had already guessed what the Anglo establishment would leave for them. In every way possible, they turned their backs on it. In that turnabout, young Chicanos motivated a large percentage of their community to present a stronger public presence. In effect, they demanded that society at large receive a new message about what it was to be Mexican. They also generated support for educational, political, and economic advancement. Public officials began addressing issues of concern to Mexicans in a serious, more respectful manner. Finally, and perhaps most important, the Chicano movement facilitated certain concessions from the Anglo mainstream. These concessions—bilingual education, Chicano Studies Programs, and affirmative action employment practices—created a setting from which a viable Mexican middle class could rise to local prominence.

A NEW REFLECTION

More than halfway through the 1980s, it is difficult to characterize the tenor of the times. Certainly Chicano leaders of the 1970s remain a model for continued activism. But like all American constituencies, Mexican Los Angeles has spent the past few years balancing its score carefully. In essence, it seems that the 1960s laid the groundwork for a series of economic advancements. It was in the 70s, after all, that a viable middle class emerged from within the community. Yet the short-term occupational gains of the last decade have been undeniably dwarfed by the economic setbacks of the early 1980s. Mexicans continued to feel the damaging effects of drastic federal budget cuts and less government support for affirmative action and bilingual education. Culturally, the past 20 years have been a time of revitalization within the community. Since 1960, energies have been directed into the arts, media, and religious institutions. But in the whip of that cultural whirlwind, the community remains tempered by a uniquely Mexican concern for cultural continuity.

In terms of language, two fascinating trends have developed over the past two decades. On the one hand, a sizeable segment of Mexican Los Angeles continues to speak Spanish. At the same time another segment of the local community continues to move toward an English-only lifestyle. In fact, many second, third, and fourth generation Mexican Americans are unable to speak Spanish. Their linguistic limitation is primarily due to the saturation of English-language media combined with a lack of formal Spanish-language education. The loss of Spanish can be most clearly seen in the city's suburbs but it is also characteristic of public housing projects in Maravilla, Venice, and other barrios throughout Los Angeles. Simultaneously, the number of Spanish-speaking Mexicans in Los Angeles is growing at an unprecedented rate. In fact, soaring immigration from Mexico and other Latin American countries has buoyed a Spanish-speaking cultural life in a manner not seen since the mid-1920s.

The spectacular revival of Spanish-language culture can be at least loosely measured by the recent proliferation of cultural service establishments such as bookstores, record shops, and movie theatres. Bookstores are an especially interesting addition to the list because they indicate the presence of a literate and well-informed Spanish-speaking public. When the demand for better-stocked Spanish-language bookstores came in the late 1970s, it was almost immediately met. In 1960, there were only one or two such bookstores

Día de los Muertos (Day of the Dead) is a centuries-old Mexican tradition. The dead are honored by fiestas, processions, and offerings of food and decorations, and friends exchange decorated sugar skulls.

(Courtesy of José Cuellar)

State Assemblywoman Gloria Molina's victory celebration, June 1982. Molina (top row, 6th from left) is the first Latina to be elected to the California state legislature. A founder and past president of Comisión Feminil Mexicana, she has held a number of significant political offices and is a long-time political activist.

(Courtesy of Rosemary Quesada-Weiner)

in all of Los Angeles. Today, there are at least a dozen spread throughout the city and several more are open for business in the county. This industry boom is partly due to the influx of well-educated Latin Americans exiled from Chile, Argentina, and El Salvador. But these customers do not constitute the bulk of Spanish-language book buyers. A substantial share of recent Mexican immigrants are more educated than their 1940s and 1950s counterparts.

The popularity of Spanish-language movie theatres also serves to indicate that the local Latin population is growing and dispersing at an astonishing rate. There are three times as many such theatres in Los Angeles today as there were just 20 years ago. Their presence is especially interesting in the West Los Angeles area. In 1960 there was only one Spanish-language theatre, and in 1980, four such theatres, three of them in the affluent city of Santa Monica.

Mainstream recreational establishments like Disneyland, Magic Mountain, and Knotts Berry Farm have glimpsed an enormous potential market within the community. Each of them makes direct marketing appeals to Mexicans in Los Angeles. As recently as 1960, Disneyland was geared exclusively toward the white, Anglo-Saxon family. Today, it joins other amusement parks in advertising Fiestas and Dias Mexicanos in local Spanish-language media. And if continually refined advertising campaigns are any measure of a profitable program, then their efforts would appear to be paying off.

Indeed, newspaper and television marketing would seem to have discovered the "Hispanic market." Because immigration and high birth rates translate into big profits for companies and advertising firms, major establishments throughout southern California court the community. It is interesting to note that the content of Spanish-language advertisements differs very little from its

English-language counterpart. As a result, expensive marketing campaigns are most effective among Mexicans who share Anglo-defined, middle class values and aspirations.

Television programming has come a long way since the late 1950s and early 60s, when small-scale Spanish-language shows bought filler air time from mainstream outlets. Today, expensive TV programs are directed at a Mexican audience. Like just about every other group, Mexicans have been fundamentally affected by television. Although few studies have actually documented the relationship between TV and Latin culture, research does indicate that the media's influence has seeped deepest into the psyche of children who spend as many as 10 hours a day in front of the screen.

Grandmother and daughter.

(Courtesy of Rosemary Quesada-Weiner)

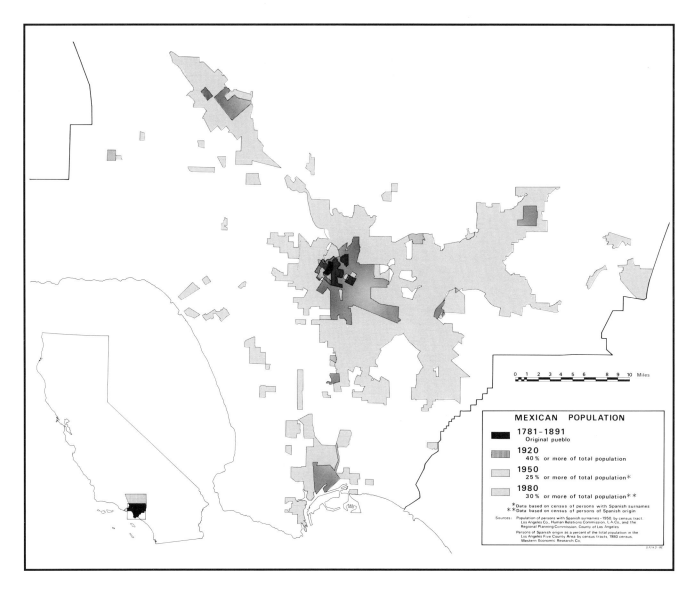

MEXICAN POPULATION

1781–1891
Original pueblo

1920
40% or more of total population

1950
25% or more of total population *

1980
30% or more of total population * *

*Data based on census of persons with Spanish surnames
* *Data based on census of persons of Spanish origin

Sources: Population of persons with Spanish surnames – 1950, by census tract.
Los Angeles Co., Human Relations Commission, L.A.Co., and the
Regional Planning Commission, County of Los Angeles
Persons of Spanish origin as a percent of the total population in the
Los Angeles Five County Area by census tracts, 1980 census.
Western Economic Research Co.

Map — Growth of urban community.

Surveys conducted on the general population suggest that television may result in a long-term weakening of family relationships. This has probably been the case among Mexican youngsters, although cultural values may figure into the equation in a manner not yet fully understood. Since TV viewing reduces the time available for communication with parents, it partially replaces them as a source of information with respect to social behavior and cultural identity. For Mexican children exposed to only Anglo-oriented programming, the traditional transmission of culture has been irretrieveably lost. Parents interested in cultural maintenance will perhaps find an answer to this problem in specialized cable stations and personalized video programming.

Whether the specific issue involves exposure to mass media, entry into the public school system, or participation in popular forms of recreation, the 1980s present themselves as years in which Mexican Los Angeles must search for alternative social influences. Thus far, the clearest alternative to mainstream cultural dominance has come from the Chicano movement. Throughout the 1960s and 1970s, Chicanos served as leaders in the revitalization of Mexican culture within the United States. Chicano artists, poets, scholars, photographers, writers, and filmmakers posed fundamental questions regarding the worth of Anglo culture and the importance of Mexican tradition. With great pride, they urged their entire community to renew its own culture and to stop imitating someone else's.

But the movement failed to solve all the cultural dilemmas that haunted its community. Perhaps the greatest problem that its leaders faced was their need to transmit an emotional message to a mass audience without losing the social content that stood behind their words. Given the fact that the community had grown extremely diverse, it was very difficult for Chicanos to create a concrete cultural program. This difficulty is reflected in the mixed reactions to Luis Valdez's play and film, *Zoot Suit*. The play's main character, El Pachuco, has generated both praise and criticism within the community. Some Mexicans see him as a defiant hero while others view him as the tragic victim of racism. If the play's controversy achieves nothing else, it points to the opposing community perspectives that sometimes obstruct a uniform platform of action.

One thing is sure: even when the city's public institutions do recognize the needs of the Spanish-speaking, they recognize them at a very slow pace. Since the passage of California's Proposition 13, cutbacks have worsened most services. Major institutions in Los Angeles County—the Department of Parks and Recreation, the County Museums of Art and Natural History, the Hollywood Bowl, and the Music Center—have changed very little in terms of their sensitivity to Mexican residents. The few changes that have taken place are obviously cosmetic. Mexicans are sometimes allowed to perform at these publicly-owned facilities but they virtually never hold policy-making positions within their administration.

Perhaps for this very reason, the community has had to creatively develop its own forms of cultural expression. In this vein, muralism stands as its most amazing artistic achievement. Just since 1970, artists such as Judy Baca, Willie Herrón, and John Valodez have completed hundreds of outside wall paintings. Most of them reflect quintessentially Mexican interpretations of religion, life before conquest, and contemporary political oppression.

Numerous teatro groups have also developed, largely as a result of the example set by *El Teatro Campesino* (The Farmworkers' Theatre). The city's long-standing tradition of Spanish-speaking drama is currently expressed in the theatrical productions of the Bilingual Foundation for the Arts. Headed by actress-director Carmen Zapata, it enjoys a level of popularity among local Spanish-speaking audiences. Nosotros, an actors group, has been formed to lobby for increased opportunity within the Hollywood film industry.

Plaza de la Raza, located in Lincoln Park, is yet another cultural outlet for the community. The entire complex was established to provide local Mexicans with exposure to and training in the arts. The Plaza's extensive cultural program of performances, exhibits, classes, and even its new cable television center are supported mainly through contributions from private foundations. Additional funds are regularly raised at gala events organized by a dedicated board of Mexican and Anglo personalities.

Among the community's many arts, there is a most decidedly avant-garde faction. Perhaps that faction was best represented in the 1970s by the art collective, *ASCO* (the Spanish word for nausea). Originally composed of four artists (Willie Herrón, Gronk, Patssi Valdez, and Harry Gamboa, Jr.), ASCO is now an umbrella group for many artists and activities.

Newspapers and magazines have been created to reflect the evolving self-concept of Mexican Los Angeles. Edited by Raul Ruíz, *La Raza* magazine stemmed from the Chicano movement. Between 1968 and 1976 it covered cultural issues of importance to the local Mexican community. Without question, *La Opinión* has been the main source of news and information for more than 50 years. Since 1970, this daily Spanish-language newspaper has renovated its style several times, always in the effort to keep pace with a constantly changing Latin community. The best example of this change may well be reflected in the paper's cultural supplement, *La Communidad*. Edited by Sergio Muñóz, *La Communidad* gained respect for its examination of topics as diverse as new wave music in East Los Angeles, the artist Rufino Tamayo, and Latin American and Chicano literature.

Even religious institutions, especially the Roman Catholic church, have been influenced by the self-directed energies of the local Mexican community. Throughout the 1960s, the Archdiocese was repeatedly criticized for its insensitivity to Mexicans. In fact, a Chicano organization called Católicos Por La Raza was specifically organized to address that insensitivity and its community leaders quickly took the lead in demanding change within the church. Although several demonstrations took place, the archdiocese did little to respond to charges of neglect. Pressure from the Vatican soon added to criticism from Latino clergy and a gradual recognition of the special needs of Mexicans and other Latino Catholics infused the Church. Largely because of the pressure brought to bear by these groups, a Latino was appointed bishop to the Los Angeles archdiocese in 1971.

WITHOUT A FINAL ANALYSIS

The community's most recent history has, in many ways, been filled with dramatic change. The values and customs that once united the Spanish-speaking residents of Los Angeles no longer serve to bind the majority of English-speaking Mexicans to their most ancient traditions. Today, new immigrants from Mexico have as little in common with the Latino upper middle class as they do with the Anglo mainstream.

But it is equally true that the past 30 years have simply repeated the process of mestizaje that began more than 100 years ago, when Spanish, Mexican, and Indian peoples each relinquished concepts of racial purity in favor of cultural transformation. The Chicano of the 1970s and 1980s stands as the newest reflection of a community that has always chosen from its myriad influences the elements of culture that best suit its immediate needs. No longer Indian but of the Indian, not Spanish but of Europe, Mexicans have emerged as the embodiment of all these cultures. Surely it must be said that they aim to resolve the complexity of their background in a way that they themselves define.

Overall, the last three decades have been filled with self-discovery for most U.S. Mexicans. They have found and exercised their strengths, solidified their own ground, and survived repeated attacks from within and without. Beyond all else, the last 30 years have shown them that they are an immovable force in Los Angeles and throughout the Southwest. Like every generation that has come before them, they are forging their path in new and unusual ways. What they will be tomorrow, they are shaping today.

NOTES

1. United States Bureau of the Census, *Seventeenth Census of the United States: 1940.*

2. Joan Moore, and Frank G. Mittlebach, *Residential Segregation in the Urban Southwest* (Los Angeles: 1967).

3. Fitzgerald, "Mexican-American Activism in the Post War Years," pp. 280-351. Also Kaye Lyon Briegel, *The History of Political Organizations Among Mexican-Americans in Los Angeles Since the Second World War* (Master's thesis, University of Southern California, 1967).

4. Briegel, pp. 11-12.

5. Acuña, pp. 333-342.

6. Briegel, pp. 48-50.

7. Ibid., pp. 50-60.

8. United States Bureau of the Census, *Eighteenth Census of the United States: 1960, Subject Reports, Persons of Spanish Surname,* Final Report PC (2)-1B, (Washington, D.C.: 1963).

9. United States Bureau of the Census, *Nineteenth Census of the United States: 1970. Subject Reports, Persons with Spanish Surname,* PC(2)-1D, (Washington, D.C.: 1973).

10. United States Bureau of the Census. *1980 Census of Population and Housing. Advance Reports. California: Final Population and Housing Counts,* PHC80-V-6. Western Economic Research Co., *1980 Population and Race Data: By Census Tracts in California* (Sherman Oaks: 1980).

11. Richard E. Meyer, "Ethnic Populations Changing Face of Los Angeles" *Los Angeles Times,* April 13, 1980, Part II, p. 1

12. Antonio, Rios-Bustamante, "A Profile of the Mexican Working Class in the United States," *Development and Socio-Economic Progress* (Cairo: 1980).

13. Briegel, p. 52.

14. Biliana C. S. Ambrecht, *Politicizing the Poor: The Legacy of the War on Poverty in a Mexican American Community* (N.Y.: 1976).

15. Juan Gómez-Quiñones, *Mexican Students Por La Raza* (Santa Barbara: 1978), p. 18.

16. Gerald Rosen, "The Development of the Chicano Movement in Los Angeles from 1967-1969," *Aztlán,* 4 (1, Spring 1973).

17. Frank Del Olmo, "68 Protest Brought Better Education," *Los Angeles Times,* March 26, 1980, Part II, p. 1. Gómez-Quiñones, pp. 30-31.

18. Acuña, pp. 366-371. Morales, Armando, *Ando Sangrando, I am Bleeding: A Study of Mexican-American Police Conflict* (La Puente: 1974).

19. Ibid., p. 388. Alberto, Juarez, "The Emergence of El Partido de la Raza Unida: California's New Chicano Party," *Aztlan,* 3 (2, Fall 1972).

20. Acuña, pp. 168-169. Luis R. Negrete, "La lucha de la comunidad mexicana por los derechos humanos de los trabajadores emigrantes," in Antonio Rios-Bustamante, ed., *Mexican Immigrant Workers in the United States* (Los Angeles: 1981).

Bibliography

I. PRIMARY SOURCES:

California Provincial State Papers, 1767-1822, Archives of California, Bancroft Library, U.C. Berkeley.

California Departmental State Papers, 1822-1884, Archives of California, Bancroft Library, U.C. Berkeley.

Padron, Los Angeles, 1790. Zoeth Skinner Eldredge, Correspondence and Papers, Bancroft Library.

Padron, Los Angeles, 1818 (1822), De la Guerra Documents, Zoeth Skinner Eldredge, Correspondence and Papers, Bancroft Library, U.S. Berkeley.

Los Angeles. Archives of the Prefecture of Los Angeles, 1834-1850. 3 Vols.

Los Angeles Aytuntamiento Records. Transcripts and Extracts from the Los Angeles Archives. 5 Vols. Bancroft Library, U.C. Berkeley.

Los Angeles. Municipal Charities Commission, *First Annual Report*. Los Angeles: n.p., 1913-1914.

_____. Municipal Charities Commission, *Second Annual Report*. Los Angeles: n.p., 1914-1915.

Los Angeles. *Report of the Los Angeles Housing Commission, February 20 to June 30, 1908*, n.p., n.d.

_____. *Report of the Los Angeles Housing Commission, June 30, 1909 to June 30, 1910*, n.p., n.d.

_____. *Report of the Los Angeles Housing Commission July 1, 1910 to March 31, 1913*, n.p., n.d.

Los Angeles. Settlement Association. *First Report*. Los Angeles: B. R. Baumgardt and Company, 1897.

Los Angeles. Social Service Commission, *Annual Report*. Los Angeles: n.p., 1916-1917.

_____. Social Service Commission, *Annual Report*. Los Angeles: n.p., 1917-1918.

United States Census Office. *The Seventh Census of the United States: 1850*. Washington, 1853.

United States Census Office. *Population of the United States in 1860: The Eighth Census*. Washington: 1864.

U.S., Bureau of the Census. *Twelfth Census of the United States, 1900: Population*, Part I. Washington, 1901.

_____. Bureau of the Census. *Thirteenth Census of the United States, 1910: Population*, Volumes I, II, IV, V, VIII. Washington, 1922-1923.

_____. *Fourteenth Census of the United States, 1920: Population*, Volumes II, IV, VIII. Washington, 1922-1923.

_____. Bureau of the Census. *Fifteenth Census of the United States, 1930: Population*, Volume I. Table 23. Washington, 1932.

United States Bureau of the Census. *Sixteenth Census of the United States: 1940. Population*. Washington: 1943.

United States Bureau of the Census. *Seventeenth Census of the United States: 1950. Population*. Washington: 1953.

United States Bureau of the Census. *Eighteenth Census of the United States: 1960. Population*. Washington: 1963.

United States Bureau of the Census. *Nineteenth Census of the United States: 1970. Population*. Washington: 1973.

United States Bureau of the Census. *Twentieth Census of the United States: 1980. Population*. Washington: 1983.

II. BOOKS:

Altman, Ida and James Lockhart. *The Provinces of Early Mexico*. UCLA, 1976.

Acuña, Rodolfo. *Occupied America: A History of Chicanos*. New York: Harper and Row, 1981.

af Geijerstam, Classes. *Popular Music in Mexico*. Albuquerque: University New Mexico Press, 1976.

Ambricht, Biliana C. S. *Politicizing the Poor: The Legacy of the War on Poverty in a Mexican American Community*. New York: Praeger, 1976.

Bakker, Elna. *An Island Called California: An Ecological Introduction to its Natural Communities*. Berkeley: University of California Press, 1971.

Bancroft, Hubert Howe. *History of California*. 7 Vols. San Francisco: The History Company, 1888.

_____. *California Pastoral*. San Francisco: The History Company, 1888.

Barnes, Thomas C. et. al. *Northern New Spain: A Research Guide*. Tucson: University of Arizona Press, 1981.

Bartra, Armando, ed. *Regeneración; 1900-1918*. México, D. F.: Ediciones Era, 1977.

Bogardus, Emory. *The Mexican in the United States*. Los Angeles: University of Southern California Press, 1934.

Blanco, Antonio S. *La Lengua Española en la Historia de California: Contribución a su estudio*. Madrid: Ediciones Cultura Hispanica, 1971.

Bolton, Herbert Eugene. (ed.). *Fray Juan Crespí: Missionary Explorer on the Pacific Coast 1769-1774*. Berkeley: University of California Press, 1927.

Botello, Arthur P. (Trs.) *Don Pio Pico's Historical Narrative*. Glendale: Arthur H. Clark Company, 1973.

Brandes, Ray (Trs.) *The Costanso Narrative of the Portola Expedition*. Newhall: Hogarth Press, 1970.

Burma, John. *Spanish-Speaking Groups in the United States*. Durham: Duke University Press, 1954.

Camarillo, Albert. *Chicanos in a Changing Society*. Cambridge: Harvard University Press, 1979.

Caughey, John Walton. (ed.) *The Indians of Southern California in 1852*. San Marino: The Henry E. Huntington Library, 1952.

Chapman, Charles E. *A History of California: The Spanish Period*. New York: Macmillan and Company, 1921.

Cleland, Robert Glass. *The Cattle on a Thousand Hills: Southern California, 1850–80*. San Marino: The Henry E. Huntington Library, 1951.

Cook, Sherburne F. *The Population of the California Indians, 1769–1970*. Berkeley: University of California Press, 1976.

Cressman, L. S. *Prehistory of the Far West: Homes of the Vanished Peoples*. Salt Lake City: University of Utah Press, 1977.

Dumke, Glenn S. *The Boom of the Eighties in Southern California*. 4th ed. San Marino, California: Huntington Library, 1955.

Donley, Michael W. *Atlas of California*. Culver City: Pacific Book Center, 1979.

Engelhardt, Fr. Zephyrin. *San Gabriel Mission and the Beginnings of Los Angeles*. San Gabriel: The James H. Barry Company, 1927.

Fogelson, Robert. *The Fragmented Metropolis: Los Angeles, 1850–1930*. Cambridge: Harvard University Press, 1967.

Forbes, Jack D. *Native Americans of California and Nevada*. Healdsburg: Naturegraph Publishers, 1968.

Francis, Jessie Davies. *An Economic and Social History of Mexican California, 1822–1846*. New York: Arno Press, 1976.

Goodman, Jeffrey. *American Genesis*. New York: Summit Books, 1981.

Gillingham, Robert Cameron. *The Rancho San Pedro*. Los Angeles: Dominguez Estate Company, 1961.

Gamio, Manuel. *Mexican Immigration to the United States; A Study of Human Migration and Adjustment*. Chicago: University of Chicago Press, 1930.

_____. *Número, procedencia y distribución geográfica de los imigrantes Mexicanos en los Estados Unidos*. México, D.F.: Talleres Gráficos Editorial, 1930.

_____. *The Mexican Immigrant, His Life Story*. Chicago: University of Chicago Press, 1931.

Gans, Herbert. *The Urban Villagers*. New York: The Macmillan Company, 1962.

Gómez-Quiñones, Juan. *Sembradores: Ricardo Flores Magón y El Partido Liberal Mexicano, A Eulogy and Critique*. Los Angeles: Aztlan Publications, 1973.

_____. *Development of the Mexican Working Class North of the Rio Bravo*. Los Angeles: Aztlan Publications, 1982.

Gordon, Margaret S. *Employment Expansion and Population Growth, The California Experience: 1900–1950*. Berkeley: University of California Press, 1954.

Grebler, Leo; Moore, Joan W., and Guzmán, Ralph C. *The Mexican-American People*. New York: The Free Press, 1970.

Griffith, Beatrice. *American Me*. Boston: Houghton Mifflin Company, 1948.

Griswold Del Castillo, Richard. *The Los Angeles Barrio 1850–1890: A Social History*. Berkeley: University of California Press, 1979.

Guinn, James M. *A History of California and an Extended History of Los Angeles and Environs*. 2 Vols. Los Angeles: Cole-Holmquist Press, 1915.

Hayes, Benjamin. *Pioneer Notes, 1849–1875*. Los Angeles: Marjorie Tisdale Wolcott, 1929.

Heizer, Robert F. (ed.) *The Indians of Los Angeles County: Hugo Reid's Letters of 1852*. Los Angeles: Southwest Museum, 1968.

Hoffman, Abraham. *Unwanted Mexican Americans in the Great Depression; Repatriation Pressures, 1929–1939*. Tucson: University of Arizona Press, 1974.

Holland, Clifton. *The Religious Dimension in Hispanic Los Angeles: A Protestant Case Study*. Pasadena, 1974.

Hutchinson, C. Alan. *Frontier Settlement in Mexican California: The Padres-Hijar Colony*. New Haven: Yale University Press, 1969.

Johnston, Bernice E. *California's Gabrielino Indians*. Los Angeles: Southwest Museum, 1962.

Jones, Oakah L. Jr. *Los Paisanos: Spanish Settlers on the Northern Frontier of New Spain*. Norman: University of Oklahoma Press, 1979.

MacLachlan, Colin and Jaime Rodriguez. *The Forging of the Cosmic Race: A Reinterpretation of Colonial Mexico*. Berkeley: University of California Press, 1980.

McWilliams, Carey. *Factories in the Field; The Story of Migratory Farm Labor in California*. New York: Little, Brown, 1935.

_____. *North from Mexico; The Spanish Speaking People of the United States*. New York: Greenwood Press, 1948; reprint ed., 1968.

_____. *Southern California Country; An Island on the Land*. New York: Duell, Sloan and Pierce, 1946.

Meinig, D. W. *Southwest; Three Peoples in Geographical Change, 1600–1970*. New York: Oxford University Press, 1971.

Moore, Joan W., and Frank C. Mittlebach. *Residential Segregation in the Urban Southwest*. Los Angeles: Mexican American Study Project, U.C.L.A., 1967.

Modell, John. *The Economics and Politics of Racial Accommodation: The Japanese of Los Angeles, 1900–1942*. Urbana: University of Illinois Press, 1977.

Morales, Armando. *Ando Sangrando, I Am Bleeding: A Study of Mexican American Police Conflict*. La Puente: Congress of Mexican American Unity, 1972.

Navarro Garcia, Luis. *Don José de Galvez y La Comandancia General de las Provincias Internas Del Norte de Nueva España*. Sevilla: Escuela de Estudios Hispanoamericanos, 1964.

_____. *Sonora y Sinaloa en El Siglo XVII*. Sevilla: Escuela de Estudios Hispanoamericanos, 1967.

Nelson, Howard J. and William A. Clark. *Los Angeles: The Metropolitan Experience*. Cambridge: Bullinger Publishing Company, 1976.

Newmark, Maurice H. *Sixty Years in Southern California, 1853–1913*. Los Angeles: The Knickerbocker Press, 1916.

Ogden, Adele. *Greater America: Essays in Honor of Herbert Eugene Bolton*. Berkeley, 1945.

Ostrom, Vincent. *Water and Politics*. Los Angeles: John Randolph and Dora Haynes Foundation, 1953.

Oxnam, G. Bromley. *The Mexican in Los Angeles*. Los Angeles: Interchurch World Movement of North America, 1920.

Packman, Ana Begue. *Leather Dollars*. Los Angeles: The Times Mirror Press, 1932.

Park, Robert E. *The Immigrant Press and Its Control*. Westport, Connecticut: Greenwood Press, 1922; reprint ed., 1970.

Perry, Louis B. and Richard S. *A History of the Los Angeles Labor Movement, 1911–1941*. Berkeley: University of California Press, 1963.

Pitt, Leonard. *The Decline of the Californios*. Berkeley: University of California Press, 1966.

Rabinowitz, Francine F. *Minorities in the Suburbs*. Lexington: Lexington Books, 1977.

Richman, Irving Berdine. *California Under Spain and Mexico, 1535–1847*. New York: Cooper Square Publishers, 1965.

Rios-Bustamante, Antonio. (ed.) *Immigration and Public Policy: Human Rights for Undocumented Workers and Their Families*. Document No. 5. Los Angeles: Chicano Studies Research Center Publications, UCLA, 1977.

_____. *Mexican Immigrant Workers in the United States*. Los Angeles: Chicano Studies Research Center Publications, UCLA, 1981.

Robinson, Alfred. *Life in California*. Santa Barbara: Peregrine Smith, Inc., 1970.

Robinson, William Wilcox. *Land in California*. Berkeley: University of California Press, 1948.

_____. *The Indians of Los Angeles: The Story of the Liquidation of a People*. Los Angeles: Glen Dawson Press, 1952.

_____. *Los Angeles: A Profile*. Norman: University of Oklahoma Press, 1968.

_____. *The Lawyers of Los Angeles*. Los Angeles: Los Angeles Bar Association, 1959.

_____. *Los Angeles from the Days of the Pueblo*. Revised with and Introduction by Doyce B. Nunis, Jr. Los Angeles: The California Historical Society, 1981.

_____. *Maps of Los Angeles: From Ord's Survey of 1849 to the End of the Boom of the 80's*. Los Angeles: Dawson's Bookshop, 1962.

_____. *Los Angeles in Civil War Days, 1860–65*. Los Angeles: Dawson's Bookshop, 1977.

_____. *Ranchos Become Cities*. Pasadena: San Pasqual Press, 1947.

Salvator, Ludwig Louis. *Los Angeles in the Sunny Seventies*. Los Angeles: Jake Zeitlin, 1929.

Shevky, Eshref and William, Marylin. *The Social Areas of Los Angeles: Analysis and Typology*. Berkeley: University of California Press, 1949.

Strong, William Duncan. *Aboriginal Society in Southern California*. Berkeley: University of California Press, 1929.

Turhollow, Anthony F. *A History of the Los Angeles District, U.S. Army Corps of Engineers, 1898–1965*. Los Angeles: U.S. Army Corps of Engineers, 1975.

Vorspan, Max and Lloyd P. Gartner. *A History of the Jews in Los Angeles*. San Marino: The Henry E. Huntington Library, 1970.

Walker, Edwin F. *Five Prehistoric Archaeological Sites in Los Angeles County*. Los Angeles: Southwest Museum, 1951.

Weber, David J. *New Spain's Far Northern Frontier*. Albuquerque: University of New Mexico Press, 1979.

Weber, Rev. Francis J. *El Pueblo de Los Angeles: An Enquiry in Early Appellations*. Los Angeles: Archidiocese of Los Angeles, 1968.

Wittenberg, Sister Mary Ste Thérèse, S.N.D. *The Machados and Rancho La Ballona*. Los Angeles: Dawson's Bookshop, 1973.

Woodward, Arthur, *Lances at San Pasqual*. San Francisco: California Historical Society, 1948.

Workman, Boyle. *The City that Grew*. Los Angeles: Southland Publishing Company, 1935.

Wrigley, Edward A. *Population and History*. New York: McGraw Hill, 1969.

Yans-McLaughlin, Virginia. *Family and Community; Italian Immigrants in Buffalo, 1880–1930*. Ithaca: Cornell University Press, 1977.

Young, Erle Fiske, ed. *Social Treatment, A Reference Manual for Social Workers in Los Angeles*. Los Angeles: Western Educational Service, 1926.

Wright, Doris Marion. *A Yankee in Mexican California: Abel Stearns 1798–1848*. Santa Barbara: Wallace Hebbend, 1977.

III.   ARTICLES:

Alexander, George. "Date Variation May Affect Migration Debate: 40,000 Year Old Tools Found in Mojave." *Los Angeles Times*, April 18, 1980.

Aschmann, Homer. "The Evolution of a Wild Landscape and its Persistence in Southern California." *Annals of the American Association of Geographers* 49 (3, September 1959).

Banon, John Francis, S. J. "Pioneer Jesuit Missionaries on the Pacific Slope of New Spain." Adele Ogden (ed.) *Essays in Honor of Herbert Eugene Bolton*. Berkeley: University of California Press, 1945.

Barrows, H. D. "Antonio F. Coronel." *Southern California Quarterly* 5 (1, 1900).

_____. "Don Ygnacio del Valle." *Southern California Quarterly* 4 (3, 1899).

Bean, Lowell John and Charles R. Smith "Gabrielino" pp. 538-549, Robert F. Heizer. *Handbook of North American Indians*. Washington, D.C., 1978.

Bean, Lowell J. "Social Organization in Native California" Lowell John Bean and Thomas F. King (ed.) *Antap: California Indian Political Organization*. Ramona, 1974.

Berger, Rainer, "Advances and Results in Radio Carbon Dating: Early Man in America." *World Archaelogy* 1975.

_____. "Thoughts on the First Peopling of America and Australia." A. L. Bryan (ed). *Early Man in America*. Edmonton, 1978.

Bogardus, Emory S. "The House-Court Problem." *America Journal of Sociology* 22 (November 1916).

Boscana, Father Geronimo. "Chinichinich" Alfred Robinson. *Life in California*. Santa Barbara: Peregrine Smith, Inc., 1970.

Bowman, J. N. "The Names of the Los Angeles and San Gabriel Rivers." *Southern California Quarterly* 29 (2, 1947).

_____. "Prominent Women of Provincial California." *Southern California Quarterly* Vol. 39, No. 2 (1957).

Camarillo, Albert. "Historical Patterns in the Development of Chicano Urban Society: Southern California, 1848-1930" Ray Allen Billington and Albert Camarillo. *The American Southwest: Image and Reality*. Los Angeles, 1979.

Camarillo, Alberto M. "Chicano Urban History: A Study of Compton's Barrio, 1936-1970." *Aztlán* (Fall 1971).

Carter, George F. "Man, Time and Change in the Far Southwest." *Annals of the Association of American Geographers* 49 (3, Part II September 1959).

Charles, William N. "The Transcription of and Translation of Old Mexican Documents of the Los Angeles County Archives." *Southern California Quarterly* 20 (2, June 1938).

Chudacoff, Howard P. "A New Look at Ethnic Neighborhoods: Residential Dispersion and the Concept of Visibility in a Medium-Sized City." *Journal of American History* 60 (June 1973).

Coalson, George. "Mexican Contract Labor in American Agriculture." *The Southwestern Social Science Quarterly* 33 (December 1952).

Coman, Catharine. "Casa Castelar." *The Commons* 7 (January 1903).

Conley, Edward M. "The Americanization of Mexico." *Review of Reviews* 32 (December 1905).

Davis, Thomas J. "Schools that Reach the Homes of Immigrants: Neighborhood Schools of Los Angeles." *American City* 17 (December 1917).

De Graff, Lawrence. "The City of Black Angels: Emergence of the Los Angeles Ghetto, 1890-1930." *Pacific Historical Review* 39 (August 1970).

Dembert, Lee. "L.A. Now a Minority City, 1980 Census Data Shows." *Los Angeles Times*, April 6, 1981.

Derland, C. P. "The Los Angeles River — Its History and Ownership." *Southern California Quarterly* 3 (1, 1893).

de Uriarte, Mercedes. "Battle for the Ear of the Latino." *Los Angeles Times Calendar*, December 14, 1980.

Esquivel, Servando I. "The Immigrant from Mexico." *The Outlook* 125 (May 19, 1920).

Fitch, John A. "Los Angeles, A Militant Anti-Union Citadel." *The Survey* 33 (October 3, 1941).

Fuller, Elizabeth. "The Mexican Housing Problem in Los Angeles." *Studies in Sociology* 5 (November 1920).

Gans, Herbert J. "The Failure of Urban Renewal." *Commentary* 39 (April 1965).

Garr, Daniel J. "Los Angeles and the Challenge of Growth 1836-1849." *Southern California Quarterly* 61 (2, Summer 1979).

Geiger, Maynard, O.F.M. "Six Census Records of Los Angeles and Its Immediate Area Between 1804 and 1823." *Southern California Quarterly* 54 (4 Winter 1972).

Gómez-Quiñonez, Juan. "The First Steps: Chicano Labor Conflict and Organizing, 1900-1920." *Aztlan* 3 (Spring 1972).

_____. "Toward A Perspective On Chicano History." *Aztlan* 2 (Fall 1971).

Gómez-Quiñones, Juan and Arroyo, Luis L. "On The State of Chicano History: Observations on Its Development, Interpretations, and Theory, 1970-1974." *The Western Historical Quarterly* 7 (April 1976).

Gonzalez, Gilbert. "Factors Relating to Property Ownership of Chicanos in Lincoln Heights Los Angeles." *Aztlan* 2 (Fall 1971).

Griswold del Castillo, Richard. "Myth and Reality: Chicano Economic Activity in Los Angeles, 1850-1880." *Aztlan* 6 (Summer 1976).

Griswold Del Castillo, Richard. "Health and the Mexican American in Los Angeles, 1850-1887." *The Journal of Mexican American History* 4 (1974).

_____. "Tucsoneses and Angelenos: A Socio-Economic Study of Two Mexican American Barrios 1860-1880." *Journal of the West* (January 1979).

Gutierrez, Felix. (Special Editor). "Spanish Language Media Issues." *Journalism History* 4 (2, Summer 1917).

Hanna, Phil Townshed. "Padrón and Confirmation of Title to Pueblo Lands." *Southern California Quarterly* 15 (1, 1931).

Hudson, Dec T. "Proto-Gabrielino Patterns of Territorial Organization in South Coastal California." *Pacific Coast Anthropological Society Quarterly* 7 (2, 1971).

Hornbeck, David. "Land Tenure and Rancho Expansion in Alta California, 1784-1846." *Journal of Historical Cartography* 4 (4, 1978).

_____. "Mission Population of Alta California 1810-1830." *Historical Cartography* 8 (1, Supplement. Spring 1978).

Juarez, Alberto. "The Emergence of El Partido de la Raza Unida: California's New Chicano Party." *Aztlan* 3 (2, Fall 1972).

Kahn, David. "Chicano Street Murals: People's Art in the East Los Angeles Barrio." *Aztlan* 6 (1, Spring 1975).

Kelsey, Harry. "A New Look at the Founding of Old Los Angeles." *California History* 55 (4, Winter 1976).

Kirsch, Jonathan. "Chicano Power." *New West* September 11, 1972.

Langellier, John Phillip. "Lances and Leather Jackets: Presidial Forces in Spanish Alta California, 1769-1821." *Journal of the West* 20 (4, October 1981).

Layne, J. Gregg. "The First Census of the Los Angeles District, Padrón de la Ciudad de Los Angeles y su Jurisdicción." *Southern California Quarterly* 18 (3-4 1936).

Leon-Portilla, Miguel. "The Norteño Variety of Mexican Culture: An Ethnological Approach." Edward H. Spicer (ed). *Plural Society in the Southwest*. New York: 1972.

Lofstedt, Christine. "The Mexican Population of Pasadena, California." *Journal of Applied Sociology* 7 (May June 1923).

Lopez, Ronald W. and Darryl D. Enos. "Spanish Language Only Television in Los Angeles County." *Aztlan* 4 (2, Fall 1973).

Marvin, George. "Invasion or Intervention." *World's Work* 32 (May 1916).

Mason, William. "The Founding Forty-Four." *Westways* (July 1976).

_____. "The Garrisons of San Diego Presidio, 1769-1794." *Journal of San Diego History* 24 (4, Fall 1978).

_____. "Fages' Code of Conduct Toward Indians, 1787." *The Journal of California Anthropology* No. 1 Summer 1975).

_____. "Los Angeles Plaza: Living Symbol of Our Past." *Terra* 19 (E, Winter 1981).

Matthews, William H. "The House Courts of Los Angeles." *The Survey* (July 5, 1913).

May, Ernest R. "Tiburcio Vasquez." *Southern California Quarterly* 29 (3-4, 1947).

McCorkle, Julia Norton. "A History of Los Angeles Journalism." *Southern California Quarterly* 10 (1915-1916).

McLean, Robert N. "Mexican Laborers in the United States." *Proceedings of the National Conference of Social Work* (1929).

"Mexicans in Los Angeles." *The Survey* 44 (September 15, 1920).

Meyer, Richard E. "Exploding Ethnic Populations Changing Face of Los Angeles." *Los Angeles Times*, April 13, 1980.

_____. "Political Impact Just Beginning: Ethnics' Influence, Particularly Latinos, to be Heavy." *Los Angeles Times*, April 13, 1980.

Miranda, Gloria. "Gente de Razón Marriage Patterns in Spanish and Mexican California: A Case Study of Santa Barbara and Los Angeles." *Southern California Quarterly* (Spring 1981).

Moore, Joan W. "Mexican Americans and Cities: A Study in Migration and the Use of Formal Resources." *International Migration Review* 5 (Fall 1971).

"Municipal Control of Charity in Los Angeles." *The Survey* 31 (October 4, 1913).

Nelson, Howard J. "The Spread of an Artificial Landscape Over Southern California." *Annals of the Association of American Geographers* 49 (3, Part II. September 1959).

_____ "The Two Pueblos of Los Angeles: Agricultural Village and Embryo Town." *Southern California Quarterly* 59 (Spring 1977).

Neri, Michael C. "A Journalistic Portrait of the Spanish-Speaking People of California, 1868-1925." *Southern California Quarterly* 55 (Summer 1973).

Oxnam, G. Bromley. "The Mexican in Los Angeles From the Standpoint of the Religious Forces of the City." *Annals of the American Academy of Political and Social Science* 93 (January 1921).

Del Olmo, Frank. "Hispanic Decade Stumbles at the Start." *Los Angeles Times*, October 16, 1980.

_____. " '68 Protest Brought Better Education." *Los Angeles Times*, March 26, 1978.

Phillips, George Harwood. "Indians in Los Angeles, 1781-1875: Economic Integration, Social Disintegration." *Pacific Historical Review* 49 (3, August 1980)

_____. "Indians and the Breakdown of the Spanish Mission System of California." *Ethnohistory.* 21 (4, Fall 1974).

Reich, Kenneth. "Latinos Push for Political Power." *Los Angeles Times*, August 17, 1981.

Rensberger, Boyce. "Bones Place First Modern Man in Southern California." *Santa Monica Evening Outlook*, p. 4, August 28, 1976.

Rios-Bustamante, Antonio. "A Profile of the Mexican Working Class in the United States." *Development and Socio-Economic Progress.* Cairo, 1980.

_____. Las clases sociales Mexicanas en Estados Unidos." *Historia y Sociedad.* Mexico, 1978.

_____. "The Once and Future Majority." *California History* 60 (1, April 1981).

Romo, Ricardo. "The Urbanization of Southwestern Chicanos in the Early Twentieth Century." *New Scholar* 6 (1977).

Rosen, Gerald. "The Development of the Chicano Movement in Los Angeles from 1967-1969." *Aztlan* 4 (1 Spring 1973).

Schiesl, Martin J. "Progressive Reform in Los Angeles Under Mayor Alexander, 1909-1913." *California Historical Quarterly* 54 (Spring 1975).

Schwartz, Harry. "Agricultural Labor in the First World War." *Journal of Farm Economics* 24 (February 1942).

Scruggs, Otey. "The First Farm Labor Program, 1917-1921." *Arizona and the West* 2 (Winter 1960).

Servin, Manuel P. "The Pre-World War II Mexican-American: An Interpretation." *California Historical Society Quarterly* 45 (December 1966).

_____. "California's Hispanic Heritage: A View into the Spanish Myth." *The Journal of San Diego History* 19 (1973).

Sokoloff, Lillian. "The Russians in Los Angeles." *Studies in Sociology* 3 (March 1918).

Spaulding, Charles B. "Housing Problems of Minority Groups in Los Angeles County." *Annals of the American Academy of Political and Social Science* 248 (November 1946).

Stanley, Grace C. "Special Schools for Mexicans." *The Survey* 44 (September 15, 1920).

Sterry, Nora. "Housing Conditions in Chinatown, Los Angeles." *Journal of Applied Sociology* 7 (November-December 1922).

Stoddard, Bessie D. "Courts of Sonoratown." *Charities and the Commons* 15 (December 2, 1905).

_____. "Recreative Centers of Los Angeles, California." *Annals* 35 (March 1910).

Sturges, Vera. "The Progress of Adjustment in Mexican and United States Life." *Proceedings of the National Conference of Social Welfare* (1920).

Taylor, Paul S. and Tom Vasey. "Contemporary Background of California Farm Labor." *Rural Sociology* 1 (December 1936).

Temple, Thomas Workman II. "Soldiers and Settlers of the Expedition of 1781, Genealogical Record." *Southern California Quarterly* 15 (1, November 1931).

_____. "Se Fundaron un Púeblo de Espanoles, The Founding of Los Angeles." *Southern California Quarterly* 15 (1, November 1931).

_____. "Supplies for the Pobladores." *Southern California Quarterly* 15 (1, November 1931).

Temple, Thomas Workman Temple, II. "Toypurina the Witch and The Indian Uprising at San Gabriel." *The Masterkey* 32 (5, 1958).

Tirado, Miguel D. "Mexican American Community Political Organization, 'The Key to Chicano Political Power,' " *Aztlan* 1 (Spring 1970).

Treutlein, Theodore E. "Los Angeles, California: The Question of the City's Original Spanish Name." *Southern California Quarterly* 55 (Spring 1973).

Vera, Ron. "Observations on the Chicano Relationship to Military Service in Los Angeles County." *Aztlan* 1 (2, 1970).

Yans-McLaughlin, Virginia. "A Flexible Tradition: Immigrant Families Confront New Work Experiences." *Journal of Social History* 7 (1974).

Young, Pauline V. "The Russian Molokan Community in Los Angeles." *American Journal of Sociology* 35 (November 1929).

Weber, Francis J. "Irish-Born Champion of the Mexican Americans." *California Historical Society Quarterly* 49 (September 1970).

Winter, Oscar Osburn. "The Rise of Metropolitan Los Angeles, 1870-1900." *Huntington Library Quarterly* 10 (1947).

Wollenberg, Charles. "Working on El Traque: The Pacific Electric Strike of 1903." *Pacific Historical Review* 42 (August 1973).

IV. DISSERTATIONS, M.A. THESES, AND UNPUBLISHED PAPERS:

Bond, J. Max. "The Negro in Los Angeles." Ph.D. dissertation, University of Southern California, 1936.

Bridge, David Alexander. "A Study of the Agencies Which Promote Americanization in the Los Angeles City Recreation Center District." M.A. thesis, University of Southern California, 1920.

Briegel, Kaye Lynn. "Alianza Hispano-Americana, 1894-1965: A Mexican American Fraternal Insurance Society." Ph.D. dissertation, University of Southern California, 1974.

_____. "The History of Political Organizations Among Mexican Americans in Los Angeles Since the Second World War." Thesis. University of Southern California. 1967.

Camarillo, Albert M. "Historical Patterns in the Development of Chicano Urban Society: Southern California, 1848-1930." Paper presented at the William Andrews Clark Memorial Lecture, University of California, Los Angeles, May, 1977.

_____. "The Making of A Chicano Community: A History of the Chicanos in Santa Barbara, California 1850-1930." Ph.D. dissertation, University of California, Los Angeles, 1975.

Cardoso, Lawrence A. "Mexican Emigration to the United States, 1900-1930; An Analysis of Socio-Economic Causes." Ph.D dissertation, University of Conneticut, 1974.

Clodius, Albert Howard. "The Quest for Good Government in Los Angeles, 1890-1910." Ph.D. dissertation, Claremont Graduate School, 1953.

De Graff, Lawrence Brooks. "Negro Migration to Los Angeles, 1930-1950." Ph.D. dissertation, University of California, Los Angeles, 1962.

Estrada, William D. "Indian Resistance and Accommodation in the California Missions and Mexican Society, 1769 to 1848: A Case Study of Mission San Gabriel Archangel and El Pueblo de Los Angeles." Paper, 1980.

French, William Foster. "A Study of Location Factors for Industrial Plants in and about Los Angeles, California." M.A. thesis, University of Southern California, 1926.

Gómez-Quiñones, Juan. "The Origin and Development of the Mexican Working Class in the United States: Laborers and Artisans North of the Río Bravo, 1600-1900," paper presented at the Fifth International Congress of Mexican Studies, Pátzcuaro, Michoacán, Mexico, October 13, 1977.

Gonzalez, Gilbert G. "The System of Public Education and its Function Within the Chicano Communities, 1920-1930." Ph.D. dissertation, University of California, Los Angeles, 1974.

Griewe, A. W. "A Study of the Habitues of the Downtown Parks of Los Angeles, With a View of Ascertaining Their Constituency, Their Social Processes, and Their Relation to the Larger Community Life." M.A. thesis, University of Southern California, 1926.

Griswold del Castillo, Richard. "La Raza Hispano Americana: The Emergence of an Urban Culture Among the Spanish Speaking of Los Angeles, 1850-1880." Ph.D. dissertation, University of California, Los Angeles, 1974.

Gustafson, Cloyd V. "An Ecological Analysis of the Hollenbeck Area of Los Angeles." M.A. thesis, University of Southern California, 1940.

Harrod, Merrill Leonard. "A Study of Deviate Personalities as Found in Main Street of Los Angeles." M.A. thesis, University of Southern California, 1939.

Herbold, Paul, "Sociological Survey of Main Street; Los Angeles, California." M.A. thesis, University of Southern California, 1936.

Hogue, Harland Edwin. "A History of Religion in Southern California: 1846-1880." Ph.D. dissertation, Columbia University, 1958.

Johnson, Charles S. "An Industrial Study of the Negro Population of Los Angeles." A Survey, National Urban League, New York, 1927.

Jones, Solomon, "The Government Riots of Los Angeles, June 1943." Thesis, UCLA, 1973.

Mazon, Mauricio. "Social Upheaval in World War II Zoot-Suiters and Servicemen in Los Angeles, 1943." Ph.D. dissertation, UCLA, 1976.

Lopez, Federico. "A Historical Analysis of Occupational and Employment Patterns of Mexican Americans in California 1950-1975." Honors Paper, UCLA. 1976.

Monroy, Douglas. "Mexicanos in Los Angeles, 1930-1941. Ph.D. dissertation, UCLA, 1978.

Munoz, Carlos, Jr. "The Politics of Chicano Urban Protest: A Model of Political Analysis," Ph.D. dissertation, Clermont. 1972.

Peñalosa, Fernando. "Class Consciousness and Social Mobility in a Mexican American Community" Ph.D. dissertation, University of Southern California, 1963.

Romo, Ricardo. "Mexican Workers in the City: Los Angeles, 1915-1930." Ph.D. dissertation, University of California, Los Angeles, 1975.

Rosales, Francisco A. "Mexican Immigration to the Urban Midwest During the 1920s." Ph.D. dissertation, Indiana University, Bloomington, 1978.

Scott, Robin Fitzgerald. "The Mexican-American in the Los Angeles Area, 1920-1950: From Acquiescence to Activity." Ph.D. dissertation, University of Southern California, 1971.